AMERICAN BUSINESS AND
POLITICAL POWER

STUDIES IN COMMUNICATION, MEDIA, AND PUBLIC OPINION
A SERIES EDITED BY SUSAN HERBST AND BENJAMIN I. PAGE

Mark A. Smith

AMERICAN BUSINESS

AND

POLITICAL POWER

Public Opinion,

Elections,

and

Democracy

THE UNIVERSITY OF CHICAGO PRESS

CHICAGO AND LONDON

Mark A. Smith is assistant professor of political science at the University of Washington.

The University of Chicago Press, Chicago 60637
The University of Chicago Press, Ltd., London
© 2000 by The University of Chicago
All rights reserved. Published 2000
Printed in the United States of America
09 08 07 06 05 04 03 02 01 00   1 2 3 4 5

ISBN: 0-226-76462-1 (cloth)
ISBN: 0-226-76464-8 (paper)

Library of Congress Cataloging-in-Publication Data

Smith, Mark A. (Mark Alan), 1970–
    American business and political power : public opinion, elections, and democracy / Mark A. Smith.
        p.   cm.—(Studies in communication, media, and public opinion)
    Includes bibliographical references and index.
    ISBN 0-226-76462-1 (cloth : alk. paper)—ISBN 0-226-76464-8 (pbk. : alk. paper)
    1. Business and politics—United States.   2. Public opinion—United States.   3. Power (Social sciences)—United States.   4. Pressure groups—United States.   5. Lobbying—United States.   I. Title.   II. Series.

JK467.S59   2000
322'.3'0973—dc21

                                                    00-008248

For Kristen, with love

CONTENTS

TABLES AND FIGURES

TABLES

FIGURES

ACKNOWLEDGMENTS

During the four years between a germ of an idea and a completed manuscript, I have incurred more than my fair share of intellectual and personal debts. This book wouldn't be the same—indeed, it probably wouldn't even be a book—were it not for discussions with and suggestions from friends, colleagues, and mentors. In the project's initial stages, Jim Stimson balanced just the right amounts of encouragement and criticism. In addition to the detailed comments he provided, Jim helped me articulate how I could address some of the big questions that motivate the study of politics. In one or another of its iterations, the manuscript was read in its entirety by Frank Baumgartner, Joe Galaskiewicz, John Gastil, Virginia Gray, Bryan Jones, David Knoke, Peter May, Don McCrone, David Olson, Steve Smith, and Frank Sorauf. Each of these individuals offered extensive written remarks that uncovered problems in reasoning, suggested additional evidence that could be collected, pointed me to relevant scholarship, and proposed revisions to improve the manuscript's readability, breadth, and coherence. Perhaps most importantly, they pushed me to reflect upon the implications of the work for students of democratic processes, popular participation, and political power. Lance Bennett, Tony Gill, Jeff Hornstein, Larry Jacobs, and Mike Ward read parts of the manuscipt, and I am grateful for their help with substantive and methodological concerns. John Hammerback marked up the entire text in a Herculean effort at the final stage of the book's evolution. John's red pen removed awkward and bulky constructions, forced me to rethink ambiguities, improved the flow both within and across chapters, and breathed much-needed life into key sections.

Officials from the U.S. Chamber of Commerce were open and candid with information. They generously allowed interviews, supplied documents, and granted permission for me to rummage through file cabinets. Hagley Museum and Library, the depository for the Chamber's archives, provided quiet surroundings during my stay there. Marge McNitch was very helpful in locating the fugitive materials I needed for the research.

On the financial side and personal side, I benefited greatly from a dissertation fellowship from the Graduate School of the University of Minnesota. My colleagues at the Department of Political Science at the University of Washington have created a warm and productive intellectual atmosphere. I feel fortunate to be part of a department that wants junior faculty to succeed and works to see that happen. The University of Chicago Press has made the publication process as painless as possible, and for that I'm grateful. John Tryneski skillfully shepherded the manuscript through various hurdles, finding excellent reviewers and offering insightful suggestions of his own. I have revised and extended analyses from an earlier article in the *American Journal of Political Science*, "Public Opinion, Elections, and Representation with a Market Economy: Does the Structural Power of Business Undermine Popular Sovereignty?" vol. 43, no. 3 (July 1999), © 1999 by the University of Wisconsin Press. I thank the publisher for permission to reuse the material as well as the article's anonymous reviewers for their comments. I also thank Claire Rasmussen for her research assistance.

My wife, Kristen Hammerback, has played every role imaginable during the research and writing: best friend, reader, editor, supporter, challenger, and entertainer. She always listened to even my most underdeveloped ideas, helping to flesh out what I was trying to say. While my confidence in the project waxed and waned, hers never wavered. During critical phases, she selflessly put our joint life on hold and patiently waited for me to finish. Midway through the writing our daughter Julie was born, allowing me to achieve necessary emotional and physical distance from the manuscript. Julie unknowingly made intellectual contributions of her own, teaching valuable lessons about power, democracy, and the need for fathers as well as scholars to test presumptions against empirical evidence.

ONE
····

Introduction

By midafternoon on June 22, 1978, champagne was flowing freely. The tantalizing smell of success had permeated the air for weeks, and now it was official: Following six failed attempts to break a lengthy filibuster, the U.S. Senate banished to committee a bill to reform the nation's labor laws. This latest twist in the high-stakes drama effectively killed the bill, bringing jubilation to the captains of commerce and industry. The business community had waged a massive campaign, built around mobilizing companies within individual states, to defeat the proposed legislation. Judging by the Senate's action, these efforts might have made the difference. The president of one major business organization, basking in the afterglow of the decision, declared it a "resounding victory for the American people."

When the year began, it was organized labor, not business, who expected to be celebrating. Virtually the same bill had cleared the House of Representatives during the previous session of Congress, leaving Senate passage the last hurdle before it would reach President Jimmy Carter's desk. Presuming support from the Democratic majority in the Senate, the nation's unions were initially confident as they pushed for some long-awaited changes in the law. The last two major statutes in the area of labor-management relations, Landrum-Griffin in 1959 and Taft-Hartley in 1947, both favored employers. Unions saw the current bill as their best chance in a generation to reverse that trend.

Business groups had other plans. Each of the four most prominent organizations representing business—the U.S. Chamber of Commerce, Business Roundtable, National Association of Manufacturers, and National Federation of Independent Business—made defeating the bill a top priority. A large variety of other corporations, trade associations, and business groups joined the effort. Even firms that typically pay little attention to politics appeared to understand the gravity of the issues at stake, and many of these firms contacted senators from their states to denounce the bill. Labor unions conducted intense lobbying of their own, but in the end business reigned victorious. After the final vote to invoke cloture failed, the intensely debated proposal for labor-law reform vanished from national politics. The Senate has not reconsidered its decision in the succeeding decades.

The bill defeated in 1978, as originally reported by the Senate Human Resources Committee, included several distinct provisions, most of them relating to the process through which unions first organize a facility. Under the legislation, companies could have continued to use work time in campaigns to persuade employees to vote against unionization, but if they did they would be required to allow the union an equal opportunity, during the working day, to present its position. Supporters contended that the current system, in which employers had full access to workers during the day but union organizers had to solicit during off-hours, gave unfair advantages to management. Representation elections (the procedure allowing workers to formally choose whether to unionize) also would have changed under the legislation. The permissible time between the union filing its petition and the actual holding of the elections would have been limited statutorily, with the timetable varying according to the situation but in no case exceeding seventy-five days. Employers feared they would lack sufficient time to counter an organization drive under an expedited schedule (Levitan and Cooper 1984, 123–28).

Many employers reacted negatively to the new penalties in the bill. If the National Labor Relations Board (NLRB)—the federal agency responsible for resolving charges of unfair labor practices—found a company to have willfully violated labor laws, that company would be forbidden from receiving federal contracts for three years. For workers the NLRB had grounds to believe were fired because of pro-union organizing, the legislation would require the board to seek a court order to reinstate them. If the evidence subsequently cleared a higher standard, the workers could receive a maximum restitution of 150 percent of the wages lost during the intervening period. Finally, if the NLRB found an employer to have refused to bargain in good faith over the first contract with a new union, the workers would be awarded compensation based upon wage increases won by other unions (Levitan and Cooper 1984, 123–28).

The bill's provisions threatened a broad range of American firms, and a diverse group of companies—large and small, unionized and nonunionized—joined together in opposition. Rather than arousing interest from only a small number of corporations or a single industry, as most bills do, this one attracted considerable attention from the business community at large. When observers noted that *business* opposed the bill, they had in mind something approximating the universe of all American firms.

The unity with which business approached the issue was widely known and reported at the time (Donnelly 1978; Fritz 1978). This was not a case where individual firms and industries acted as autonomous units, each independently pursuing its own narrow concerns. Instead, a multitude of corporations, trade associations, and other business organizations took nearly identical positions. Scholarly accounts have pointed to this unity as the most important reason why the bill failed (Akard 1992, 607, 609; Levitan and Cooper 1984, 134–35). Because so many diverse firms and industries overcame their frequent political disagreements to collectively oppose the legislation, the argument runs, their unified efforts achieved success.

COMMON ASSUMPTIONS THAT UNITY LEADS TO STRENGTH

The prevalence of unity, then, may have greatly enhanced the capacity of business to block the bill to reform the nation's labor laws. Behind this particular claim lies the more general premise that when companies achieve solidarity, they become especially powerful in determining government policies. "United we stand, divided we fall" is both folk wisdom and a reasonable expectation about the operation of business power. If unity within business does translate into immense political power, then the prospects appear remote for ordinary citizens to affect what government does when business coalesces on a single position.

The logic behind such an ominous assumption was stated clearly by Dahl (1958, 465), who wrote that the "political effectiveness" of any group, meaning its ability to steer authoritative decisions in its favor despite resistance from other groups, depends upon its "potential for unity." Although Dahl's formulation could apply to all kinds of groups, the distinctiveness of business requires that scholars carefully scrutinize the ability of the nation's private companies to acquire power through solidarity. No other part of society can rival the organizational and financial resources at the disposal of business firms. If these resources are deployed in unison on behalf of collective ends desired by nearly all companies, then business might easily secure its political prizes and steamroller citizen demands. Useem (1984, 6) summarizes the argument nicely: When major corporations "are feuding and atomized, their political impact tends to be inconsistent, at times contradictory, and thus neutralized. When less divided and better organized for collective action, however, they can be very effective in finding and promoting their shared concerns."

Analogies to the realm of commerce make this assumption seem entirely reasonable. When corporations cooperate—or, to use the legal term, "collude"—in their commercial activities, the consequences are infamous: lessened competition, price increases, the stifling of innovation, and most importantly, higher profits. Since the late nineteenth and early twentieth centuries, when Populist and Progressive reformers such as President Theodore Roosevelt vowed to quash the trusts, antitrust policies have sought to prevent or dismantle such collusive agreements. U.S. laws, for example, forbid executives of competing corporations from discussing prices with each other. When the antitrust issue rose to national prominence many decades ago, most people realized that owners and managers who covertly coordinated their pricing and production benefited themselves at the expense of consumers.

It should be no surprise that scholarly observers have expected similar consequences if corporations cooperate in the political realm. Any possibility for a democracy responsive to the needs and wants of the general public would likely depend upon differences of interest that balance segments of business against each other. In the absence of these conflicts, the voice of the public could be substantially muted and its influence sharply restrained. For the cases where the policies collectively desired by business enterprises differ from those supported by the public, business preferences appear likely to prevail because of the overwhelming force generated when vast corporate resources are applied toward common ends. Certainly no one would expect unified business interests to win every battle and the mass public to be completely irrelevant, but the power of business should be extensive and the influence of ordinary citizens only marginal. If business is politically fragmented, however, the resources of its competing segments could offset each other and thus permit the political system to be more responsive to the preferences of the public.

The notion that American firms gain power by sharing political goals is the kind of intuitive assumption that seems to require no discussion—even in the typically skeptical world of academic research. Some scholars (Dahl 1958, 465; Levitan and Cooper 1984, 6; Useem 1984, 6, 9; Mizruchi 1992, 42) briefly state the assumption and then quickly proceed to develop themes based upon the unexamined first premise; others do not bother acknowledging that their arguments rest upon the unstated assumption. The syllogism that business unity produces business power and threatens representative democracy has achieved the status reserved for only the most widely held assumptions: It appears so self-evidently true that no one has seen the need to thoroughly examine it. The near-sacrosanct premise has even worked its way into the body of knowledge considered appropriate for introductory college courses on American Government, for textbooks often confidently assert that unity makes groups such as business more powerful.[1]

A long tradition of American political thought invites scholars to accept the unity-leads-to-strength assumption. From the earliest days of the nation's existence, political leaders worked to envision and create a representative democracy that would not be jeopardized by concentrations of power. Moved by the colonies' experiences with the English monarch and by philosophical arguments about dividing up authority, framers of the U.S. Constitution sought to reduce opportunities for consolidating power. Madison's famous answer, advanced in *The Federalist No. 10,* required extending the sphere of the republic to incorporate a large territorial space and a diverse society with many competing interests. Such an arrangement, he argued, would erect barriers to block the coalescence of a single faction that could usurp either majority or minority rights. By encouraging the formation of many different factions, the political system would prevent any one of them from overrunning the others.

After ratification in 1789, the Constitution permanently enshrined the American belief that power amassed in the hands of a few subverts democracy. The fear of concentrated power, whether in a monarch or a strong national government, prompted a constitutional design that diffused control over policy across several branches and levels of government. While the Constitution's solution satisfied the framers, unforeseen circumstances eventually intervened as the formerly agrarian society

1. See, for example, Gitelson, Dudley, and Dubnick (1998, 235); Wayne et al. (1997, 244–45).

evolved into an industrial one. Massive corporations came to dominate the economic landscape at the turn of the twentieth century, raising new concerns about concentrated power. This major transformation of the economy challenged many cherished American ideals, among them the very possibility of democracy. The emergence of trusts controlling single industries introduced the menacing danger that they might join together politically. Woodrow Wilson, writing in *The New Freedom* (1913), voiced the Progressive-era view that monopolies corrupt democratic government by amassing power sufficient to resist attempts to regulate them. Others joined his anxious call for political responses to this new threat to democracy.

Trepidation about power resting in any large and centralized institution remains embedded in the nation's core values to this day. Within American political discourse, one can invoke a jaundiced view of virtually any institution simply by labeling it "big." Americans retain deep-seated suspicions of big business, but they also respond negatively to images—whether accurate or not—of big labor and big government (Lipset and Schneider 1983). Given a choice between either centralized or decentralized structures of authority and decision-making, most Americans probably would choose the latter.

SCHOLARLY DEBATES OVER THE EXISTENCE OF BUSINESS UNITY

The fear that concentrated power undermines democracy, then, predates the American republic and comprises an enduring component of its political culture. A belief that business unity would beget business power represents a natural extension of this tradition. Hence a long-standing controversy in the social sciences has focused upon whether elites, or the owners and managers of business firms in particular, actually attain unity. Clawson, Neustadtl, and Weller (1998, 168) pinpoint the key matter of contention: "For at least the last thirty years, the central question in academic debates about business power has been whether or not business unifies to promote a common agenda."

To argue about whether unity exists presupposes that something important rests upon the answer. Scholars, trained to hesitate before venturing beyond the evidence at hand, sometimes refrain from discussing the broader significance of their work. The profound implications of research on the potential for unity, though, need only a small push to rise to the surface. Debates about whether or not, or the degree to which, firms coalesce around common political aspirations are really debates about the extent of business power and the opportunities for a properly functioning democracy. One would be hard-pressed to find a topic more deserving of careful examination.

Complicated though their answers may be, entrants to the controversy over unity gain guidance from their common starting point. An agenda for research follows naturally from broad consensus on the consequences unity would bring. If all observers agree, at least implicitly, that a popular democracy responsive to the citizenry would yield to substantial business control should unity materialize, then discussion can focus upon the second-order question of whether firms actually unify. That ensuing question has stimulated dueling points of view, each marked by seminal writings, perceptive discoveries, and distinguished adherents.

The contestants in the decades-long debate over unity are well known. Pluralists have argued that groups and elites, including business firms, do not form a cohesive whole. On matters resolved through politics, segments of business routinely oppose each other (see especially Truman 1951, 251, 256; Epstein 1969, 226–28, 239–41; Berle 1963, 13; Rose 1967). Part of the pluralist perspective rests on the idea that social and economic groups other than business wield countervailing power, but one of the primary tenets points to dissension within the business ranks. Pluralists avert concerns regarding the consequences of unity by claiming that it never arises in the first place. If firms do not exhibit solidarity in practice, we need not worry about the hypothetical likelihood that unity would lead to business power so strong as to subvert representative democracy. Paralleling the American founders' belief that dividing government authority through constitutional design would check concentrations of power, pluralists see economic competition among firms and industries producing similar restraint.

The pluralist position has been countered by elite and class theorists, whose viewpoints merge in the argument that business approaches politics as a collective. Before business enters politics, any preexisting conflicts between firms are resolved through myriad social, political, and economic relationships (see especially Mills 1956, 18–20, 62–68, 120–25; Miliband 1969; Domhoff 1978, 61–127; Domhoff 1983, 24–37). Recent work has sought to specify more precisely the mechanisms and conditions through which agreement among firms is or is not achieved (Mizruchi 1992; Prechel 1990; Akard 1992). If widespread consensus prevails, either most of the time or under certain circumstances, then it appears that business becomes extremely powerful and the outlook for representative democracy becomes bleak. By advancing a claim about interfirm alliances that contrasts with the pluralist notion of conflicting preferences, elite and class theorists reach a vastly different conclusion about whether business can peacefully coexist with democracy.

THE APPROACH TAKEN HERE

Despite the extensive research and intricate argument this debate has spawned, there has been no sustained investigation of the premise underlying concerns about unity. Scholars disputing the actual level of agreement among firms are nevertheless guided by the same assumption that widespread unity, should it emerge, leads to increased corporate power and a diminished capacity for average citizens to affect policies. I will argue that this assumption completely misses the mark. That is, unity does not increase the direct influence of business and reduce democratic control by the citizenry. Instead, unity coincides with the opposite results. Issues marked by a common business position are precisely those for which government decisions are affected most strongly by election outcomes and the responsiveness of officeholders to their constituents. Policies match the collective desires of business only when citizens, through their policy preferences and voting choices, embrace ideas and candidates supportive of what business wants. To bolster its odds of winning in politics, business needs to seek backing from the broader public.

My assessment of the ways business, when unified, does and does not influence policies will strike many readers as surprising and controversial. To support my argument, I will devote several chapters to developing its theoretical foundations and corroborating it with empirical evidence. Throughout the book I focus upon the lawmaking process, where Congress and the president, building upon proposals originating in legislative committees or in executive branch departments, determine the framework for national policy. Given that the study strives to understand how the practice of democracy—rule by the people— operates when business unifies, it makes sense to examine the decisions collectively reached by incumbent officials who must win public support during elections. The legislative process represents the forum where elections have the greatest opportunity to ensure that policy reflects the public's values and preferences.

Lawmaking also provides an appropriate focus for my investigation because business is so keenly attentive to it. Raising revenues through taxation, which the legislature and chief executive must undertake to pay for the programs they oversee, affects profit margins. Regulatory legislation legitimizes some kinds of corporate behavior while outlawing others, inevitably drawing business into lawmakers' orbits. Federal social welfare programs, which alter employers' relationships with their employees, are authorized and financed by congressional statutes. Because of its obvious importance to profit-seeking companies, lawmaking presents an attractive venue for exploring the workings of representative democracy when firms achieve unity.

I begin the investigation in chapter 2 by presenting a set of theoretical reasons why public opinion and election outcomes might influence federal policymaking. That influence is especially pronounced, I argue, when an issue elicits a unified position from private enterprise. Issues generating a consensus within business tend to be politicized, meaning that they are ideological, partisan, and highly salient among the public. As a result, those issues provide officeholders with incentives to respond to constituent preferences and also heighten the consequences of elections. Disputing conventional wisdom, I claim that when unified, business possesses only modest direct leverage over policymaking.

The unity-leads-to-strength premise that I challenge implies a set of contrary predictions. When business unifies, according to this premise, legislative decisions will reflect such business actions as lobbying, the temporary service of corporate leaders in government, contributions to political campaigns, and participation in policy discussion groups where favorable ideas are developed. Moreover, the preferences, beliefs, and values of ordinary citizens will have little impact upon the authoritative decisions reached by government officials.

To uncover evidence that could substantiate or refute my central thesis, I first identify a set of issues marked by a high degree of business unity. Chapter 3 seeks to isolate the full universe of federal legislative debates over the last few decades that were characterized by substantial unity. My intention is to conduct a study whose findings will have a high degree of generalizability by applying to all of American national politics for a long time span and in a large number of distinct policy domains. In chapter 4, I show that issues generating unity among firms tend to have specific attributes that increase the public's influence on lawmaking and decrease the chances for business to dictate policy decisions.

After developing annual indicators of the favorability of lawmaking to business, I begin the empirical analysis in chapter 5. Subjecting my expectations to a systematic test, I attempt to determine what can best explain the patterns of legislation on unifying issues. The findings match my predictions: Public opinion and election outcomes strongly determine the likelihood that business preferences prevail during the legislative process. A theoretical position claiming that business unity leads to a politics run by elites, whereby ordinary citizens merely stand on the sidelines, appears difficult to reconcile with this evidence.

I address business influence that arises through overt means, a form of direct power, in chapter 6. Using my explanatory model featuring public opinion and election outcomes, I add several avenues for firms to affect policymaking directly through actions such as joining businesswide associations and making campaign contributions to candidates and parties. The results indicate that the overt mechanisms of power are only mildly successful. After these additions to the model, public opinion and election outcomes stand as the most important determinants of whether business sees its preferences furthered or hindered in the political arena.

Chapter 7 incorporates into the analysis the possibility that elected officials' needs to facilitate private investment critically constrain their range of decisions. These economic imperatives, defined here as a form of business power that could directly affect policymaking, would bias legislative decisions toward the policies endorsed by business and away from those it opposes. Such a process would impede the capacity for public opinion and election outcomes to affect policy choices. I analyze and evaluate these expectations, finding them to be inaccurate.

My argument, then, is that rather than being undermined by business unity, representative democracy becomes most responsive to citizen preferences and least vulnerable to dominance by business interests when firms agree on their preferred policies. While large enough to be observable in many cases, I contend, the direct power of business is not the main cause of policy decisions. The reasons unified business positions either win or lose are traceable not to any kind of direct leverage that business exerts, but rather result most importantly from the impacts of public opinion and election outcomes. Instead of instigating the most dire prospects for popular democracy, business unity coincides with the best opportunities for citizens to make a real difference for policymaking. The channels of representation that connect citizens to government provide the American public with the means to guide congressional and presidential lawmaking.

Based upon the findings of this study, the most effective political strategy for a unified business community involves influencing public opinion. By doing so successfully, business could achieve favorable policies by relying upon the linkages between constituent preferences and officeholders' decisions, without the need for direct influence upon elected officials. This form of power is indirect because business works through the citizenry rather than going straight to policymakers. To illustrate how business might indirectly influence policymaking, in chapter 8 I propose a mechanism for business to shape public beliefs on the critical question of the appropriate size and scope of government. The evidence suggests that in the last two decades, corporate America has helped cause, at least to some extent, changes in public desires regarding what government should and should not do. I conclude by arguing that during instances when business realizes internal unity, its most effective influence arises not through any direct impact upon elected officials, but rather through its capacity to shape public opinion.

TWO

Business Unity and Its Consequences for Representative Democracy

If unity leads to strength, establishing the universal presence or absence of business-wide agreement would produce far-reaching implications for questions of power and the promise of democracy. Showing that business creates a broad alliance would seem to jeopardize our intuitive conception of a working democracy, while demonstrating the presence of divisions within business would allow the possibility that democracy could be achieved in practice. This seemingly obvious payoff invites investigators to envision a single alignment of preferences that encompasses the most important issues and extends over time.

Accordingly, scholars have usually embraced one—and only one—of three competing perspectives, of which two see unity failing to arise while the other posits the prevalence of widespread unity. This chapter describes each perspective and the attendant category of issues it proposes. There are solid grounds to believe that each kind of issue embodies distinctive characteristics that determine the process through which legislative decisions are reached. By considering the political forces affecting congressional and presidential action within the categories, I will explain why issues that unify business show a dynamic contrary to what social scientists have assumed.

A TYPOLOGY OF POLICY ALIGNMENTS AMONG FIRMS

The first of the perspectives views issues as largely *particularistic,* meaning that small subgroups of companies or industries pursue their own specific interests without involving the rest of American business. In the limiting case, only one firm enters a policy debate. This viewpoint is developed in the school of thought traceable most notably to Cater

(1964), McConnell (1966), and Lowi (1979) that contends that policymaking occurs within insulated arenas. These institutional settings, often called "subsystems," "subgovernments," or "iron triangles," serve as forums where a limited number of private- and public-sector actors cooperate to reach mutually beneficial decisions. The interest groups that participate exert significant influence on the issues most important to them.

For the role of business in politics, these factors mean that policy issues usually evoke concern from just a few firms or from only one industry. Home builders, for example, intervene in decisions regarding housing policy, while utilities become key players in the regulation of electricity prices. If American business truly is characterized most prominently by the pursuit of narrow interests, then each segment of business expends political resources on matters of special concern to it. The diversity of particularistic issues means that firms and industries normally do not oppose each other, but neither do they join forces to benefit business as a whole.

The second perspective emphasizes tensions within the business community, claiming that issues are primarily *conflictual*. Two distinct groups of scholars each assert systematic divisions among firms. Pluralists (Truman 1951; Rose 1967; Epstein 1969; Dahl 1961) claim that firms and industries routinely find their interests to be divergent. During virtually any political struggle, one can identify segments of business on all sides. Trucking and railroad companies disagree on transportation policy, for example, while importers battle exporters over tariffs. Pluralists reason that the conflicts among firms, when combined with American institutional arrangements such as the separation of powers and the diffusion of policy authority across the local, state, and federal levels, produce multiple power-centers that no single group can dominate simultaneously.

Relative autonomy neo-Marxists (Poulantzas 1973; Offe 1984) offer a proposition similar to the pluralist notion of conflicts within business, but they base that claim on a different line of logic. These scholars maintain that firms are too narrow-minded to cooperate on behalf of their common interests. While the collective needs of private companies might seem to induce cooperation, conflicts arise because of differing profit rates across factions of capital. Policies facilitating profit-making in one sector may introduce impediments in others, causing individual firms and sectors to oppose each other in politics. Only the state, which maintains autonomy from the day-to-day pressures brought by parochial segments of capital, can rationalize and uphold the capitalist system.

Within the third perspective on the level of agreement among firms, policy debates are *unifying* because business advances a single position on important issues. Power elite theorists (Mills 1956; Prewitt and Stone 1973; Dye 1995) portray leaders of major institutions as holding a common worldview that leads to unity among corporations. On issues ranging from foreign policy to social welfare programs to taxation, business enters politics as a cohesive force. Disputing the pluralist contention that power is diffuse, elite theorists find power to be concentrated in few hands. While the composition of the power elite varies somewhat within different formulations of the thesis, the owners and managers of large corporations always constitute a central element. These individuals, by virtue of their organizational positions, wield momentous influence over public policy.

Ruling-class theorists (Domhoff 1967, 1978, 1983) and instrumental Marxists (Miliband 1969) also posit the existence of unity among private companies. They differ from elite theorists by giving more attention to class structure and economic interests in creating a unified business outlook. On a deeper level, all of the scholars finding issues to be unifying agree that consensus within business does not represent the natural state of affairs, but rather arises through identifiable means. That is, firms often begin with divided loyalties, but a variety of institutions and processes integrate business views into a coherent whole. Mechanisms posited to promote unity include corporate leaders' common social origins, experiences, and intermarriage (Miliband 1969; Domhoff 1983), organizations that contemplate the long-term interests of business (Peschek 1987; Domhoff 1978), commercial banks centrally located within corporate networks (Mintz and Schwartz 1985), overlapping boards of directors (Useem 1984; Mizruchi 1992), and equity-holding by institutions and by one company in another (Mintz and Schwartz 1987).

The three perspectives lead respectively to three distinct possibilities for the political behavior of business: Firms either promote a narrow conception of self-interest, battle each other openly, or band together to pursue collective goals. Depending upon the positions of various companies and industries, issues are particularistic, conflictual, or unifying.[1]

1. Although my three-point classification system overlaps Lowi's (1964) typology of distributive, regulatory, and redistributive issues, the two frameworks differ in important ways. While Lowi's labels correspond in part to the divisibility of policy

Within each category issues need not share any qualities beyond the pattern of interfirm alignments. Unifying issues, for example, are simply those on which diverse firms and industries can stand together. The motivation for such an uncomplicated scheme derives from the book's theoretical underpinnings. Because concerns about the consequences of business unity are not limited to issues with any specific content, I construct a policy type as broad as the concept of interest.

THE COEXISTENCE OF PARTICULARISTIC, CONFLICTUAL, AND UNIFYING ISSUES

Social scientists often perceive only one of the three categories, implicitly assuming or explicitly claiming that other kinds of issues are either rare or trivial. It is apparent, however, that one can identify actual legislative debates fitting into each category. Clearly, there are instances when narrow segments of business pursue influence on the particularistic issues most important to them (Browne 1988; Engler 1961). Similarly, one can point to cases characterized by either conflicts (Bauer, Pool, and Dexter 1963; Cox 1996) or unity (Whitt 1982) among firms.

The abundant examples of diverse alignments of preferences have led some scholars to abandon monolithic descriptions of political issues. Lowi (1964) made the first call for recognizing multiple patterns by presenting a policy typology similar to the one offered here. Heinz et al. (1993) uncovered a variety of business configurations across the agriculture, energy, health, and labor domains, while Mizruchi's (1992) investigation of testimony before Congress found variation in the overlap between the positions of leading corporations. Baumgartner and Jones (1993), by showing that particularistic policy subsystems can persist for decades only to be completely reconstituted when new actors and understandings intrude, demonstrated that even the same issue can produce different alignments over time.

Given these empirical realities, forcing all policy debates into only one of the three categories produces a distorted portrait of American

---

outputs, mine simply indicate the nature of business alliances and divisions. As a result, policies with quite different substantive content fit into the same category within my framework. For example, besides issues regarded as class-based, many others not often understood to be "redistributive," such as consumer protection and similar policies commonly called "regulatory," fall into my unifying category. Similarly, particularistic issues are not restricted to the kinds of taxation and spending policies that Lowi calls "distributive."

politics. All three types of issues exist, sometimes even simultaneously. For example, the Texaco Corporation might seek a tax break for itself, join a battle waged between fellow fossil-fuel extractors and renewable energy producers, and contribute to a business-wide effort to reform product liability laws, all at the same time. Similarly, diverse companies share desires for lower marginal tax rates even as they divide on more specific provisions of the tax code such as exemptions for various kinds of capital.

The coexistence of all three kinds of issues does not imply, though, that they occur in equal proportions. Indeed, the evidence presented in chapter 4 will show that unifying issues occur only rarely. It is well known that the business community in the United States, on the whole, is fragmented in comparison to other industrialized countries (Vogel 1978; Wilson 1990). Noting that American firms develop a consensus only infrequently, however, is quite different than saying that they never combine forces (Vogel 1989).

As Lowi (1964) suggests, the theoretical lens one employs to explain policy outcomes should depend upon the category of issues being examined. The pluralist perspective, for example, could help us understand the resolution of conflictual issues, but it is unlikely to offer similar insights into particularistic issues. Likewise, policymaking on particularistic issues within an insulated and obscure subsystem calls for a different explanatory approach than decisions on unifying issues that engage congressional leaders and the president, attract the news media, and involve the business community mobilized behind a single position. Reflecting my interest in the tension between popular sovereignty and business power when firms attain unity, I devote most of my attention to unifying issues. To explore the joint political influence of all American companies, one has to examine those cases for which it is meaningful to speak of business as a collective. Focusing upon unifying issues, though, does not require denying the existence of particularistic and conflictual ones.

THE ORIGINS OF BUSINESS UNITY

When studying the conditions that might make an issue unifying, researchers have uncovered several possible factors. Prechel (1990) and Akard (1992) emphasize that unified policy preferences develop when firms experience a common economic threat to profits. Periods of economic decline facilitate business unity, while upturns in the economy

eliminate the common threat and therefore lead to fragmented preferences. Other scholars point to social and political relationships among
firms that encourage the congealing of preferences. These mechanisms include overlapping corporate boards (Useem 1984; Mizruchi
1992), common social experiences of corporate executives (Mills 1956;
Domhoff 1983), and commercial banks acting as intermediaries (Mintz
and Schwartz 1985). Cathie Martin (1995) offers convincing evidence
that interfirm policy networks within the health care domain, through
which managers gain access to broader political ideas through Washington offices and discussion groups, help to build consensus.

With the exception of interfirm policy networks, these factors do
not change across issues. At any given moment, the overall state of the
economy is a constant. Similarly, interlocking directorates and the social
connections between executives could vary across companies or over
time, but they do not vary across issues. For this reason, these forces
cannot explain why, during the same period, oil depletion allowances,
telecommunications reform, and consumer protection might attract
three different alignments—particularistic, conflictual, and unifying,
respectively. Economic conditions and social relationships among firms
might predispose business toward unity, but they cannot comprise a
complete explanation.

An alternative explanation embraced by scholars such as Levitan and
Cooper (1984) and Vogel (1989), which emphasizes attributes specific
to each issue, offers the most fruitful approach for my purposes. To
discover whether businesses will unify on a policy proposal, one should
examine the consequences the proposal would produce and its impact
on various firms. Issues differ on those attributes, which helps explain
why at any point in time some issues attract a business-wide position
while others do not.

The incidence of a policy's benefits and costs across firms helps
determine whether it becomes unifying. A policy proposal must affect a
variety of companies in similar ways, either positively or negatively, to
elicit a unified business position. Policies meeting that criterion normally
alter the overall degree of government involvement in the marketplace.
If a policy proposal would noticeably change government capacity
to manage the economy, it may affect many different companies in
comparable ways and hence spark unity. Policies that do not alter
government authority in a systematic way probably will not register
similar impacts throughout the business world. As a result, those policies
usually will generate particularistic or conflictual alignments.

A policy's benefits and costs across firms frequently are readily apparent. Consider a typical particularistic issue benefiting a single industry, such as whether agribusiness should receive subsidies to produce ethanol. Regardless of how it might be resolved, the issue does not materially affect the reach of government and therefore is irrelevant to the vast majority of companies. No matter what networks or institutions potentially could promote extensive unity, it is extremely difficult to motivate unaffected firms to join together with agribusiness and hence make the issue unifying.

By way of comparison, a bill to increase regulation of product warranties would strengthen government's presence in the economy, a change that would impose compliance costs upon many different manufacturers and service providers. In this case a high degree of unity follows directly from the nature of the issue under consideration. One can easily identify other policy proposals that fit a similar pattern; for example when single-industry regulation of prices and entry yielded in the 1970s to multi-industry regulation of pollution, workplace safety, and hiring practices, the number of unifying issues therefore rose as well. Unity across additional issues resulted from the simple fact that the new style of regulation altered the scope of government and affected many different companies in similar ways.

The objective interests of the business community, though, are not always so obvious. Throughout the twentieth century the U.S. business community has embraced the principle of limited government (Sutton et al. 1956; Krooss 1970), but such an outcome was by no means assured. Historical circumstances were important in that the American corporation matured before the American state (Vogel 1978). In industrialized nations that developed under different conditions, business leaders tolerate and even desire stronger government oversight of the marketplace than do their American counterparts (Wilson 1990).

While the politically conservative views that exemplify the American business community were not preordained, they nevertheless have emerged and endured. Issues important to a small number of firms or industries, which usually only marginally affect the overall capacity of government, typically produce a particularistic or conflictual policy alignment. Reflecting the evolution of political ideology within business, issues affecting the federal government's authority across a range of industries attract a high degree of unity. When the size and scope of government is at stake, business frequently unifies.

WHY POPULAR SOVEREIGNTY IS HARMONIOUS WITH BUSINESS UNITY

The typology of particularistic, conflictual, and unifying issues provides a means of classifying all policy debates attracting attention from one or more segments of business. As more than just an organizing device, though, the typology leads to otherwise hidden insights. Once the three kinds of issues are recognized as distinct, their characteristics can be studied and compared. If the characteristics of each kind of issue vary, the forces affecting the corresponding legislative decisions will likely vary as well. That is, particularistic issues probably involve a different range of actors, institutions, and decision-making procedures than conflictual issues, which in turn follow different processes than unifying issues. By encouraging investigation of these processes, the typology can facilitate an understanding of whether popular sovereignty is compatible with business unity.

Proceeding without the benefit of the typology, the pluralist, elitist, and ruling class theories assume that highly undesirable consequences ensue when firms enter politics as a cohesive bloc. Each theory presumes that a unified business alliance will normally achieve its political goals, thereby weakening the impacts of the public's voice. Unifying issues, then, are expected by prevailing theories to pose the strongest threats to popular sovereignty. I will advance and defend the antithetical claim that unity among firms corresponds with the best, rather than the worst, conditions for citizens to affect what government does. While implausible upon first glance, this contention gains credence when we examine the attributes of the issues comprising the typology. Three attributes of issues—their ideological, partisan, and salient nature—stand out for their importance in determining how legislative decision-making progresses. By comparison to particularistic and conflictual issues, unifying ones are far more likely to possess these attributes. That likelihood creates major consequences for the power of business and the linkage between public preferences and legislative action.

UNIFYING ISSUES ARE IDEOLOGICAL

One of the defining characteristics of unifying issues is that they blend into prominent ideological fault lines. Within the United States, the ideologies of modern liberalism and modern conservatism offer competing perspectives on the proper responsibilities of government. These broad orientations structure the thinking and behavior of officeholders, political activists, and electorates. Since the New Deal, liberalism and conservatism have split sharply on the appropriate role of the federal government and the desired level of spending. These ideologies supply a means to determine whether federal agencies should regulate more or less, whether the welfare state should expand or contract, and whether or not labor laws should strengthen the bargaining leverage of workers. Those are precisely the sorts of issues that evoke unity among firms. For this reason, unifying issues are highly ideological and fit cleanly into the liberal-conservative dimension of political struggles.

Particularistic and conflictual issues, however, frequently cannot be neatly mapped onto the ideological spectrum of left and right. One is unlikely to find an ideological rationale for why a narrow economic interest should be either advantaged or disadvantaged through public policy. The program though which the U.S. Forest Service subsidizes the timber industry by building roads in national forests, for instance, embodies no clear ideological thrust. Nor can the broad themes within liberal and conservative belief systems easily apply to disputes internal to business. When deciding conflictual issues, such as the extent to which commercial and investment banks may impinge upon each other's traditional territory, elected officials often cannot gain much guidance from their ideological convictions.

Why does it matter that unifying issues tend to be ideological? This ideological character means that House members, senators, and presidents possess the ability to assess and respond to public opinion. If officeholders want to determine majority preferences within the elec-torate that brought them to power, they can construct an interpretation using available information about the overall ideological sentiment in the constituency. While few individuals maintain integrated belief systems (Converse 1964), aggregates behave quite differently. At the level of districts, states, or the nation, ideology can be clearly identified and measured (Erikson, Wright, and McIver 1993; Stimson 1999). Aggregate ideological dispositions vary meaningfully not only across geographic units, but also over time within those units and over time within the nation as a whole. No one doubts, for example, that Alabama is more conservative than Massachusetts or that the nation was more conservative in 1955 than in 1965.

It is this ideology within electorates, rather than the ideology within isolated individuals, that matters most to politicians. Every elected official knows whether the constituency she represents is generally liberal, moderate, or conservative. That datum adorns readily available

reference works like the *Almanac of American Politics* that seem ubiquitous in the offices of politicians, lobbyists, and political consultants.
When a policy choice must be made on an ideological issue, elected
officials often already sense or know the majority sentiment within their
constituencies.

For example, suppose a senator must vote on a unifying issue, such
as a budget package that raises corporate taxes and increases spending
on social programs. Even without any specific information regarding
constituents' views on this particular piece of legislation, the senator
knows whether she represents a liberal state or a conservative one. She
can use that knowledge to estimate the most common position voters
would take if they possessed sufficient information about the package
at hand. If the senator so chooses, she can incorporate this estimation
of majority opinion into her own decision on the matter.

Evidence indicates that the ideological views of constituencies do,
in fact, influence how representatives in Congress behave. When one
measures and compares on a left-right scale the ideological positioning
of members of the House of Representatives and the citizenry in their
districts, one finds a very high correspondence between them (Erikson
and Wright 1997; Brady et al. 1999). Conservative districts have representatives who vote conservatively in office, while the reverse is true for
liberal districts. These findings are at once both obvious, in that most
people would have expected them, and highly consequential, for they
establish a clear link between citizens and government. Of course, this
process of incorporating popular sentiment only works to the extent that
a policy choice can be easily understood in ideological terms—which
is frequently the case when unifying issues are on the table.

Using information on the constituency's ideological tendencies becomes more difficult if the senator must vote on particularistic or conflictual bills, for those bills often do not fit into liberal and conservative
belief systems. To determine what constituents want, elected officials
frequently must rely only on information specific to the policy being considered. This information may be costly to collect, unreliable, or perhaps
even nonexistent. For the unifying issues that invoke ideological themes,
though, they can use specific information about the legislation and also
general information about the constituency's ideology. The availability
of both kinds of information should increase elected officials' accuracy
when they estimate majority sentiment. That accuracy translates into
greater opportunities for public viewpoints to guide decision-making.

When an issue is ideological, politicians in Congress and the White

House also can benefit from knowing something about national opinion, particularly changes in it. If opinion throughout the country shifts
in a certain ideological direction, then most likely opinion is moving
in the same direction within individual districts and states. Through
a variety of sources, including dialogue with their colleagues and staff,
reports in the news media, and a perusal of polling data, elected officials
can determine whether the country's "mood" is becoming more liberal
or conservative (Stimson, Erikson, and MacKuen 1995). In the late
1970s, officeholders hardly needed to look beyond the successful ballot
initiative to roll back property taxes in California to grasp the conservative changes among the electorate. During the previous decade, as
President Lyndon Johnson laid the foundation for the Great Society,
expansions of federal authority seemed much more likely to meet public
approval. When broad shifts occur in the ideological sentiment of the
population, politicians can—if they so desire—alter policies in a corresponding manner. Some especially strong incentives, discussed later in
the chapter, should make that possibility a reality for unifying issues.

UNIFYING ISSUES ARE PARTISAN

In representative democracies, political parties serve as a central linkage
mechanism connecting citizens to government. Parties are unparalleled
by other organizations in their ability to mobilize voters, sponsor candidates for election, and raise issues for public discussion. Within the
United States, the two major parties focus more on winning elections
than on upholding coherent policy stands. In keeping with that motivation, the Democratic and Republican parties each incorporate a diversity of viewpoints—a diversity that often results in their advancement of
indistinguishable positions (Page 1978). In addition, neither party can
dictate the behavior of officeholders who win elections by running under
the party's label. House members, senators, and presidents all desert
their parties at times to embrace positions the other party typically
champions.

One must be careful not to push these generalizations too far. Recognizing that the two major parties embrace internal diversity does
not mean that they are interchangeable. Although officeholders do
not maintain complete party loyalty, it does not follow that partisan
affiliations bear no relationship to lawmaking. Understanding when
political parties will instigate a redirection in policy requires determining when they will offer distinctive programs and maintain relatively
high discipline.

Distinguishable programs and high discipline happen most frequently when the issue in question includes ideological concepts, thereby tapping into splits between the contemporary Democratic and Republican parties. By being more likely than particularistic and conflictual matters to stir ideological passions, unifying issues show a greater tendency to be partisan. For example, debates over regulatory and social welfare programs, which frequently attract a unified business position, also demarcate much of the New Deal legacy that has separated the parties (Ladd and Hadley 1975). Decisions over the total amount of taxes and spending, which often unify business in favor of lower levels, have incited divisions between the parties in the last few decades.

On particularistic and conflictual issues, however, the Democratic and Republican parties' positions often blend together. No one was surprised when the parties did not offer coherent alternatives during a particularistic debate in 1959 to provide federal assistance for constructing commercial fishing vessels. Likewise, a 1990 proposal to require cable television systems to carry local broadcast stations may have caused cable companies to battle the major networks, but the Democratic and Republican parties did not diverge on the matter. When officeholders consider particularistic and conflictual issues, strong divisions between the parties are uncommon.

In contemporary usage, the word "partisan" often carries negative connotations. Reflecting Americans' long-standing unease with organizing politics through parties, elected officials who behave according to their partisanship are often perceived to be blindly following the party line. Such a view overlooks the positive consequences that result when political parties present clear alternatives to the electorate. Individual candidates, who often run campaigns that emphasize their résumés or personal qualities more than their stands on issues, normally cannot achieve a level of clarity on policy matters comparable to that of parties. Without parties staking out positions, it becomes more difficult for citizens to use their votes to systematically alter the course of government policy.

Whether elections bringing new parties into office will actually change policy, then, depends upon the issue in question. Partisan turnover in governing institutions likely will not produce new policy directions on particularistic and conflictual matters for which the parties do not offer the electorate alternative programs. However, elections modifying the partisan balance in Congress and the presidency will critically affect areas, such at those marked by business unity, that separate the parties.[2] The strength of each party helps determine whether business will win or lose on unifying issues. Higher numbers of Republicans in office will lead to more legislative victories for business at large, while the election of more Democrats will instigate more of the policies business opposes.

Consider, to take one example, the congressional elections of 1994. Republicans seized simultaneous majorities in both chambers of Congress for the first time in four decades. The election probably prompted few systematic policy shifts on nonpartisan issues, among which particularistic and conflictual issues were disproportionately represented. After the election, the greatest changes occurred on questions that had divided the parties for decades (Gimpel 1996). Topics such as taxation, the generosity of social welfare programs, and the scope of federal regulation rose to the top of the congressional agenda. In each case, the average Republican position fell considerably to the right of the average Democratic position. Most importantly for the argument advanced here, the policy changes surfaced on the kinds of issues that frequently unify a diverse array of firms. For this reason, the 1994 elections appear to have affected the political fortunes of business as a collective.

This result does not imply that the Democratic Party is antibusiness—it would be inconceivable for a competitive party to be "against" any large segment of society, whether it be business, labor, or religion. Rather, the policy changes that follow important elections simply indicate that the Republican Party more often advocates ideas corresponding to what business wants. That core difference between the parties heightens the impact of the ballot box. Through their choices during elections, voters affect the likelihood that unified business interests will later prevail in public policy.

UNIFYING ISSUES ARE SALIENT

Besides being ideological and partisan, unifying issues frequently register high salience among the public. In part, unifying issues become salient because they already possess the other two characteristics. Contending ideological divisions on a policy matter, which reduce the complexities that excite experts into more easily understood elements,

2. In addition to distinguishing themselves from the competition, parties also can promote new policies by converging at the median voter (Downs 1957). While both parties often do move toward the middle, for unifying issues the more common route to policy change occurs because the parties present distinctive programs.

clarify the issue's relation to prominent belief systems. By underscoring recognizable themes, discussion on unifying issues among officeholders, policy experts, and interest groups can attract people's attention. When ordinary citizens see how an issue connects to their fundamental values, they become more interested in the outcome.

In a manner similar to ideological divisions, partisan cleavages also create substantial visibility for unifying issues. Campaigns often highlight the questions that separate the parties, disseminating information on those questions to the public. During the legislative process, Democratic and Republican officeholders normally debate the issues that divide them rather than those for which party differences are negligible. This leads to ideological and partisan discussion in the halls of Congress and the White House, in television newscasts and daily newspapers, and within some friendship circles, families, and workplaces. Reflecting their ideological and partisan nature, issues linked to a common business preference become widely visible to the public.

Other factors also add to the salience of unifying issues. When a policy proposal attracts the same position from many different firms, it probably addresses questions of national importance that arouse other parts of society as well. Unions, citizen groups, and nonprofit organizations frequently advocate positions at odds with business interests when lawmakers consider initiatives in the labor or social welfare domains. Environmental and consumer groups often oppose the collective business position on regulatory policies. These competing interest groups, often organized into a broad-based coalition, counter at least some of the pressure brought by business. Pluralist theory has often been interpreted as implying that opposing groups bring truly neutralizing pressure; that notion has long since been discredited, and rightly so. In its place a different understanding, that countermobilization changes the balance of forces but does not equalize them, has gained adherents (McFarland 1992).

Interest group participation on multiple sides of an issue, particularly when business stands opposed by a coalition of other groups, leads to another consequence as well. By stimulating diverse groups to become involved, unifying issues entice journalists seeking interesting stories. Issues that engage broad segments of society can meet the criterion of newsworthiness (Gans 1979), and the dramatic battles that often accompany those issues elicit additional attention from the mass media. Media coverage spurs public visibility for the issues themselves and for policymakers' responses. The volume of news stories on proposals for

Social Security reform in 1983, to take one prominent case, raised public awareness of the problem addressed and the solutions considered. This was a unifying issue, as the business community largely supported the eventual package enacted into law (Light 1985).

A final way unifying issues become salient is through the institutional venues that resolve them. When a wide cross-section of firms expresses common preferences, the matter usually cannot be decided within insulated policy subsystems. Maintaining a subsystem requires an issue perceived to be narrow and of concern to few political actors. If those qualities exist, the institutional setting for decision-making affords little involvement by the public or even by congressional leaders and the president (Baumgartner and Jones 1993). When an issue draws interest from the business community at large, though, many actors participate in the policy process. Because of the sizable stakes, the intervention of a variety of groups, and ideological and partisan divisions, the debates over what course of action to take attract congressional leaders, the political parties, and the president. Both corresponding to and resulting from the concern they command from the most prominent government officials, unifying issues spark attention from the broader public.[3]

Why does it matter that policy disputes marked by business unity tend to be highly salient among the public? Salience is critical for two reasons. First, when issues become visible, people gain the information necessary to form preferences. Second, salience creates incentives for elected officials to respond to those preferences. Working in conjunction with each other, these two reasons strengthen the ability of citizens to shape legislative policies.

The first consequence of salience, the dissemination of information people need to form preferences, has been emphasized by theorists ranging from Mill (1859) to Arendt (1965) to Zaller (1992). Collective deliberation results in alternative perspectives on the underlying problem, the principles involved, and the appropriate government response. By joining this dialogue at work, at home, or in a variety of social groups, some people will determine their own preferences. Even inactive participation, achieved when citizens are merely present in those settings or when they receive and assimilate political information through the news media, allows some citizens to connect their existing values to the issue at hand (Page 1996).

3. Under the right circumstances, particularistic issues can reach high salience as well (Baumgartner and Jones 1993; Arnold 1990), but this is usually more likely for unifying issues.

Without opportunities for deliberation and learning, public opinion either does not exist or exhibits considerable ambiguity. Under these conditions, public opinion can offer only imprecise guidance for political leaders. Elected officials, after all, cannot respond to unformed opinions; at best, they can attempt to anticipate the opinions that would develop if citizens learned about the matter. Such a pattern is common among low-profile particularistic and conflictual issues. By contrast, the broad discussion frequently achieved on unifying issues creates and disseminates the information necessary for many citizens to determine their preferences. In addition, as argued earlier, the ideological nature of unifying issues lowers the information barrier because elected officials can infer opinions on the topic in question from the public's overall ideological tendencies. As a result, when making decisions on a unifying issue lawmakers can, if they so choose, accurately represent public views.

As its second consequence, salience creates electoral incentives that bring this possibility to fruition, leading lawmakers to pay careful attention to public opinion. To hold elected officials accountable for their actions, constituents need information about what those officials are doing. Through the discussion and debate on unifying issues, citizens can learn about their representatives' behavior, a possibility that officeholders consistently recognize. When an issue is currently salient, or potentially could become salient during the next election through the publicity activated by challengers or interest groups, incumbent politicians face incentives to anticipate and respond to public opinion (Arnold 1990). Risk-averse officeholders intending to seek reelection, aware that some constituents can gain the information necessary to allocate punishments and rewards at the voting booth, become more likely to heed public opinion as an issue's salience increases.[4]

Through the process of responding to public opinion, elected officials need not reverse previous positions or violate their own preferences. In the more likely case, legislators, presidents, and other officeholders strategically shade and modulate their actions. At the margins, a politician can realize electoral gains by shifting toward the positions backed by the public. Such behavior decreases the number of incumbents defeated at the polls. Yet, and this point is critical, politicians shifting their positions according to public opinion cause policymaking to change

4. See also Burstein (1998), Geer (1996), B. Jones (1994, chap. 5), and Page and Shapiro (1983) on why salience encourages elected officials to incorporate public opinion into their decision-making.

even without the intervening mechanism of elections (Stimson, Erikson, and MacKuen 1995). When many officials move modestly in the same direction at the same time, the cumulative result can be substantial changes in aggregate policy choices.[5]

The effectiveness of the electoral motive in stimulating responsiveness does not require that all or most individuals closely follow politics, correctly perceive their representatives' positions, and vote accordingly during elections. Instead, the incentives for politicians to respond to public opinion simply require electorates as a whole to hold representatives accountable. As more than just the sum of their parts, electorates possess qualities that individuals typically do not: high levels of information, a tendency to react in expected ways to political events and trends, and the capacity to punish officeholders who behave in ways contrary to public opinion (Converse 1990; Erikson, Stimson, and MacKuen forthcoming; Page and Shapiro 1992). Officeholders whose support within their constituencies falls only a few percentage points, a possible outcome when votes on high-salience issues prove unpopular in the constituency, can move from winning the next election to losing it (Brady et al. 1996).

The consequences of salience follow from Schattschneider's (1960) astute observation that increasing the scope of conflict transforms any political struggle. When officeholders reach decisions in an insulated environment, a pattern common among particularistic and conflictual issues, the public usually possesses only minimal knowledge of the subject area, the options actively considered, and the eventual decisions. With officeholders lacking incentives to consider current or prospective public opinion, they gain more discretion in their decisions, but they also become more likely to cater to business interests.[6] In this case, it is not really "business" but rather segments of business, such as the General Motors Corporation or the pharmaceutical industry, that exert influence.

Issues that unify diverse companies and industries, however, frequently stimulate extensive debate that allows public opinion to form.

5. The same result would be achieved if legislators view themselves as delegates dispatched by their districts or states to represent constituency views. These legislators would need no electoral incentive, for their self-perceptions would automatically induce them to monitor and incorporate constituents' opinions (Wahlke et al. 1962; McCrone and Kuklinski 1979).

6. See Redford (1969), Wilson (1980), and Thurber (1991) for similar arguments.

High visibility in turn precipitates a close connection between what citizens want and what government does. It should be noted that the strong impact of the public voice does not imply that all citizens participate equally or have equal influence, because they clearly do not (Verba, Schlozman, and Brady 1995). When we consider the public as an aggregate and examine the most widespread preferences, however, we should find that the public provides substantial direction for lawmaking on unifying issues.

BUSINESS UNITY, THE PUBLIC, AND BUSINESS POWER

In some ways, it is surprising that any issues promote popular representation. The framers of the U.S. Constitution did not seek a majoritarian political system that would quickly and efficiently respond to the people. Instead, they designed explicitly countermajoritarian institutions, such as a restricted franchise, indirect elections, and a distant presidency. In the intervening centuries American institutions evolved such that nearly all adult citizens gained suffrage, senators became elected through statewide contests, and presidents sought a closer connection to the people than the framers envisioned (Wiebe 1995; Tulis 1987). Notwithstanding those changes, policies that reflect public preferences remain far from inevitable. Such will always be the case when representatives serve as elected intermediaries between citizens and government.

But while responsiveness to the people is uneven, it becomes most pronounced on unifying issues because of their ideological, partisan, and salient nature. Public opinion and election outcomes therefore should strongly affect the likelihood that business, when unified, will either win or lose in politics. Of course, public preferences need not clash with what business wants. Through their issue opinions and voting choices, citizens often endorse ideas and candidates supportive of probusiness policies. Nor does the distinctive character of unifying issues mean that business must lose. Indeed, the positions on which firms share agreement frequently match the eventual legislative decisions. Instead, the argument developed here emphasizes that the *reasons* a unified business community sees its desires either furthered or hindered are traceable to the contours of public opinion and the results of elections.

Because of those factors, business normally cannot use its political or economic resources to cause policies to deviate substantially from public desires. That is, direct forms of business power, which will be addressed empirically in chapters 6 and 7, do not account for the general patterns of outcomes on unifying issues.[7] While it would be foolish to claim that the political and economic pressures brought by business add up to naught, the reasoning developed in this chapter implies that business's direct forms of power yield considerably lower returns than social scientists have usually expected.

A very different pattern holds for conflictual and, especially, particularistic issues. Because these issues typically lack the attributes of being ideological, partisan, and salient, elections usually do not precipitate policy changes, public opinion is often imprecise or else nonexistent, and officeholders face little incentive to react to any majority views that do exist in the constituency. Under these conditions, individual companies and industries have greater opportunities to steer legislative decisions in their favor. Another relevant factor is that on particularistic issues, the businesses seeking beneficial policies often face only limited, if any, opposition from other groups. While issues where firms or business sectors encounter absolutely no opposition appear to be rarer than was once believed (Heinz et al. 1993; Berry 1998), the level of competition on particularistic issues nevertheless pales by comparison to what occurs on unifying issues where other groups regularly mobilize against business. That contrast helps explain why it is easier for narrow segments of business to achieve their aims on particularistic issues than for business as a whole to dictate policy decisions on unifying issues.

Resulting from the myriad differences between unifying issues on the one hand and particularistic and conflictual issues on the other, the workings of democracy markedly differ across the categories of issues. Rather than breaking down on issues where business is unified, as social scientists on all sides of the debate over unity have concluded, democracy faces its greatest threats when business *does not* unify. On the flip side, it is the unifying issues that are most propitious for popular representation and least amenable to control by business. Several theoretical orientations have reached the opposite conclusions by assuming that unity leads to strength. That assumption is probably justified, *ceteris paribus*. Business unity, however, decidedly does not materialize with all else being equal. Instead, unity occurs alongside other factors that increase the scope of public guidance for policymaking and simultaneously limit the amount of direct business influence.

7. Burstein (1998) makes a similar point about the minimal direct effects of interest groups and social movements on the history of legislation regarding equal employment opportunity, a salient issue where elected officials appear to have responded to changes in public opinion.

The same forces that lead to business unity, then, also infuse an issue with attributes that enhance the potential for representative democracy. When a policy proposal would alter the responsibilities of the federal government in ways affecting many diverse firms, that proposal often leads to a unified business position and also tends to become ideological, partisan, and salient. Unity among firms therefore corresponds with a politics heavily responsive to the citizenry, but unity does not cause that outcome. Hence it would be mistaken to say that business unity, abstracted from the factors that appear beside it in practice, strengthens democracy. Similarly, because the existence of unity is not itself a causal agent driving policy decisions, business would not become more powerful through increased infighting.

A unified business community would gain power, however, if it can shape public opinion at the early stages of the political process. That kind of power, arising at least one step removed from actual policymaking, is indirect. If public opinion is favorable to business before concrete issues emerge, then unified business preferences become more likely to prevail in subsequent government actions. Chapter 8 contains an extended discussion of how business has influenced public opinion by using think tanks as an intermediary. Since the early 1970s, the American business community has contributed large sums of money to conservative think tanks. Corporate-financed think tanks, by attracting attention from the mass media and spreading their ideas widely, can affect public opinion in ways beneficial to business. Because of their perceived credibility and independence, analysts at think tanks apparently enjoy a greater persuasive ability than do official spokespersons for corporate interests. Thus through think tanks, a subtle source of indirect power over lawmaking, the business community can eventually shift policy decisions in its favor.

The effect of business efforts to mold public opinion, the evidence will suggest, reaches a magnitude strong enough to be noticed but not so strong as to indicate that business has completely convinced the citizenry to support its demands. That is, business shows an ability to influence public opinion rather than dominate it. The difference between influence and domination has important theoretical implications. It means that public opinion is more than just the refracted preferences of business, for public opinion is also caused by factors largely unrelated to business preferences—such as people's experiences in families and communities, social and economic trends, competing interests that speak through the news media, and reactions to previous government policies.

While unifying issues allow the strongest opportunities for a close connection between citizens and government, the capacity of public opinion to guide policy depends upon the specificity of the decisions examined. Most legislation embodies both principles and details; public opinion almost inevitably will have a greater impact on the former than the latter. The welfare changes enacted in 1996, which brought forth unified business support, provide an apt illustration. The driving motivation behind the legislation was a desire by backers to eliminate Aid to Families with Dependent Children as an entitlement and shift to a system of temporary assistance programs controlled by individual states. While many scholars and policy experts challenged the merits of welfare reform, public opinion followed its own path. Polling and other data indicate that the package, taken in its entirety, won approval from most of the public (Cammisa 1998, chap. 3). Within that broad consensus, many details were necessary to flesh out the legislation, such as the methods by which state agencies would measure the numbers of people moving from welfare to work. Public opinion was more ambiguous on these details, leaving lawmakers and administrative agencies considerable discretion.

Given the extensive debate that accompanies some issues, public opinion on certain occasions can offer guidance to lawmakers on both principles and details. The creation of Medicare in the 1960s, as shown by Lawrence Jacobs's (1993) analysis, provides one noteworthy example. The public possesses enough information to form opinions on the provisions of some legislation, and at other times policymakers can make educated guesses about what will and will not attract public support. Even on unifying issues, though, public opinion cannot possibly cover all contingencies. The closer one moves to the specific and technical provisions within legislation, the less likely that public opinion either has crystallized on a preference or can be accurately estimated (Weissberg 1976). Consequently, policymakers can most readily ascertain what citizens want at a broad level.

During 1969 and 1970, for example, President Richard Nixon and congressional leaders such as Senator Edwin Muskie recognized deep public support amidst business resistance to stringent air pollution programs. Partially in response to public pressures, the legislative and executive branches designed nonincremental legislation that greatly expanded federal authority to control air pollution (Jones 1975). Yet for some details, such as whether to control new emissions through a technology mandate or through a performance standard, policymakers could only guess at public opinion because most Americans simply had not engaged the issue at that level of specificity. While politicians often can sense whether constituents favor the general approach of a bill, anticipating the degree of public support for particular provisions poses a nettlesome challenge. The greater the specificity with which elected officials attempt to determine current or prospective public opinion, the lower the accuracy of their assessments.

As a result, political leaders and their staffs will always enjoy discretion when they fashion policies. This is especially true on low-salience particularistic and conflictual issues, but political leaders also exercise discretion on high-salience unifying issues. On unifying issues, the public's role extends far beyond Edmund Burke's vision of a citizenry that merely called attention to problems and then deferred to political leaders on solutions. But public opinion usually lacks sufficient specificity for officeholders to fully write legislation by simply determining what the public wants. For this reason, public opinion on unifying issues will produce a stronger effect on the overall flow of government action than on every provision contained within a policy initiative.

Election outcomes carry impacts similar in specificity to those of public opinion. That is, election outcomes strongly influence the principles motivating legislation on unifying issues. When Democrats win elections, solutions to societal problems will allocate government a larger responsibility than when Republicans win elections. Republicans will be more inclined to stress private solutions and to minimize government involvement in the marketplace, thereby allowing greater autonomy for businesses. Within these broad parameters, however, election outcomes begin to recede in importance. The details within any given decision will depend upon a complex interaction involving a variety of political actors.

One may wonder which is more important: the principles underlying legislation or the precise details? Attempting to answer that question is like asking whether a ranch would be better defined by the fence that establishes its boundaries or the grass the cattle feed upon. Both principles and details are critical, and each loses its meaning without the other. Policies cannot be enacted without spelling out some details, but without a framework of principles those details will not blend together in any systematic way. Both principles and details merit scrutiny by social scientists.

The next chapter will argue in greater depth that when business unifies, agreement centers on the principles and general outlines of legislative proposals. Different segments of business may prefer the same overall approach to problems even as they disagree on how to implement the particulars. For this reason, I focus upon policymaking at a broad level. When examining the consequences of business unity, it seems apparent, one should focus the investigation at the level where unity occurs.

When it comes to specific provisions, especially technical ones, the interests of various companies and industries often diverge. This makes the corresponding debates over those provisions particularistic or conflictual. While business as a whole may support a bill requiring regulatory agencies to conduct cost-benefit analyses, for example, different companies and industries will likely advance competing perspectives on provisions specifying the ways costs and benefits will be measured. These details, inserted or deleted with little public knowledge or interest, are where policymakers enjoy the greatest discretion and where business influence should be most apparent. Because business typically splinters when it comes to details, the influence we observe is usually exerted by certain firms or industries rather than business at large. Business normally unifies, then, at the level where public opinion is most clear and election outcomes produce the greatest impacts. Thus we have another reason for claiming that unifying issues manifest a high capacity for public guidance and limited potential for business control. To substantiate these claims I must first identify unifying issues, a task I undertake in the following chapter.

THREE

Identifying Business Unity

As we have seen, issues can be classified as particularistic, conflictual, or unifying according to the prevailing alliances and divisions within business. Because my theoretical interests center upon cases marked by agreement among a wide cross-section of firms, I need a means to isolate those cases for further study. Exploring the consequences of unity first requires specifying the concrete issues where it arises. Accordingly, this chapter presents a method of determining when business has unified.

The natural starting place in a search for unity is to examine the positions espoused by individual business enterprises. The alignment of preferences among firms, which in principle could be observed for any piece of legislation, indicates the presence or absence of unity. Each company can express indifference, support, or opposition to a bill's passage. If a sizable majority of firms maintains a collective position either for or against passage, then the issue is an instance of business unity.

What empirical procedure could be used to categorize policy questions as predominantly particularistic, conflictual, or unifying? One might begin by imagining the information that could resolve the matter decisively. Assume that for each bill introduced, the alliances and divisions within business are known *a priori*. Two pieces of information define each firm's location in the debate: its level of interest and its position. Firms vary in their levels of interest, from caring deeply to caring not at all about a given issue. Among the interested firms, their positions on a bill could range from strongly opposed to strongly supportive. If one possessed prior knowledge of the relevant information, the location of all companies along the two dimensions of interest level and position taken could be plotted for each bill. The clustering among the firms would determine whether an issue is best described as particularistic, conflictual, or unifying.

Table 3.1 shows the classifications resulting from different configurations within business of both interest levels and positions. Consider a bill attracting little attention from most firms but serious interest from a small number of them. For this configuration the few firms expressing concern hold a common view on the bill, either in support or opposition. Take, for example, a proposal to ban cigarette advertising on billboards. Tobacco companies and advertising agencies would oppose the bill, but the issue remains distant from most firms' day-to-day operations. Such a bill is particularistic in orientation. Relatively few companies participate in the debate, but those actually advancing a preference by and large maintain similar viewpoints.

Other policy debates are characterized not by cohesion within a segment of business but rather by widespread dissension. Whether a small or large number of firms care about the outcome is not relevant for these cases. In the defining feature of conflictual issues, the interested firms express a diversity of positions. A large portion of the firms with a stake in the debate favors one side, yet many firms take an opposing stance.[1] The 1996 congressional debate over telecommunications deregulation, for example, exposed major cleavages among local phone companies, long-distance carriers, cable providers, and computer firms. If different segments of business oppose each other, a bill is conflictual.

Instead of sowing dissension, some bills instigate alignments whereby a broad assortment of firms both voices interest and tends toward the same position. In these cases large segments of business express a

Table 3.1 The Nature of Firm Alliances and Divisions

TYPE OF ISSUE	LEVEL OF INTEREST	CONSISTENCY IN FIRMS' POSITIONS
Particularistic	low among most firms, high among small number of firms	unity among the small number of interested firms
Conflictual	high among at least some firms	divisive among the interested firms
Unifying	high among many firms	unity among a substantial majority of the interested firms

1. For my purposes, the term "conflictual" describes issues marked by dissension within business, not within society at large. The alignments of other interest groups or parts of society do not enter into the typology of particularistic, conflictual, and unifying issues.

collective sentiment either in support or in opposition. A bill designed to increase unionization throughout the economy, for instance, would be opposed by a wide variety of companies. The configuration of interest levels and positions taken differs from the particularistic case in that many firms, rather than very few, care about the outcome. Bills of this sort fall into the unifying category.

If the investigator knew beforehand the levels of interest and positions of all companies, classifying a given issue as primarily particularistic, conflictual, or unifying would be straightforward. A project attempting to understand how business unity affects the practice of representative democracy could simply select for analysis the group of unifying issues. While political reality as it can be observed poses practical research challenges, defining the research ideal facilitates thinking about the next-best alternative for identifying unifying issues. Whether or not all firms' interest levels and positions are known in advance, the objective in locating unifying issues remains the same: One has to isolate policy debates that (1) elicit attention from many different firms, and (2) attract a rough consensus in the firms' positions.

That task could be solved by examining the policy positions of organizations that presume to speak for business. Two such organizations sometimes mentioned are the Council on Foreign Relations and Conference Board. The problem with using these groups as indicators of business unity, though, is that their membership rolls are comprised of individuals; companies themselves do not join. Because there is no large-scale base of companies who pay dues, corporations cannot easily "vote with their feet" if the organizations do not follow their wishes. Indeed, neither mission statements nor the constraints of satisfying a membership dictate that these groups rest their actions upon an assessment of what a cross-section of companies prefer. Instead, the groups hold and sometimes exercise the freedom to express sentiments independently from what most companies actually want.

A search for business unity can more fruitfully turn to membership organizations, where large numbers of corporations regularly participate in deliberating and deciding upon policy positions. Membership organizations within business, by definition, are explicitly established to represent dues-paying companies. The most useful membership organization for determining when unity exists would be an encompassing one that enrolls a diverse array of companies. Such an organization, by virtue of its varied constituency, would aggregate myriad firms and industries into a cohesive whole and thus reflect the perspectives prevalent throughout business. If this organization could take one policy position that satisfies the various elements of its constituency, then substantial unity would certainly mark that issue; its inability to decide upon a position would indicate that a business consensus cannot be forged.

Does such an organization exist? The United States certainly contains an abundance of business associations, but most of them are narrowly based. Groups with names like the American Wire Producers Association or the National Association of Brick Distributors do not even attempt to integrate the general business population; they simply advocate the interests of their member firms. Other organizations are reasonably inclusive yet still fall short of representing business as a whole. While much more diverse than a trade association, the National Association of Manufacturers, as its name would suggest, cannot reasonably be expected to advocate vigorously the preferences of the service, agriculture, construction, and retailing sectors of the economy. The National Federation of Independent Business and the American Business Conference specialize in the concerns of only small business and medium-sized high growth firms, respectively. The Business Roundtable and the Committee for Economic Development enlist large corporations but make no attempt to cater to companies not part of their membership or contributor bases.

One organization, however, stands apart from the rest. Among all business associations in the country, the U.S. Chamber of Commerce carries by far the largest and most diverse membership. While no group can truly speak for all of private enterprise, the Chamber comes closer than any other association in representing the overall business viewpoint. The Chamber provides the nearest approximation to an organization whose mission statement and financial constraints require it to discover, integrate, and articulate policy preferences from throughout business.

THE U.S. CHAMBER OF COMMERCE AS THE VOICE OF BUSINESS

The U.S. Chamber of Commerce is composed of both organizational and individual members. The membership of state, local, and regional chambers has always given the Chamber a truly national flavor. Multitudes of trade associations belong to the Chamber, making it to a large extent an organization that aggregates the common concerns of other business organizations. The Chamber also serves a constituency of individual businesspeople and of companies of all sizes, from small businesses to Fortune 500 corporations. The companies and trade associations span many industries and sectors, including manufacturing, finance, construction, retail, mining, transportation, and services. The U.S. Chamber of Commerce, in short, represents the overall business viewpoint through its varied membership.

The Chamber's original bylaws state that the organization participates in issues "national in character, timely in importance, and general in application to business and industry" (Childs 1930, 110). This definition of mission matches my conception of unifying issues. As a rule the organization does not join political frays over particularistic issues consequential for only one firm or industry. In line with the Chamber's purpose to advocate the concerns of business as a collective, its efforts are reserved for cases marked by genuine consensus among the membership.

No doubt the Chamber's help would be welcomed by narrow segments of business that seek particularistic benefits from government, but this sort of indulging could quickly compromise the organization's central goals. If the Chamber were to participate in a policy debate significant to just a small portion of its membership, other factions would likely demand similar intervention for their special concerns. Meeting these particularistic demands would divert scarce resources from the Chamber's mission of marshalling and exerting political influence on issues important to the business community at large.[2]

Throughout its history the Chamber has resisted entering policy debates that energized only one component of the membership (Childs 1930; Mundo 1992, chap. 4). Before taking an official position, the Chamber requires that an issue affect a wide spectrum of firms. When an industry lobbies Congress for a unique subsidy, for example, the Chamber remains neutral. Instead, trade associations and individual corporations wage their own political battles on particularistic issues. This distinction in respective goals leads to a convenient division of labor, with trade associations and corporations using many of their resources on narrow issues while the Chamber mobilizes the business community on wide-ranging issues. Belonging to the Chamber allows

2. Interview with Stephen A. Bokat, Vice President and General Counsel, U.S. Chamber of Commerce, 18 December 1997 (hereafter Bokat interview).

segments of business to contribute to joint efforts for the cases marked by shared preferences.[3]

Besides avoiding particularistic issues, the Chamber also eschews positions when the issue at stake is conflictual and its members are internally divided. In some cases the Chamber has been criticized from within business for remaining neutral during momentous policy debates. One journalist expressed the criticism metaphorically in the title of his article: "Chamber's Ponderous Decision Making Leaves It Sitting on the Sidelines" (Lanouette 1982). The reason for the Chamber's strategy goes beyond simple fidelity to its mission; facing strong financial pressures to avoid jeopardizing future dues, the Chamber cannot afford to lose any part of its membership by taking a position favoring one faction over another. The Chamber would rather remain silent during debates on conflictual issues than risk alienating some members, an outcome that would hinder subsequent political efforts on the unifying issues that define its core purpose.[4]

Commenting upon the Chamber's internal decision-making, Bauer, Pool, and Dexter (1963, 332–40) note that there must be "quasi-unanimity" among members to spark the organization's involvement in an issue. The Chamber gives minority factions within its membership significant veto power over decisions, thereby establishing a high threshold for unity. Given uncertainty about whether an issue is conflictual or unifying, the Chamber typically considers it conflictual and remains neutral; when faced with internal dissension, it takes no action at all. For this reason, when the Chamber does declare a position, one can be confident that American firms generally possess a common perspective. Instead of participating in all of the political issues each year affecting some company or industry, the Chamber conserves its resources for the few dozen characterized by substantial unity in business preferences.

Martin (2000) aptly describes the deliberative procedures of the U.S. Chamber of Commerce and other umbrella associations as a "least common denominator politics." In requiring consensus before moving forward, the Chamber often tends toward inaction and loses any ability to lead the business community in new directions. These outcomes, Martin shows, have weakened the potential for business to rally behind

3. Interview with Jeffrey H. Joseph, Vice President of Domestic Policy, U.S. Chamber of Commerce, 17 December 1997 (hereafter Joseph interview).

4. Interview with Martin A. Regalia, Vice President of Economic Policy and Chief Economist, U.S. Chamber of Commerce, 18 December 1997 (hereafter Regalia interview).

recent initiatives seeking public-private partnerships to improve the efficiency of health care delivery and enhance the skills of the workforce.

If one defines democratic procedures to be those that facilitate majority rule, the Chamber's operations fall far short, because they require supramajorities before taking action. For a researcher seeking to determine when unity exists, however, the high threshold set by the Chamber yields significant dividends. Namely, when the Chamber abandons its frequent silence to announce support for or opposition to a bill, there are solid grounds to infer that American business is predominantly unified behind the position. The policy positions of the Chamber can be used to identify empirically those instances of relatively high unity. In effect, the Chamber performs a task that otherwise could be addressed only in theory by assuming prior knowledge of firms' interest levels and positions taken.

Of course, one could not conclude that every single company shares agreement when the Chamber expresses a position. If 100 percent of U.S. firms must stand on the same side of an issue for it to qualify, unity would never surface in practice. Outside of hypothetical proposals, such as a bill to nationalize all of private enterprise, the interests of some firms will always clash with the rest of the business community on any specific issue. One could envision, for example, consulting firms specializing in mediation and dispute resolution that could profit handsomely from labor laws favorable to unions. Rather than requiring complete and total unanimity, a unifying issue simply needs a large majority of companies to hold a common position. A minority of dissenters does not obscure the overall pattern.

Unity therefore should be conceived as lying along a continuum. Once we reject a conception of unity as an all-or-nothing proposition, we can move to the more fruitful endeavor of identifying issues with the highest *degree* of unity. Given this notion of unity as a continuum, the policy positions espoused by the U.S. Chamber of Commerce become valuable data. If one imagines a latent dimension with complete fragmentation at one pole and total unity at the other, the Chamber's stands are much closer to the latter. The Chamber does not and cannot achieve total unity, but its positions fall toward that end of the continuum.

Through its decision-making process, the Chamber strikes a balance between requiring widespread consensus among its membership and not demanding a threshold so high as to eliminate any manifestations of unity. Chamber officials resist specifying the precise supramajority necessary for the organization to proclaim a position because the number sometimes varies. One staff member, however, suggests as a reference point that the Chamber likes to see at least 80 to 85 percent of its membership on the same side. As that figure drops to 75 or 65 percent, the organization tends to stay neutral.[5] Another staffer stresses that the Chamber's cautious procedures are designed to identify consensus when it occurs. Consensus normally means much more than a majority but less than unanimity.[6]

An examination of all of the Chamber's positions over time would probably uncover exceptions to its ability to identify consensus. Sporadic errors are likely within any organization that must gather and assimilate so much information about members' policy preferences. A minority of problematic cases, though, would not jeopardize the validity of the Chamber's policy declarations when considered as a group. Most importantly for my purposes, the Chamber does not systematically err in finding the perspectives most prevalent among the business community at large. In the realm of social science, an indicator need not perfectly tap the desired latent concept to facilitate finding answers to theoretically important questions.

DECISION-MAKING WITHIN THE U.S. CHAMBER OF COMMERCE

In reading thousands of pages of the Chamber's testimony before congressional hearings, one cannot avoid noticing how infrequently its witnesses venture beyond their prepared statements. When House members and senators probe further by asking whether the Chamber supports or opposes proposals or amendments not explicitly mentioned in the remarks, the witnesses typically respond that the Chamber has not developed a position. When witnesses intend to declare the Chamber's views on a bill or a particular segment thereof, they do so candidly in their prepared statements, but they strongly resist wading into uncharted waters. This pattern of behavior reflects the constraints under which the Chamber operates. Decisions to endorse or oppose a legislative proposal are reached through careful deliberation to determine that members are unified. The Chamber does not permit its witnesses before congressional hearings to address proposals that have

5. Regalia interview.
6. Interview with Harvey Alter, Manager of the Resources Policy Department, U.S. Chamber of Commerce, 18 December 1997 (hereafter Alter interview).

not been discussed in the organization's formal process for arriving at decisions.[7]

To ensure that policy positions correspond to the consensus business viewpoint, the Chamber throughout its history has granted members notable voice in internal governance (Childs 1930; Mundo 1992, chap. 4). Referenda of the Chamber's organizational members frequently have established the group's official positions. In recent years, regular surveys of the membership have given information to Chamber staff about where the members fall on issues receiving attention in Congress.[8] Delegates from the membership have discussed, debated, and ratified policy positions at the annual convention since the Chamber's creation in 1912. The Chamber's policy committees, which determine the bulk of the organization's stances on a day-to-day basis, include representatives from different elements of the membership.

The point here is not that the Chamber works like the classic New England town meeting, but simply that it invites sizeable participation from its membership, particularly in comparison to other interest groups and especially to other business organizations. As Mundo (1992, chap. 4) notes, the organization probably could not survive without incorporating its members into decision-making. By involving its diverse membership in deliberations that set its positions, the Chamber can help avoid taking stands opposed by part of its constituency. The participation of members helps to ensure that the Chamber takes action only when there is a consensus within business.[9] Even when decisions must be reached without large-scale consultation of the Chamber's constituency, the policy committees, board of directors, and staff use available information and precedents to find the common ground supported throughout the business community.[10]

The Chamber's commitment to follow the broad priorities upon which its members can agree sometimes leads it to release vague policy statements unattached to any specific legislation. Such statements are revealing not so much for what they say but rather for what they imply—namely, that business has not unified for or against any current

7. Joseph interview.

8. Interview with David Voight, Director of the Small Business Center, U.S. Chamber of Commerce, 17 December 1997 (hereafter Voight interview).

9. Interview with Martin Lefkowitz, Director of Economic Trends, U.S. Chamber of Commerce, 25 September 1996 (hereafter Lefkowitz interview).

10. Interview with Neil E. Trautwein, Manager of Health Care Policy, U.S. Chamber of Commerce, 16 December 1997 (hereafter Trautwein interview).

legislation on the matter in question. At other times business does unify on concrete legislative proposals, and the Chamber's declarations correspondingly change from abstract expressions to endorsement of or opposition to specific proposals. When responding to legislation before Congress, though, the Chamber can be no more precise than its methodical procedures allow. As the most important guidepost for understanding the Chamber's positions, business more frequently unifies on general principles than upon legislative details (Epstein 1969, 50–53; Bauer, Pool, and Dexter 1963, 332–40; Wilson 1973, 310–12).[11]

When declaring positions on legislation, therefore, the Chamber frequently either supports or opposes congressional bills wholesale. For the most part the organization does not undertake the kind of line-by-line scrutiny typical of many interest groups. Concerning specific details inside a bill, the Chamber's members often splinter into different subgroups. It is far easier to generate unity on the question of whether a bill as a whole, rather than every single provision, benefits American business at large. As one former Chamber staffer said of the organization: "If they got into the business of making trade-offs or proposing amendments, they'd be pitting one part of their membership against another, and they can't do that." (Kirkland 1981, 156)

The centerpiece of President Reagan's economic program, the omnibus budgetary bills enacted in 1981, provides a striking illustration of these points. The bills contained extensive tax and spending cuts—most notably reductions in marginal tax rates and accelerated depreciation for investments—supported across multitudes of companies and industries. Business was solidly unified behind the general outlines of the Reagan program. Buried within the final bills enacted into law, however, were many particularistic sections consequential only for narrow segments of business. One provision, known as "safe harbor" leasing, permitted unprofitable companies to sell their tax breaks to profitable ones. That provision generated a huge windfall for companies in traditional smokestack industries who were feeling pressure from international competition.

Championing the deep business support for the overall program, the Chamber endorsed the Reagan tax and spending packages as a whole. The organization was officially neutral, however, on the various particularistic provisions benefiting narrow segments of business. This

11. Interviews with Chamber staff members substantiated this claim. The Chamber officials added, though, that the prevalence of consensus on principles but not details is a tendency rather than an ironclad law (Alter interview; Bokat interview).

case exemplifies the Chamber's typical decision-making patterns. In attempting to represent the totality of American business, the Chamber adopts positions only at the level where unity exists. Because business supported the general tax and spending cuts, the Chamber worked to push them through Congress but remained silent on the specific provisions that lacked unity among its members.

A single bill, then, can contain unifying as well as conflictual and particularistic dimensions. Insertion of the safe harbor section into the 1981 tax legislation benefited heavy industries, but business writ large neither gained nor lost as a result. By contrast, final passage of the Reagan program, especially the tax reductions for many different companies, was a triumph for business as a collective. Eliminating the safe harbor provision would not have tarnished the victory. Similarly, enactment of a bill opposed by a wide range of firms would represent a defeat even if the bill contained a particularistic component desired by one industry.

The Chamber's strategy to influence the legislative process points to the limitations on its decision-making. Because the Chamber tends to find unity, when it appears, within the broad outlines of a bill rather than on specific provisions, the organization is not especially effective at the "inside" lobbying game and historically has devoted relatively few resources to it (Kirkland 1981; Goldman 1972). On this matter, it is telling that an organization with a $70 million annual budget and 900 employees maintains only 10 full-time lobbyists.[12] The Chamber has never been known for an ability to shape the specific provisions and wording of bills when House members and senators strike deals and add amendments during the legislative process. The same factors that restrict Chamber witnesses from going beyond their prepared statements also limit the organization's capacity to engage in the give-and-take of legislative politics. Constrained by the need to ensure that its members concur, the Chamber usually cannot respond rapidly to the fast-paced changes legislators propose to either facilitate or harm a bill's chances for passage. The sometimes-lengthy process of finding the policy ideas upheld throughout business restricts the Chamber's ability to participate in the bargaining often necessary to fashion congressional majorities.

12. Data on the budget for fiscal 1997, the number of employees as of early 1998, and the number of full-time lobbyists come from the Comptroller's Office, Department of Human Resources, and General Counsel within the U.S. Chamber of Commerce, respectively.

From its founding the Chamber has elevated most of its resources to enlisting companies and business organizations within individual constituencies to bring pressure upon House and Senate members.[13] Adding to its reputation for "outside" lobbying, the Chamber was a notable pioneer among interest groups in developing the computer capacity to track its members and to encourage them to contact their legislators (Loomis 1983). During the 1980s the Chamber created a closed-circuit television network to mobilize its members on short notice, and both friends and foes in Congress have long recognized the organization's capacity to stimulate vast quantities of correspondence from its membership (Gordon 1975; Goldman 1972). The guiding philosophy is that House and Senate members respond more favorably to pressure from businesses in their home localities than to arguments from Chamber staff located in Washington.[14] The Chamber's members participate in these efforts only if they share the organization's viewpoint, giving the Chamber another reason to accurately represent its heterogeneous constituency.

POTENTIAL PROBLEMS IN IDENTIFYING UNIFYING ISSUES

There are instances when the Chamber develops a stance on issues that, by directly affecting only one industry, might appear to be particularistic. During the 1950s and 1960s, for example, a series of bills sought to establish a program of federal compensation for workers suffering from exposure to nuclear radiation. On the surface the bills appeared to affect only the nuclear power industry. The Chamber contended at the time, however, that the proposals would set a precedent for additional federal control of workers' compensation insurance, a program that formerly operated almost entirely at the state level. Believing that future federal involvement would have produced unwelcome consequences for a variety of firms, business collectively opposed the proposals to prevent the possibility from arising. Whether this case, or any other for that matter, portended a "slippery slope" requires a judgment best left in the hands of interested political actors. If the motive for Chamber members' opposition to the bills on workers' comp was to ward off further efforts in the future, then the bills should be classified as unifying.

13. Bokat interview; Voight interview; Deakin 1966, 30–32, 131–32; Hall 1969. Chamber officials stress, though, that some direct lobbying is necessary to complement the grassroots mobilization of individual firms and business groups.

14. Joseph interview; Lefkowitz interview.

The Chamber has sometimes been charged with favoring either big business or small business. Selective information could be marshaled to support either view, but only if one overlooks contradictory evidence. For example, the Chamber draws the bulk of its membership from small firms. In the last few decades, it has worked hard to attract additional small companies, particularly by creating and promoting its Small Business Center. Yet its board of directors, which sometimes decides how to apply the organization's previous policy statements to specific legislative proposals under review, has always been dominated by representatives of large- and medium-sized corporations and business groups. The largest corporations, moreover, continue to provide most of the organization's revenues through its sliding-scale recommendations for dues.

The Chamber's policy stances show concern for firms of all sizes. On the one hand, the Chamber has consistently opposed antitrust policies that would harm large corporations but could substantially benefit their smaller competitors. Similarly, it has vigorously advocated tax revisions, such as investment tax credits and accelerated depreciation, that aid big business but often do not apply to small firms. Yet many of the Chamber's other positions reveal strong concern for the interests of small business. The Chamber has regularly opposed increasing or extending the minimum wage, which greatly affects small companies but produces much more modest impacts upon larger ones. The organization also has fought to weaken regulatory laws by exempting companies with few employees. When considered in their entirety, the Chamber's positions (described later in the chapter) demonstrate a reasonable balance between big and small business.

The Chamber's core stands in areas like regulatory policy, labor, and public lands have persisted for decades, giving the organization strong continuity from one period to the next. Business lobbyists and members of Congress, in fact, have often viewed the Chamber as being overly predictable, which is a natural consequence of its notable consistency (Levitan and Cooper 1984, 21; Balz 1976, 1106–7). It would be inaccurate, however, to say that the Chamber's positions are *completely* consistent over time. During 1993, for example, the Chamber was seen to be shifting leftward and toward big business (Victor 1993). This perception was driven largely by the fact that the Chamber endorsed health care reform with a requirement for companies to provide insurance for employees, a position that reversed its longstanding opposition to federally mandated benefit packages.

When the full record is scrutinized, though, the revisions in the Chamber's positions become conspicuous as exceptions from a norm of stability. For the vast majority of stands taken in 1993, the inertia of the Chamber's history proved dominant. As it had in the past, the Chamber supported legislation to require economic impact statements for all new regulations, to restrict unfunded mandates on subnational governments and the private sector, and to give the president line-item veto authority. Similarly, the Chamber opposed legislative efforts to strengthen the Clean Water Act, to prohibit hiring of permanent replacement workers during a strike, and to restrict mining on federal lands. All of these positions could have been easily predicted from the organization's previous declarations.

The expectation of constancy in the Chamber's positions helps explain why legislators, lobbyists, scholars, and political analysts quickly recognize the shifts that do occur. Much as one notices a successful third party candidate because of the backdrop of persistence in the two-party system, the Chamber's sporadic changes draw attention against its usual pattern of stability. In noting the cases of change, one should be careful not to generalize from them to the entire platform advocated by the organization; before any global interpretations can be offered, shifts on particular issues must be placed in the context of all of the Chamber's positions. When this broader context is examined, the Chamber's enduring center of gravity becomes apparent. Even in 1993, a year seen by many to mark a break from the past, the continuity in the Chamber's positions stands out far more than the changes.

Perhaps resulting from the Chamber's balancing act, neither big business nor small business has been entirely pleased with its behavior. In the last few decades, large corporations grew sufficiently dissatisfied to form the Business Roundtable to advocate their interests exclusively. Small business took parallel action in revitalizing the National Federation of Independent Business. The Chamber's membership continued to grow even after these groups increased their profiles in the 1970s, indicating that the organization does successfully represent a business-wide constituency despite the difficulties. Addressing the needs of both large and small companies necessarily poses a challenge, but the Chamber manages this tension to the fullest extent feasible. In an analogous situation, a politician sometimes drawing fire from elements of both the left and the right is probably promoting the centrist policies that best express the majority opinions among the population. The criticism of the Chamber articulated now and then by both big business and small business suggests that the organization does an adequate job finding the common ground among the largest possible number of business enterprises.

An occasional Chamber decision might lead one to question the extent to which it taps business unity. Like any organization that depends upon participation by its members, the Chamber can be led astray from consensus positions if energetic but unrepresentative segments of the membership participate while others do not. On certain issues, factions with disproportionate representation on the board of directors and policy committees have been known to influence the Chamber's positions (Hall 1969). By comparison to the set of all the Chamber's positions, however, those instances are infrequent.

UNCOVERING INSTANCES OF HIGH BUSINESS UNITY

The discussion so far explains why the policy declarations of the U.S. Chamber of Commerce can be used to identify cases of high business unity. Once the relevant issues have been isolated, it then becomes possible to measure the extent to which lawmaking favors business. As a first step toward this measurement, I collected every position of the Chamber over the last four decades. In an attempt to conduct a thorough search, I gathered information from both the Chamber's headquarters in Washington and from its archives at Hagley Museum and Library, located in Wilmington, Delaware.

I examined diverse materials, many with overlapping information, to uncover policy positions. Four kinds of documents were particularly useful: letters the Chamber sent to members of Congress, descriptions of the organization's stands in various newsletters the Chamber regularly distributed to its members, the Chamber's testimony before congressional hearings, and roll call votes that the Chamber has used to construct ratings of House and Senate members since 1965. My study of these and other documents yielded a massive amount of information. The resulting compilation of issues is, to my knowledge, the complete set of policy questions on which the Chamber took a position during the last few decades.[15]

15. I cannot be certain that I have identified all of the Chamber's positions. What I can claim is that I spent many months combing the existing records of the organization and coding the information I found, and I included every position uncovered. My

For the purposes of this project, an "issue" denotes a legislative proposal that the Chamber potentially could support or oppose. While the term "issue" often refers to a broad cluster of related questions addressed in public policy, a more specific meaning is intended in the remainder of the book. For example, a proposal to restrict programs requiring affirmative action in federal contracting constitutes an issue according to my usage. The broader concepts of "affirmative action" and "race" extend beyond the conceptual apparatus employed here. Within many other lines of research, the more expansive definitions would be appropriate.

My data set of unifying issues derives from the lawmaking side of government, thereby tapping the main interaction between Congress and the president. Career civil servants and appointed officials within the executive branch, who often draft bills for introduction in Congress, should also be considered integral to the legislative process. To be counted as a unifying issue, an item must reach the formal agenda (Cobb and Elder 1983), meaning that it passes two criteria. First, each proposal must be embodied within a tangible bill or provision thereof that the Chamber either supports or opposes explicitly. If, for example, the Chamber sends a letter to members of Congress or the president requesting that the antitrust laws be relaxed, that does not count as an agenda item. Nor do the generalized statements the Chamber often makes qualify as issues unless the Chamber connects them to specific legislative proposals. Restricting attention to bills or provisions follows from my objective to explain the substantive lawmaking of Congress and the president. As for the second criterion, an item must receive some kind of formal consideration during the year, which includes discussion or action on the bill during hearings, committee markup, floor votes, or conference committee. This requirement eliminates bills that members of Congress introduce, sometimes repeatedly over a long time span, despite knowing that the bills have no chance of even being considered. In other words, items defined as part of the legislative agenda must clear a minimum requirement of political feasibility. Appendix A describes several other coding rules to identify issues. Applying those rules to the complete set of the Chamber's policy positions creates a

---

efforts benefit from the fact that the Chamber's strategy in influencing legislation emphasizes mobilizing its members rather than the inside lobbying of legislators behind closed doors. To successfully implement an outside strategy, the Chamber has to publicize its positions, a task that typically leaves behind a paper trail.

set of 2,364 issues from 1953 to 1996,[16] or an average of 54 issues per year.[17]

THE SUBSTANCE AND TONE OF THE CHAMBER'S POSITIONS

Studies of business influence in politics often mention the U.S. Chamber of Commerce (e.g., Bauer, Pool, and Dexter 1963; Wilson 1981; Domhoff 1978; Vogel 1989). No one, however, has analyzed the full range of its positions. The data collected here provide the opportunity to peer into the Chamber in a comprehensive manner.

An exploration of its internal documents reveals that the Chamber has participated in practical politics throughout the post–World War II period. Every year the Chamber has taken stands on a few dozen issues and communicated its views to legislators through letters, personal meetings, and testimony at hearings. Some observers have called the Chamber a purely defensive organization that knows what it opposes but not what it supports. The data point to a very different interpretation, for over the last four decades the Chamber has regularly both supported and opposed legislation. Of all the Chamber's policy positions from 1953 to 1996, 49 percent were in support of bills or provisions thereof while 51 percent were in opposition. Thus, the Chamber plays defense only a trivial amount more often than it plays offense.

As one would expect from knowing the basic outlines of American political eras, the frequency with which the Chamber attempts either to promote or block legislation varies somewhat by decade. During the 1950s, 1980s, and 1990s, the Chamber's positions were in support 51 percent, 53 percent, and 59 percent of the time, respectively. The Chamber was on the defensive more often during the 1960s and 1970s, when 40 percent and 46 percent of its positions supported legislation.[18]

16. I chose the beginning date of the data collection to correspond with the periods of availability for the measures of public opinion and election outcomes to be described in chapter 5.

17. The magnitude of this number might lead one to believe that a high degree of unity occurs frequently, but such an inference would be inaccurate. In chapter 4, I show that the fifty-four instances of substantial unity per year represent only a very small component of the annual volume of legislation that Congress considers.

18. During these periods the Chamber acquired a reputation, appropriately, as an organization more often trying to stymie legislation than to advance it. As the political context changed, though, the Chamber took a greater proportion of positions in support of bills.

The overarching portrait emerges clearly: Throughout the last few decades, the Chamber has continually demarcated both what it stands for and what it stands against.

A careful scrutiny of the Chamber's positions indicates that the organization does not alter its guiding philosophy in any major way according to the pressures of the moment. The Chamber normally does not, for example, embrace a less ambitious agenda and compromise on key principles during a hostile political environment. The Chamber is not inclined to embrace a bill certain to pass if that bill conflicts with its previous orientation on the matter, and the result is a strong continuity in the Chamber's positions. One could examine its statements on consumer regulation in the 1960s, for instance, and predict quite accurately its statements during the 1990s. The Chamber has continually opposed strong federal efforts to protect consumers by regulating business practices.

When evaluated in their entirety, the Chamber's positions follow a consistent pattern over the years. Proposals to expand regulatory and social welfare programs usually have met Chamber opposition,[19] as have tax increases and labor laws favorable to unions. On the flip side, the Chamber has supported stronger corporate autonomy from the regulatory and social welfare state. The Chamber also has endorsed tax cuts and laws that strengthen the hand of management over workers. On questions of whether policy authority should be vested in the federal government or in the states, the Chamber usually has favored the states. Reflecting business preferences, the Chamber has opposed placing requirements on government contractors and advocated allowing private development on public lands.

CONSERVATISM AND THE U.S. CHAMBER OF COMMERCE

The Chamber's various positions aggregate into a fairly cohesive worldview. When business attains a high level of unity on a policy question, thereby motivating the Chamber to become involved, the resulting positions usually embody principles understood as classically liberal

19. The Social Security and unemployment compensation programs are exceptions to this tendency. Reflecting the fact that the business community had come to view those programs relatively favorably by the 1950s, the Chamber has often supported extensions to new workers and benefit increases, although usually the organization's preferred expansions were more limited than those desired by many members of Congress.

or, within contemporary usage, as conservative. This pattern does not imply that all elements of business embrace conservative viewpoints all the time. Individual firms and industries overlook their frequent support for limited government and free markets when a specific form of government intervention would serve their interests. Special preferences in the tax code, which exempt certain kinds of income from taxation, provide perhaps the paradigm case. Much of the complexity of the federal tax system stems from unique provisions, sometimes applicable to only a single corporation, that Congress and the president have created over the years. Corporations and trade associations continually attempt to gain and protect these exemptions. The spending side of the ledger can confer parallel advantages that businesses readily seek. Many spending programs in areas like defense, agriculture, and transportation create direct subsidies for private companies. Special benefits alternatively can be created through the instruments of trade policy, as Adam Smith discerned centuries ago, where firms can win protection through means like tariffs, import quotas, and non-tariff barriers. Regulatory policy, too, can bestow advantages upon narrow business interests. Industries such as trucking, telecommunications, and utilities have often sought policies to restrict the entry of new competitors and guarantee existing companies a targeted rate of return on capital.

These instances of businesses pursuing and defending government involvement in the marketplace are plentiful and probably account for the majority of business-government interactions. For my purposes, they are noteworthy in another sense: They are usually particularistic or conflictual rather than unifying. Tax exemptions, subsidy programs, trade protections, and industry-specific regulations usually apply only to certain segments of capital, often at the expense of others. Policies and programs that unify business have very different characteristics. Rather than being marked by the seeking of benefits through government action, as is frequently the case with particularistic and conflictual issues, unifying issues most commonly (though certainly not always) reflect a sentiment among businesses for a government whose management of the economy is circumscribed and restrained. When firms achieve unity, they are normally on the side of weaker rather than stronger government.

This pattern greatly affects the character of the Chamber's positions. The Chamber's membership, generally representative of business at-large, dictates where the organization falls on the ideological spectrum. Several major studies of the opinions held by business owners and managers during the twentieth century have found them to be, on the whole, conservative (Sutton et al. 1956; Krooss 1970; Prothro 1954; Silk and Vogel 1976). Although that finding is not surprising, the studies have been remarkably consistent in showing that the conservative attitudes persist over time. While certainly not a monolith, American businesspeople do manifest certain tendencies. Silk and Vogel (1976) observed 360 high-ranking corporate executives who participated in a series of three-day meetings to discuss the role of business in society and politics. Drawing upon their observations, they write: "Businessmen share a deep skepticism about the ability of government to do anything efficiently, and they believe that whenever possible the achievement of society's objectives is better left in their own hands" (46). As pressures of international competition intensified in the 1990s, some managers of large corporations warmed to the prospect that well-designed government programs—provided that they build upon a framework of markets—can promote economic efficiency and stimulate productivity gains among the workforce (Martin 2000). When this rethinking within pockets of business sparked businesswide support for specific proposals, such as school-to-work and training legislation, the Chamber's positions evolved as well. Thus the central tendency within the business community in recent years should be seen as conservative but not reactionary, supportive of some state-led reforms that involve a strong business role but opposed to new programs that involve centralized government direction.

Vogel (1978) offers an explanation for why American business has long been more conservative than its counterparts in other industrialized nations. Only in the United States, he observes, did the rise of the large corporation predate the growth of significant government authority. While European and Japanese governments often helped finance and build large business enterprises, the corporation developed with less assistance within the United States. The federal government's interactions with business have largely been confrontational rather than cooperative, particularly in the area of regulation—a point that Graham Wilson's (1985) analysis of worker health and safety programs nicely demonstrates. According to Vogel (1978), then, historical circumstances explain the adversarial relationship between business and government in the United States (see also Jacoby 1991 and Chandler 1980). In advocating the interests of business at large, the U.S. Chamber of Commerce follows traditions deeply rooted in American history.

The Chamber has occasionally been called a reactionary organization, but this charge may have been affected by the personal viewpoints of those advancing the claim. It is natural for all kinds of people—journalists, scholars, politicians, and other political actors—to unknowingly and inaccurately perceive the center of the ideological spectrum to be closer to themselves than it really is. Biased perception of this sort often leads to the erroneous conclusion that anyone offering ideological views different than one's own must be far from the mainstream. In the same manner that many conservatives observe the positions of the AFL-CIO or American Civil Liberties Union and incorrectly accuse those organizations of representing only the far left, some left-leaning observers mistakenly see the Chamber as speaking solely for the right fringe of American politics.

Related to the claim that the Chamber advances only a far-right ideology is the perception in some quarters that the Chamber adopts different political positions than other, more moderate segments of the business world. This impression frequently contains a belief that the Chamber reflects a small-business, hardline mentality while the more reasonable advocates of big business uphold moderate positions and seek to work with, rather than against, government. In the last few decades, the Business Council and the Business Roundtable are the organizations allegedly embodying the more reasonable mentality most clearly. McQuaid (1982, 1994), for example, contrasts the Chamber with these other two groups in precisely the manner described above.

Scholars often discuss the Business Council and the Business Roundtable as a single unit, for their high overlap in membership and preferences renders them virtually sister organizations. Domhoff (1983, 136) writes that their members "are in effect the same small group of corporate executives taking part in two different activities," with the Council emphasizing behind-the-scenes discussions with senior government officials and the Roundtable stressing out-in-the-open lobbying. Given the tendency for the Roundtable to leave the more extensive public record, it is easier for researchers to track its policy stands. Any compilation of the Roundtable's positions, though, would also provide considerable insight into the sentiments held by the Council.

To determine whether the U.S. Chamber of Commerce expresses unrepresentative viewpoints, as suggested by some observers, its record of policy stands can be compared to those of the Business Roundtable. When one considers the totality of both organizations' platforms, the occasional differenes between them can be properly understood as deviations from the usual pattern of agreement and cooperation. The misperceptions about the Chamber's ideology and its relationship to the larger business community, while understandable, rest upon two inaccurate inferences.

First, as noted earlier, the Chamber is not an ultraconservative organization in service of only the far right. Instead, the Chamber has represented the more pedestrian kind of American conservative thought throughout the postwar period. The point is not that the Chamber's positions have an intrinsic normative merit, but simply that they coincide with perspectives prevalent among conservative citizens and politicians. There is a difference between embracing conservative positions and espousing ideas pervasive among the extreme right wing, and the Chamber does the former rather than the latter.[20]

Second, despite some interpretations to the contrary, the Business Roundtable does not expound a centrist philosophy. Instead, the Roundtable—like the Chamber—typically voices positions consistent with standard American conservatism. In mistakenly perceiving divergent ideological outlooks between these groups, some analysts have been led astray by the two organizations' quite different approaches to gaining influence. The Chamber operates under a constraint to find unity within its varied constituency. Because of its mission and its financial incentives to promote all segments of business, the Chamber's leaders lack the authority to bargain extensively during the legislative process. Instead, the Chamber normally maintains fixed positions while attempting to mobilize its membership. This gives the organization an appearance of ideological rigidity, a perception consonant with its often strident tone, but the Chamber's positions only demonstrate its exquisite care in determining whether unity exists and the difficulty in assessing membership support for potential compromises.

The Business Roundtable, by contrast, does not have members in the usual sense. Instead, the organization consists only of the chief executive officers from about 200 of the nation's largest corporations. Founded in 1972, the Roundtable attempts to bring corporate executives directly

20. Poole and Rosenthal's (1997, chap. 8) analysis of the ideological positions of eight interest groups supports this observation. Through their scaling techniques, they find that nearly all of the interest groups examined attempt to pull House members and Senators toward ideological polarization by promoting ideologies more extreme than those found in Congress. The U.S. Chamber of Commerce, whose ideological positions fall within the range observed in Congress, is the sole exception in their analysis.

in contact with important policymakers. High-ranking politicians and staffers in Congress and the White House, the Roundtable's leaders believe, are likely to respond favorably to the sentiments expressed by CEOs.

In contrast to the Chamber's role as an outsider, the Business Roundtable plays the role of the quintessential insider. The tactics that prove effective for the former often do not apply to the latter. A bombastic style, for example, can help the Chamber rally a broad base of business either for or against a proposal, but that approach may prove ineffective at the negotiating table. Anyone participating in policy formation and bargaining soon learns that compromise sometimes is a prerequisite for political success. The Roundtable reacts to the context of the situation, recognizing that there is a time to hold firm and a time to introduce a fallback proposal. Through this strategy, the Roundtable seeks not only to influence congressional and presidential action on bills receiving formal attention, but also to join negotiations before key legislative and executive officials reveal their proposals publicly. To forestall undesirable proposals or to gain a lessened benefit when the preferred one appears unlikely to pass, the organization sometimes will accept a watered-down version. Such practical compromises appear to attach the Roundtable to a moderate orientation, but appearances can be deceiving.

When the executives from the Roundtable believe that legislation they oppose will eventually pass, they attempt to fashion a more favorable bill. We should not mistake a willingness to compromise, however, for centrist beliefs. There is a big difference between what corporate executives would actually prefer from the political process and what they perceive to be the best results they can achieve. The Roundtable sometimes will settle for half a loaf, while the Chamber will insist on the whole loaf, but this distinction does not imply that the two organizations' underlying positions differ.

During the first two years of the Bush administration, for example, Washington insiders expected enactment of legislation to strengthen civil rights laws by overturning recent Supreme Court decisions. The Business Roundtable, hoping to prevent incorporation of provisions that could seriously restrain management practices regarding employee relations, participated in negotiations with the White House and Congress to seek an agreeable compromise. The Chamber of Commerce, suspecting the development of unfavorable legislation, announced early opposition to overturning the Court's rulings. Eventually the talks stalled and the Business Roundtable pulled out, joining the Chamber to oppose the legislation later enacted into law. The differences between the Roundtable and the Chamber stemmed largely from strategy, not preferences.

OVERLAP BETWEEN THE U.S. CHAMBER OF COMMERCE AND THE BUSINESS ROUNDTABLE

The convergence between the two organizations can be demonstrated systematically. Like the Chamber, the Roundtable promotes its own recommendations and expresses views on concrete bills or provisions before Congress. Because both organizations have supported and opposed many legislative proposals since the early 1970s, their positions can be compared to identify instances of agreement and disagreement. The Business Roundtable is more selective than the Chamber in that the former addresses only a handful of issues per year while the latter tackles a few dozen. Among the issues important to the Business Roundtable, however, the Chamber expresses interest in nearly all of them. The policy stands of the two organizations therefore provide a valid basis of comparison.

Two organizations that truly uphold different ideological outlooks would be expected to disagree sometimes. To determine the frequency of disagreement, I gathered every position of the Roundtable from 1972 to 1996 that I could locate. Information came from the Roundtable's testimony before Congress, the business press such as *Business Week* and *Fortune,* and Washington-oriented periodicals such as *Congressional Quarterly Weekly Report,* the *Washington Post,* and the *New York Times.* During the mid- to late 1970s, the Roundtable opposed such proposals as a consumer protection agency, labor law reform, and hospital cost controls. The organization supported ideas such as civil service reforms, capital gains tax cuts, and price decontrol of oil and natural gas. During the early 1980s, the Roundtable supported the Reagan tax and budget cuts, regulatory reform, loosening of antitrust laws, and limits on product liability. Among the proposals opposed in the late 1980s were bills to control acid rain, to mandate plant-closing notification, and to require employers to provide health benefits. In the 1990s, the organization has supported the balanced budget amendment, Superfund reform, and requiring regulatory cost-benefit analyses.

The Roundtable's positions correspond to a high degree with the Chamber's. In fact, for the 135 instances when both organizations address the same proposal, they agree on 96 percent of the cases while standing on opposite sides only 4 percent of the time. Moreover, this strong overlap defines the entire period since the Roundtable's formation. During the 1970s, 1980s, and 1990s, the rates of agreement are 96 percent, 95 percent, and 100 percent, respectively. In each decade, then, the Chamber and the Roundtable have advocated different sides of an issue in no more than one out of twenty cases. When the complete set of positions is studied, it becomes clear that the Chamber has not vacillated in and out of alignment with the Roundtable. There is no evidence to substantiate any serious divergence in their ideological perspectives.

Supplementing the data presented here, several Chamber officials stated during interviews that significant disagreement between the Chamber and the Roundtable occurs only rarely.[21] Sporadic scholarly assertions to the contrary notwithstanding, both organizations express viewpoints typical of American conservatism. Such a finding simply mirrors the conservative sentiment within business as a whole. The U.S. Chamber of Commerce and the Business Roundtable do sometimes devote their greatest quantity of resources to different issues. The Chamber might stress one issue while the Roundtable prioritizes another even though their positions on both issues are congruent. In addition, as noted earlier, the Roundtable tackles fewer issues at any given moment than does the Chamber. Still, by almost anyone's definition, the 4 percent rate of disagreement on issues addressed by both organizations has to be considered low.[22]

Certainly there are business organizations more open than the Chamber or the Roundtable to a stronger government role in promoting economic growth and the health, safety, and productivity of workers. The Committee for Economic Development, for example, has championed such beliefs at certain times in its history (Collins 1981). More recently, leaders from companies well known for their progressive stances—such as Ben and Jerry's, the Body Shop, and Levi Strauss & Company—founded the reform-oriented Business for Social

21. Trautwein interview; Joseph interview; Voight interview; Regalia interview.

22. Although I have not systematically collected the data to allow a similar comparison between the Chamber and the National Association of Manufacturers (NAM), during the course of the study I came across many of the latter organization's positions. My impression is that disagreement between the Chamber and NAM is even rarer than disagreement between the Chamber and the Roundtable. Among all three peak associations, harmony and cooperation prevail far more often than dissension and conflict.

Responsibility (BSR). The evolution of BSR is revealing, though, as its decision to invite mainstream corporate leaders into the organization has undermined its ability to articulate bold views (Jacobs 1998).

Even as a watered-down version of the organization it began as, Business for Social Responsibility does remain a voice of dissent. Yet BSR has failed to shift the center of gravity in the business community. When compared to the business world at large, BSR's differences emerge starkly. BSR thus stood alone among business organizations in supporting the Family and Medical Leave Act (Jacobs 1998), showing how truly unrepresentative it is. The U.S. Chamber of Commerce, by contrast, reflects the predominant perspectives within business. While the policy positions of the Chamber are not a perfect indicator, they do serve to isolate issues high on the unity continuum. A more detailed examination of these issues is therefore in order.

FOUR

A Portrait of Unifying Issues

The federal deficit easily ranked among the most noteworthy policy controversies of the 1980s and early 1990s. For some observers, the annual deficit and resulting debt formed the legacy of President Ronald Reagan, who won sharp increases in the defense budget and significant cuts in taxes; for others, the deficit symbolized the rapid growth in spending on entitlements. For more than a decade, politicians wrangled not only over the deficit's causes, but over whether it really mattered to the nation's economic health and, if so, how best to resolve the never-ending problem.

One proposed solution would amend the Constitution to require Congress to offset taxes and spending dollar-for-dollar every year. Although seen by many policy analysts as a gimmick that postponed the tough choices of raising taxes or lowering expenditures, the balanced budget amendment, as it came to be called, retained the political virtue of simplicity. The business community generally endorsed the idea, making the amendment a unifying issue, and diverse companies and industries worked together on many occasions to lobby Congress for passage. Embodying the prevailing perspectives within business, the U.S. Chamber of Commerce strongly supported the balanced budget amendment.

Arousing extended discussion and impassioned appeals, the legislative battles were highly ideological, partisan, and salient. When their party controlled the House and Senate, enough Democrats voted against the balanced budget amendment to keep it from receiving the necessary two-thirds majority in each chamber. After Republicans took control of Congress in 1994, they promised a prompt vote on the amendment as part of the Contract with America. While easily clearing the House in 1995, the amendment fell one vote short in the Senate, signaling what in retrospect appears to be its final burial. In a noticeable partisan split, the amendment attracted the support of 98 percent of Senate Republicans but only 27 percent of Senate Democrats. The ratings of Americans for Democratic Action (ADA), an interest group often used as a barometer of liberalism, tell a similar story of ideology. On a scale from 0 to 100, Senate opponents received an average ADA rating of 85 while supporters scored an average of only 24.[1] Many American citizens, as one would expect for a unifying issue, were familiar with the broad parameters of the debate over the balanced budget amendment. A March 1995 poll asking how closely people had followed news stories on the amendment found 57 percent responding either "very closely" or "fairly closely."[2] Both reflecting and amplifying the salience of the issue, the news media covered it extensively. The evening news on CBS reported on the legislative action in 1995 on six occasions, while the *New York Times* gave it front-page coverage five times.[3]

Previous chapters argued that unifying issues tend to be ideological, partisan, and salient; the balanced budget amendment certainly fits that mold. The question naturally arises: Was the amendment typical among unifying issues in having those characteristics, or was it an aberration? This chapter moves beyond advancing theoretical propositions into substantiating them with evidence. The findings herein show that unifying issues are indeed highly ideological, partisan, and salient. After presenting these findings, I will classify into various policy domains the 2,364 unifying issues identified through the positions of the U.S. Chamber of Commerce. The classifications will help illuminate the substantive content of the issues. Finally, I will measure legislative decisions on each unifying issue. After this scorecard has been constructed, subsequent chapters will explore the reasons why business, when unified, wins or loses in legislation.

1. The figures were calculated by the author from ratings released by Americans for Democratic Action.

2. The poll, conducted by Princeton Survey Research Associates, is archived as question USPSRA.033095, R06D in the online database at the Roper Center for Public Opinion Research.

3. The days for CBS were January 27 and March 1 through March 5, 1995. The *New York Times* front-page coverage fell on January 26 and 27 and March 1 through 3, 1995.

THE IDEOLOGICAL AND PARTISAN NATURE OF
UNIFYING ISSUES

An ideological issue separates liberals from conservatives while a partisan one divides Democrats and Republicans. On these kinds of issues, politicians' behavior can be accurately predicted using only information about their general ideological and partisan affiliations. To determine whether unifying issues are ideological and partisan, one can analyze patterns of voting in Congress. Volumes of previous research have found that when congressional members must publicly choose "yea" or "nay" on a roll call vote, their own ideological and partisan preferences strongly affect their decisions. Poole and Rosenthal (1997) show that throughout two centuries of congressional voting, a scaling procedure based upon a single dimension—which can be interpreted as the liberal-conservative continuum—performs extremely well in explaining outcomes on roll call votes. Given knowledge of a House or Senate member's general ideological outlook and the content of a given vote, one can predict with high accuracy whether the member will choose yea or nay on that particular decision. Research on Congress also has long used the partisan affiliations of House and Senate members to explain the distribution of yeas and nays across roll calls (Collie 1985). Thus, we know that if a decision reaches the point of a roll call vote, ideology and party factor heavily into the outcome.

Decision-making in Congress, however, often presents no need for a recorded roll call vote. Both congressional chambers have developed procedures to dispatch quickly the routine and noncontroversial actions expected to be approved or rejected by a majority so large as to approach unanimity. Minor legislation can be summarily passed through the method of unanimous consent; as long as no member objects, this timesaving device allows legislation to be approved expeditiously by dispensing with a formal vote. In both chambers, actual voting most commonly occurs through an unrecorded voice vote in which the presiding officer sequentially asks the "ayes" and the "noes" to express their votes verbally (Froman 1967; Smith 1989). Based upon the quantity of noise generated by each side, the presiding officer determines whether the vote has carried. Neither the votes of individual members nor the aggregate totals on each side are recorded.

For the vast majority of actions decided by a voice vote, a strong or even overwhelming majority favors one side (Oleszek 1989). Matters at all controversial can be easily routed to a roll call vote if a small proportion of House or Senate members so requests. Similarly, when the voice vote is ambiguous because of noise on both sides, any House member can immediately demand a division vote, also known as a standing vote, whereby both sides alternatively rise to be precisely counted. If a voice vote decides the fate of a bill or amendment, meaning that members did not request another voting procedure, we can infer that the outcome was lopsided in one direction.

Decision-making by unanimous consent or voice vote, therefore, demonstrates a near consensus, indicating that the matter at stake is inherently nonideological and nonpartisan. If all or nearly all House members or senators reach the same decision, the outcome cannot be explained by the distribution of ideological and partisan affiliations. When Senators Jesse Helms and Ted Kennedy—plus all of their colleagues—fully agree on a decision, they clearly did not interpret it through ideological and partisan lenses. This principle distinguishes issues requiring voting by roll call or division from those passing by unanimous consent or a voice vote.

A simple test follows as a result. If issues marked by business unity usually need the former procedures that often create splits while the average issue is routinely dispatched through the latter procedures that reflect consensus, then unifying issues must be disproportionately ideological and partisan. By requiring roll call or division votes, which are widely known to depend upon ideology and partisanship, unifying issues would meet the criteria of separating liberals from conservatives and Democrats from Republicans.

An example illustrates the point. On April 28, 1960, the House of Representatives considered just one unifying issue, a bill to increase the federal government's role in housing construction. Because the bill passed 214–163 through a roll call vote, one can infer that members' ideological and partisan preferences shaped their choices. Among all other bills and amendments that day, none of which were unifying, 81 percent were quickly resolved through either unanimous consent or a voice vote. With decision-making usually proceeding by consensus, ideology and party could have only limited impacts upon the outcomes. If April 28, 1960, was representative of the period from 1953 to 1996, then unifying issues must be disproportionately ideological and partisan.

To determine whether reality matches my expectation, I compared decision-making on the population of unifying issues and a sample of all issues before Congress. The first population consists of floor decisions on unifying issues, primarily bills and resolutions but also some amendments. I counted for each congressional body and each year from 1953 to 1996 the number of decisions reached through (1) roll call or division votes, and (2) unanimous consent or voice votes.[4] I then divided the number resolved through roll call or division votes by the sum across both categories. This calculation yields for each house the yearly proportion of decisions settled through methods depending heavily on ideology and party. When averaged across the years, the House and Senate decide unifying issues via roll call or division votes 76 percent and 64 percent of the time, respectively. Most of the time, then, unifying issues require decision-making procedures that allow ideology and party to strongly influence the outcome.

The second population includes all floor decisions reported in the *Daily Digest* of the *Congressional Record*.[5] For each year from 1953 to 1996, I randomly selected five decisions from both the House and Senate, thereby leading to a sample size of 220 for each body.[6] As before, I classified decisions as either roll call/division or unanimous consent/voice.[7] For each house of Congress, I then calculated the average yearly proportion of decisions resolved by either roll call or division. The House and Senate produce average proportions of only 29 percent and 25 percent, respectively. These figures highlight important facets of congressional legislating: for a substantial majority of decisions, ideology and party do not noticeably affect the outcome because a consensus cuts across ideological lines and partisan affiliations. The

4. For the infrequent occasions when they are used, teller votes are grouped with roll call and division votes. As a practical matter, none of the unifying issues were ever resolved by unanimous consent.

5. Passage of multiple bills or amendments with a single action counts only once. I exclude from the population unanimous consent requests by members to extend remarks in the *Record*, dispense with quorum calls, and the like, which are not reported in the *Daily Digest*. My sampling framework also excludes private bills and unanimous consent agreements in the Senate.

6. To select a decision, I first determined a day of the year by randomly choosing a number between one and 365. If no floor decisions occurred on the chosen day, then another day was randomly selected until a usable one surfaced. By subsequently choosing a random number between one and the number of floor decisions on that day, I pinpointed a specific decision. I repeated the process to gain a sample of five votes per year per chamber.

7. I counted voice votes reconsidered as division or roll call votes with the division/roll call category because this additional information suggests that the original voting margin was reasonably close.

estimates add precision to what congressional scholars (Froman 1967; Smith 1989; Oleszek 1989) have long known, namely that Congress routinely dispenses most floor decisions with little debate or dissension.

The foregoing analysis reveals that unifying issues, by comparison to the average issue, are far more likely to rely upon the nonconsensual procedures that uncover splits according to ideology and party. While unifying issues in the House and Senate reach roll call or division votes 75 percent and 65 percent of the time, the comparable estimates for the average issue are only 29 percent and 25 percent. One can infer, therefore, that ideology and party become especially important when a unifying issue is under consideration.

UNIFYING ISSUES: SALIENT BUT RARE

The theoretical perspective developed in previous chapters predicts that unifying issues will be not only ideological and partisan but salient as well. How can one detect empirically the presence or absence of the latter attribute? Given the inability of citizens to observe personally the officials making decisions—members of Congress, the president and his staff, and the executive branch officials who author some bills—lawmaking on an issue usually cannot become salient without coverage by the news media. Extensive media attention brings information about the issue to the public, allowing some citizens to formulate preferences and learn about their representatives' behavior. The volume of media attention, then, is a valid indicator of an issue's salience.[8]

The approach used here compares the media coverage prompted by unifying issues, expected to be substantial, with the coverage given to a control group consisting of all issues. For this comparison I measure salience as a dichotomy indicating whether, at least once during the year, lawmaking on the issue reaches the front (first) page of a pre-eminent newspaper, the *New York Times*. Other media outlets typically follow the lead of elite media such as the *New York Times, Washington Post* and the network news (Graber 1989), making coverage in the *Times* a reasonable measure of an issue's national salience. My predictions would be confirmed if unifying issues are disproportionately likely to attract front-page coverage.

From the population of unifying issues, I selected 210 by randomly

8. See also Baumgartner and Jones (1993), Sharp (1994), and Edwards, Mitchell, and Welch (1995) on using media coverage to measure salience.

choosing five from each year between 1953 and 1994.[9] To determine whether each item reached the front page during the specified year, I combed the annual *New York Times Index*, developing new searching categories for every issue. Of the 210 issues, 72 of them—or 34 percent of the total—reach the high threshold of appearing on the *New York Times* front page. Many of the others attracted articles elsewhere in the newspaper.

The control population consists of all legislation actively considered by Congress. To sample from this population, I used the database of congressional hearings constructed by Frank Baumgartner and Bryan Jones (Baumgartner, Jones, and MacLeod forthcoming), who have coded all 70,000 congressional hearings from 1949 to 1994. In determining the relevant population, I narrowed their database to nonappropriations referral hearings. By excluding oversight hearings that do not consider actual legislation, I impose the same criterion used to identify unifying issues. Namely, only bills reaching the formal congressional agenda should be eligible to be chosen. Appropriations hearings were excluded because of the challenges, noted in appendix A, that spending bills sometimes pose for determining the positions of the U.S. Chamber of Commerce.

Alternating between the House and Senate, I sampled five hearings from each year to produce a total of 210 cases. Using both the Congressional Information Service's online index and *Congressional Quarterly Almanac*, I created descriptions of all bills considered during the chosen hearings. I subsequently devised appropriate searching categories and checked the *New York Times Index* for possible front-page coverage.

Within the control sample, only 5 percent of the issues reach the front page. This figure probably overestimates the salience of the population of all congressional issues for two reasons. First, salient bills, by producing unusually large numbers of hearings from different committees and subcommittees, have additional chances to appear in the sample. Second, and more importantly, the hearings database from which the control sample is drawn includes entire bills rather than their detailed provisions. This second reason is consequential because, as noted in chapter 3, business unifies most frequently on bills as a whole. Specific provisions, sometimes addressed through amendments, are normally particularistic or conflictual. At the same time, those specific provisions

9. The control population, to be described shortly, does not include 1995 and 1996. Hence the comparison must be restricted to 1953–1994.

are less likely to attract media coverage, which typically focuses on the broad themes of bills. Hence a comparison using bills but not provisions has little effect upon the estimated salience of unifying issues but inflates the salience of the control population by dropping items unlikely to garner media attention.

Even if the 5 percent figure for the salience of the control population was not an overstatement, it would remain much lower than the 34 percent calculated for unifying issues. The limits of public and media attention dictate that salience cannot be spread across large numbers of issues simultaneously. Unifying issues, for reasons described in chapter 2, are disproportionately salient. That attribute should have major implications for the power of business and the scope of popular representation.

Of course, salience should probably be conceived as a continuum rather than as a dichotomy. The measure of front-page coverage, in establishing a high cutoff point, serves to isolate the upper reaches of the salience continuum. However, it cannot calibrate gradations, and many of the unifying issues that fall short of front-page coverage nevertheless do attract moderate levels of visibility. By yielding a rough comparison, though, the dichotomy does establish the distinctiveness of issues marked by business unity.

We now know that unifying issues have an increased likelihood of being salient, but an additional question remains: How often do unifying issues arise in the first place? The population of unifying issues consists of an average of 54 per year. Without a frame of reference, these data cannot tell us whether, within the entire realm of legislative politics, unity happens frequently or only rarely. The sample of control issues chosen above allows a preliminary answer to this question. Of the 210 cases sampled from the population of all congressional hearings, only 7 percent also belong to the set of unifying issues. Based upon this information, we would estimate that 7 percent of all issues are unifying.

This figure probably exaggerates the true prevalence of unifying issues for the same reasons that the control population overestimates salience. Namely, by incorporating bills but not provisions, the control population increases the odds of selecting both unifying issues and issues with high salience. Thus the actual proportion of all issues that are unifying is surely less than 7 percent—but even 7 percent would be a very low figure. The remaining 93 percent include all the particularistic and conflictual issues. Within the context of all legislative action, according to this finding, consensus within business does not materialize very often.

Additional evidence based on the work of Mayhew (1991) can demonstrate the tendency for unifying issues to be salient but rare within American politics. Mayhew seeks to determine whether, as conventional wisdom holds, divided government inhibits the ability of Congress and the president to pass truly important legislation. To answer this question, he first identifies important legislative acts through leading newspapers' wrap-up stories written as Congress adjourns and through the retrospective evaluations of policy experts. Incorporating information from both sources, he develops a set of steps for systemically identifying the most important acts from 1946 to 1992.[10] Through these procedures Mayhew catalogs laws of critical importance, a concept strongly related to the salience of legislation. It is difficult to draw public attention to a trivial matter that seems remote from people's lives. By contrast, a matter of clear national importance will typically be discussed in the news media and followed by many citizens. Mayhew's list of the most important laws therefore serves as a reasonable proxy for a list of the most salient ones.

Through his various sources, Mayhew finds 245 acts of critical importance from 1953 to 1992.[11] One hundred thirty-one of these, comprising 53 percent of the total, were marked by business unity. For the majority of important acts, firms share agreement on whether passage would benefit or harm them. In other words, on a list of the most important acts from the last few decades, unifying issues outnumber particularistic and conflictual issues *combined*. Substantively important laws exhibit a high likelihood of producing business unity either in support or in opposition.

The differences in importance, and hence in salience, between unifying and other kinds of issues grow starker when we consider that agreement among firms occurs only infrequently. From 1953 to 1992, exactly 14,044 separate acts, or roughly 350 per year, were signed into law (Ornstein, Mann, and Malbin 1996, 165). The majority of these laws were irrelevant to most Americans and can only be classified as

10. The hardback version of the book runs from 1946 to 1990, while the paperback version includes an epilogue applying his methodology for 1991–1992.

11. Mayhew examines only enacted legislation, rather than the full spectrum of congressional action, but his classification scheme nevertheless yields information useful for exploring the characteristics of unifying issues.

having low substantive importance. Even the best-informed observers would find among the laws enacted in a given year hordes that they have neither heard of nor care about.

That reality reflects the fact that particularistic and conflictual issues, which typically find little interest among ordinary citizens, far outnumber unifying issues. Of the 14,044 laws enacted from 1953 to 1992, only 462—or 3 percent of the total—are characterized by unity within business. Thus, while just 3 percent of all enacted laws, unifying issues comprise 53 percent of the most important and salient ones. Although they occur only infrequently, unifying issues are especially likely to attain high salience.

POLICY DOMAINS PROMINENT AMONG UNIFYING ISSUES

The path thus far in the chapter has taken us through the internal rules and proceedings of Congress. A valuable payoff has resulted from the effort, for we see strong evidence that unifying issues tend to be ideological, partisan, and salient. Chapter 2 proposed that unifying issues possess those characteristics and the data now provide confirmation.[12] This corroboration of chapter 2's predictions is no small matter, as important implications for how lawmaking unfolds should result from the characteristics of unifying issues.

Before constructing a model to explain the outcomes of unifying issues, it will be instructive to explore the content of the policy debates attracting a business consensus. What kinds of issues over the last few decades have stimulated unity among diverse firms and industries? Have unifying issues appeared most often in certain areas of public policy? To answer these questions, I classified each issue into one of fourteen mutually exclusive policy domains; each domain is then divided into several subcategories (table 4.1).

The table displays the main categories in order of their frequency, and each subcategory is accompanied by an illustrative example. I urge readers to examine this list to gain a sense of the issues that garner a business consensus. The list offers contextual information that makes more concrete what otherwise might seem to be an undifferentiated data set.

12. These findings show a kind of construct validity for using the positions of the U.S. Chamber of Commerce as indicators of business unity. Because the issues identified through the Chamber have attributes matching theoretical expectations, usage of the Chamber's positions passes a test of construct validity.

Table 4.1 Policy Content of Unifying Issues

POLICY DOMAIN	ILLUSTRATIVE EXAMPLE AND YEAR
Regulation 25%	
Consumer (4%)	require truth in packaging (1966)
Antitrust (3%)	require government notification of mergers (1956)
Environment (3%)	strong water pollution control programs (1972)
Miscellaneous (2%)	prohibit polygraph testing (1986)
Benefit plans (2%)	simplify pension regulation (1991)
Agency rulemaking (2%)	require regulatory cost-benefit analyses (1996)
Energy prices/entry (2%)	deregulate natural gas prices (1983)
Discrimination (2%)	expand coverage of civil rights statutes (1985)
Wages/prices/credit (1%)	authorize wage and price controls (1971)
Worker health/safety (1%)	protect whistleblowers on safety violations (1990)
Transportation prices/entry (1%)	loosen transportation rate regulation (1963)
Securities/financial (1%)	expand securities regulations (1955)
Lobbying (1%)	strengthen lobbying registration requirements (1967)
Social welfare programs 15%	
Education/job training (3%)	provide federal aid for education (1953)
Public works/development (2%)	public service jobs for the unemployed (1971)
Health (2%)	government health insurance for the elderly (1965)
Housing/urban affairs (2%)	construct more public housing (1955)
Unemployment compensation (2%)	streamline unemployment compensation (1980)
Miscellaneous (1%)	subsidies for state child care programs (1988)
Social security/disability (1%)	raise and index social security benefits (1970)
Welfare (1%)	streamline food stamps program (1976)
Veterans (1%)	extend benefits to peacetime veterans (1960)
Worker's compensation (1%)	federal standards for worker's compensation (1973)
Natural resources/public lands 9%	
Development on public lands (2%)	authorize development in Alaskan wilderness (1987)
Land/wildlife preservation (2%)	expand national wilderness system (1957)
Land/water projects/ cleanup (2%)	clean up toxic dumps via Superfund (1980)
Miscellaneous (1%)	establish mining and minerals policy (1969)
Federal/state issues (1%)	require states to plan land use (1974)
Energy (1%)	subsidize development of synthetic fuels (1976)
Taxation 8%	
Corporations (5%)	repeal investment tax credit (1969)
Individuals (2%)	increase tax incentives for saving (1979)
General (1%)	corporate and personal income tax cuts (1981)

Continued

Table 4.1 *Continued*

POLICY DOMAIN	ILLUSTRATIVE EXAMPLE AND YEAR
Government organization/management 8%	
Miscellaneous (3%)	establish middecade census (1973)
Reorganize/study agencies (3%)	study comparable worth for federal jobs (1985)
Postal service (1%)	increase rates to cover postal deficit (1957)
Labor 7%	
General labor laws (3%)	overturn state right-to-work laws (1966)
Minimum wage/overtime (1%)	increase minimum wage (1961)
Strike/dispute intervention (1%)	deny food stamps to striking workers (1975)
Mandated benefits (1%)	require family and medical leave (1993)
New unionization (1%)	collective bargaining in public sector (1972)
Miscellaneous federal spending 6%	
Generic federal spending (2%)	extend revenue sharing (1975)
Agriculture (2%)	reduce farm price supports (1958)
Omnibus spending bills (1%)	cut federal spending (1982)
Business subsidies (1%)	fund Super Sonic Transport (1971)
Trade/export promotion 6%	
Miscellaneous (2%)	disallow MFN status for China (1990)
Export subsidies (2%)	expand Export-Import Bank (1968)
Trade agreements (1%)	authorize multilateral trade negotiations (1979)
Procurement 4%	
Miscellaneous (2%)	reform federal procurement procedures (1977)
Contractor profits/wages (2%)	require contractors to pay prevailing wages (1956)
Foreign policy 4%	
Foreign aid (2%)	contribute to development banks (1963)
Miscellaneous (1%)	economic sanctions against South Africa (1984)
Treaties (1%)	authorize negotiations for patent treaty (1969)
Federally run enterprises 3%	
Federal energy production (2%)	expand Tennessee Valley Authority 1955)
In-house vs. contract out (1%)	require more private sector contracting (1984)
Budget rules 3%	
Rules to restrict spending (2%)	set statutory limits on federal spending (1980)
Budget amendment/item veto (1%)	allow a line-item veto (1995)
Elections 2%	
Miscellaneous (1%)	voter registration at government offices (1975)
Campaign finance (1%)	public funding of congressional elections (1973)
Justice system 3%	
Expedite justice (2%)	restructure bankruptcy courts (1983)
Patents (1%)	reform patent system (1967)

Note: The main policy domains are followed by their constituent subcategories. Each subcategory's percentage indicates its share of the 2,364 issues marked by business unity from 1953 to 1996. Category totals do not sum to 100 percent due to rounding error.

The domain of regulation easily ranks first and contains 25 percent of all unifying issues. Vogel (1989) devoted extensive attention to regulation in his analysis of business power over time, so its prominence here would be expected. Among unifying issues in this category, proposals dealing with consumer, antitrust, and environmental regulation are especially numerous. The regulation domain includes initiatives to ensure truth in packaging (1966), establish strong water pollution control programs (1972), simplify pension regulation (1991), require regulatory cost-benefit analyses (1996), and protect whistleblowers on safety violations (1990).

The category of social welfare programs ranks second with 15 percent of the unifying issues. This domain includes education/job training, public works/development, health, housing/urban affairs, and several other components. Examples of legislation in these areas include bills to provide federal aid for education (1953), construct more public housing (1955), streamline the unemployment compensation program (1980), and implement federal standards for workers' compensation (1973).

After the areas of regulation and social welfare programs, the other domains encompass considerably fewer issues. Natural resources/public lands, taxation, government organization/management, and labor contain 9 percent, 8 percent, 8 percent, and 7 percent of all unifying issues, respectively. Those categories include bills to expand the national wilderness system (1957), increase tax incentives for saving (1979), study comparable worth for federal jobs (1985), and raise the minimum wage (1961 and other years).

The remaining categories are miscellaneous federal spending, trade/export promotion, procurement, foreign policy, federally run enterprises, budget rules, elections, and the justice system. Those domains contain legislative proposals to extend revenue sharing (1975), authorize multilateral trade negotiations (1979), require contractors to pay prevailing wages (1956), establish economic sanctions against South Africa (1984), and allow a line-item veto (1995). It is notable that foreign policy includes such a small share of unifying issues, just 4 percent of the total. Foreign policy has often been recognized as a domain dominated by conflicts among firms (McLelland and Woodhouse 1966), so its rarity among the set of unifying issues is expected. The data thus dictate that a study of unifying issues focus largely on domestic policy.

A BRIEF TOUR OF THREE POLICY AREAS

Given their shared characteristics, it makes sense to generalize across unifying issues in seeking to understand the legislative process. Abstracting the common forces shaping their resolution, though, introduces the danger that the tangible legislative struggles in the data set, each with its own colorful history, will be overlooked. This danger can be mitigated by investigating further some of the policy areas marked by business unity. To facilitate greater awareness of the issues under study, I will present brief overviews of postwar lawmaking in three areas containing many instances of business unity: employment policy, labor-management relations, and air pollution. The discussion will not only allow additional familiarity with the kinds of issues evoking business unity, it will also illustrate the earlier finding that unifying issues stand among the most important and salient disputes in all of American politics.

EMPLOYMENT POLICY

Though its failure to overcome a Senate filibuster occurred slightly before the period under examination, the Full Employment Bill of 1945 cast a shadow over later initiatives regarding employment policy. The legislation would have guaranteed a job to everyone wanting to work, a promise backed by a commitment to social spending to achieve full employment. Faced with a bill that would have greatly expanded the federal government's management of the economy and increased the bargaining leverage of labor, business predictably unified in opposition. Subsequently the more general and less targeted levers of fiscal and monetary policy became the means accepted by economists and policymakers to promote employment (Mucciaroni 1990; Weir 1992). Over time Keynesian deficit spending faded as an option, though Keynesian tax cuts did gain sporadic attention. The Tax Revenue Act of 1964 that significantly reduced marginal tax rates, championed by the Kennedy Administration as a means to stimulate employment, enjoyed generally strong backing from business.

In the late 1950s and early 1960s, legislation authorizing and providing appropriations for area redevelopment emerged as one potential way to increase employment. The loans and grants, mostly opposed by business as an unnecessary expansion of federal power, were used to construct and repair local public facilities. Under what was called public service employment, enlisting the federal government to create jobs directly gained support in the late 1960s from the liberal-labor coalition inside and outside Congress. During the recession of 1971 this approach was enacted into law over the objections of business, and grants began flowing to localities to do the hiring. The Comprehensive Employment and Training Act of 1973 (CETA) authorized public service employment on a permanent basis. Business, maintaining relatively high unity, continued to oppose the idea.

Potentially more sweeping legislation soon appeared in the form of the Humphrey-Hawkins bill, first introduced in 1974. The legislation, similar to the Full Employment Bill of 1945, would have secured a right to a job for everyone wanting to work and would have pledged the federal government to spending the necessary money to achieve full employment. As had been the case three decades earlier, business strongly resisted the proposal, contending that the resulting scope of government oversight of the economy would be counterproductive. The core principles of Humphrey-Hawkins were never enacted into law, though a substantially watered-down version passed in 1978.

At about the same time, businesses joined together to endorse President Carter's Private Sector Initiative Program, which extended CETA but added greater private involvement in job creation and ceded additional authority to state and local governments. That approach was taken one step further through the Job Training Partnership Act of 1982. This new legislation, also supported by business, incorporated local business leaders into planning and administering the programs. As another means to stimulate development in depressed areas, the Reagan Administration proposed creating enterprise zones, tracts that would feature tax incentives to attract private investment. Business unified behind certain versions of the enterprise zone concept, though it has not been enacted into law on a large scale.

LABOR-MANAGEMENT RELATIONS

Probably no issue gains as much attention from business as its relations with labor. In 1959 the broad business community backed the Landrum-Griffin Act, which placed restrictions on unions in areas such as the procedures to elect union leaders. The legislation also curbed the capacity of unions to employ boycotts and picketing in support of striking workers from other unions. During the 1960s business coalesced against respective bills to expand the powers of the National Labor Relations Board and to repeal states' authority to enact right-to-work laws. Should it have been enacted, the latter legislation would have effectively repealed much of the Taft-Hartley law that had governed labor-management relations ever since its passage in 1947. The bill ultimately passed the House of Representatives but fell victim to a Senate filibuster in 1965 and 1966.

Business unified to support an unsuccessful 1970 proposal to transfer judicial and prosecuting powers from the NLRB to federal judges and U.S. Attorneys, officials business expected to be friendlier to the management side of disputes. A bill to legalize the practice of picketing an entire construction site when a union's grievances stemmed from a single subcontractor, which a united business community opposed, passed both chambers of Congress in 1975 but died after the president vetoed it. Similar bills had received attention in Congress over the previous two decades. Another business-opposed bill in 1975, which would have given national unions more control over the collective bargaining of local chapters, passed the House of Representatives but not the Senate.

In the key struggle of 1977–1978, unified business interests squared off against unions on a bill to reform labor laws. Business groups joined together in 1984 behind a bill to ban the use of union dues for political purposes—an issue that disappeared for a time before making a strong resurgence in the late 1990s. A 1995 bill, which would have granted greater leeway for employers to establish employee committees and task forces, passed the House but went no further. Unified businesses supported it; labor, fearing the legislation would open the door to company unions, mobilized against it.

AIR POLLUTION

Prior to the 1960s, the federal government's role in controlling air pollution consisted of conducting research and supplying technical assistance to state and local governments. Potential proposals to regulate emissions of nitrogen oxides, particulate matter, lead, and other agents never appeared on the congressional agenda. Even the original Clean Air Act, enacted in 1963, demanded little more of federal agencies than using publicity to promote cooperation between state governments and industry. As befitting the lack of substantive debates over air pollution for most the nation's history, business did not unify for or against any legislative proposals before the last years of the 1960s. Those years saw a rapid transformation of the issue that drew business into its orbit.

In 1967 business united against legislation that would have established federal air quality standards; presumably the standards would have been followed by regulatory policies to achieve them. The legislation failed in Congress, which instead passed the business-supported Air Quality Act that left devising standards for air quality firmly in the hands of states. The idea of national standards continued to attract congressional attention, however, and reappeared in the Clean Air Act Amendments of 1970. That legislation, the central pillar of national policy on air pollution, mandated reductions in certain kinds of emissions, gave the newly created Environmental Protection Agency (EPA) oversight over state plans designed to meet the national standards, and permitted citizens to sue the EPA if the agency was not fulfilling its enforcement duties. The law signaled a shift in control over air pollution from states to the federal government and sparked unified business resistance, though business groups including the U.S. Chamber of Commerce recognized the immense public support for the legislation and chose not to spend much effort opposing it (Jones 1975).

In the mid-1970s the dominant question regarding air pollution was whether areas already exceeding the standards would be allowed to degrade to the level the standards seemed to permit. The Supreme Court had ruled that the EPA must prevent significant degradation—which might result from new industrial development—in areas currently conforming to air quality standards. A set of Clean Air Act amendments enacted in 1977, which business opposed, codified this ruling.

As the 1980s began, scientists raised new concerns about the consequences that rain with a high level of acidity produces for wildlife, lakes and streams, and human structures. "Acid rain," as it came to be called, results when water droplets mix with air pollutants, especially sulfur dioxide, nitrogen oxides, and hydrocarbons. Proposals to combat acid rain appeared in Congress, and when they mandated curbing industrial emissions business unified in opposition. The Reagan administration joined business groups in contesting new air pollution regulation; it was not until 1990 that the Clean Air Act was strengthened to include, among other provisions, policy tools to address acid rain (Bryner 1993).

MEASURING THE OUTCOMES OF UNIFYING ISSUES

Now that we have acquired a feel for unifying issues and seen that they include some of the milestones of postwar lawmaking, we can proceed to the next stage of the analysis. Future chapters will attempt to explain legislative outcomes on the 2,364 unifying issues. To prepare for this explanation, I traced each issue through the legislative process and recorded the final resolution. Several sources were helpful in this effort, including *Congressional Quarterly Weekly Report, Congressional Quarterly Almanac,* the Congressional Information Service's online index of congressional hearings and documents, the electronic database *Legislate,* and the Chamber's own internal documents. Potential outcomes include reaching the agenda but proceeding no farther, passing one house of Congress but not the other, or enactment into law.

How should these data be measured and analyzed? Legislative decisions will eventually be the dependent variable that I seek to explain. Measurement procedures for the dependent variable, though, must be synchronized with those for the independent variables. The independent variables described in subsequent chapters either have a natural periodicity of one year or else cannot be measured uniquely for each issue and must be aggregated on an annual basis. Elections bringing new officials to office, for example, affect many different policy areas simultaneously and hence do not vary across the issues considered in a given year. Such variables as public opinion and lobbying cannot be measured for each of the 2,364 issues but rather must be aggregated. To match the independent and dependent variables over the same interval, I will construct indicators of lawmaking by aggregating the legislative action on all bills falling within a given calendar year.

Measuring lawmaking on a yearly basis may not be as easy as it appears upon first glance. In particular, one might wonder whether a decision at a given moment could be compared with a decision during another era with a different context. These difficulties cannot be overcome entirely, but they are mitigated by the continuity across time in the U.S. Chamber of Commerce's guiding ideology. Because legislative actions will always be measured here relative to what the Chamber wants, and the core principles that determine the Chamber's positions do not change much over time, it becomes possible to construct a measure to compare outcomes from different years.

Mitchell (1997) argues convincingly that any thorough explanation of business power must consider both wins and losses, and that approach will be followed here. The best measure of policy would include all aspects of legislative activity. Scholars sometimes focus only on the final product—the actual laws enacted—while overlooking the earlier stages of the legislative process. Yet examining bills that fail somewhere along the institutional obstacle course, by far the most likely outcome for any piece of legislation, affords insights that might be missed if the analyst investigates only successful bills (Edwards, Barrett, and

Peake 1997). Many observers suspect that business gains its greatest power through its ability to block legislation, a pattern that can be uncovered only by including business-opposed bills that died. Similarly, a comprehensive perspective on business power needs to consider bills business supported that nevertheless ended up in the graveyard of legislative politics. Analyzing only the bills that pass could lead to major errors in inference; a satisfactory explanation of lawmaking should address what does not pass in addition to what does.

Merely placing an item on the congressional agenda can be a critical first step, for political conflicts change once an issue attracts attention (Schattschneider 1960). Public opinion often cannot crystallize until an issue is actively considered and citizens gain opportunities to respond to competing perspectives on the matter. Moreover, new proposals constantly appear on the congressional calendar; it takes time for policymakers to evaluate them and for coalitions to form. It is no surprise, then, that in the postwar period few important laws were enacted the year they were initially introduced. For example, establishing Superfund to require industry to help pay for cleaning up toxic waste dumps—a unifying issue—was considered by a congressional committee as early as 1975 yet was not written into law until 1980. Including the creation of Superfund in the analysis only the year it passed would miss much of the story.

Because no single measure could adequately cover the entire scope of legislative action, the analyses in the next three chapters use multiple indicators. The indicators tap several elements of lawmaking that students of public policy regard as important, such as what gets on the agenda, who prevails on floor votes, and who prevails in terms of enacted legislation. All stages of the legislative process are included, from the earlier ones where most bills die to the later ones where some bills become laws. To capture the full range of activity, I created six different annual measures, each scored such that higher values reflect policy decisions more favorable to business:

1. *Agenda composition.* Of the total number of agenda items (i.e., all bills or provisions marked by either business support or opposition that receive formal consideration in Congress), the proportion supported by business.[13]

2. *Out of committee.* Of the total number of business-related items reaching

13. All six indicators are subsequently multiplied by 100 to yield scores with theoretical ranges from 0 to 100.

some stage beyond the committee level (i.e., bills that were reported and/or received a floor vote), the proportion supported by business.

3. *Passed one chamber.* Of the total number of business-related items passing either the House or the Senate or both, the proportion supported by business.

4. *House margins.* Of all relevant votes on the floor of the House, the average proportion of voting members taking the probusiness side.[14]

5. *Senate margins.* Of all relevant votes on the floor of the Senate, the average proportion of voting members taking the probusiness side.

6. *Enactment scorecard.* Of the total number of business-related items signed into law, the proportion supported by business.[15]

THE FAVORABILITY OF POLICYMAKING TO BUSINESS

Figure 4.1 displays the values of the indicators from 1953 to 1996. For each indicator, scores have a theoretical maximum of 100 and a minimum of 0. High and low points on the graph indicate policymaking that is relatively favorable and unfavorable to business, respectively. Probably the most striking feature of figure 4.1 is the common movement of all six indicators. Indeed, they so closely track each other that it is difficult to tell them apart; they appear to be all measuring the same construct.

The inability for the naked eye to distinguish among the six indicators is, in fact, an interesting finding. This pattern demonstrates the analytic parsimony gained from treating them collectively, as a single measure of lawmaking, instead of individually. Most scholars would agree that all stages should be studied; the question is whether the best approach would perform six discrete investigations or else undertake one summary assessment. On theoretical grounds one might construct reasons to study independently each aspect of the legislative process, leading to six different analyses. As an empirical matter, though, outcomes for the various stages are so heavily intercorrelated as to render separate

14. Voice votes are counted as passing with complete unanimity, but voice votes that merely ratify amendments added by the other chamber are not included. When there are multiple floor votes in the House or Senate on the same item, such as votes for initial passage of a bill and then a vote on the conference report, the score for the individual item is constructed by averaging across these votes. Each item, that is, counts only once in the computation of the overall score for the year.

15. Simple resolutions requiring a vote in only one congressional chamber, and no presidential signature, are not counted within the "Enactment Scorecard," but they are included within the other indicators. Constitutional amendments need to pass both bodies of Congress by the requisite two-thirds margins to be coded as being enacted.

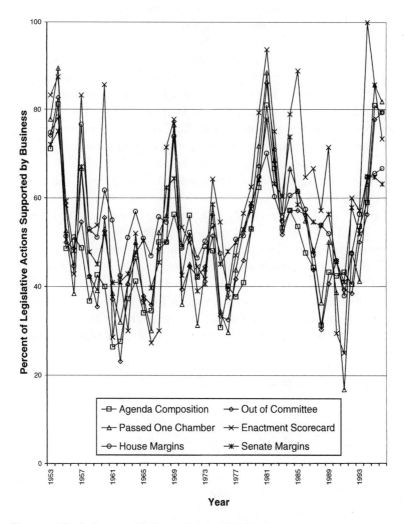

Figure 4.1 Six Indicators of Policymaking on Unifying Issues

analyses redundant and inefficient. The high intercorrelations mean that studying the stages together rather than separately benefits from a major technical advantage: Each indicator undoubtedly has measurement error associated with it that would make a statistical estimation using only that indicator problematic. A dimensionality analysis undertaken on all six can generate a more reliable and valid indicator of the underlying concept than could be gained from only one of them.

A principal components estimation, whose results are presented in table 4.2, indicates that a single dimension explains 85 percent of the variance in the six indicators. Thus, a one-factor solution fits the data very well, which is expected given the large amount of common movement revealed in a visual examination of figure 4.1. The communalities, which range from .77 to .96, show that all indicators relate strongly to the latent dimension. The data support an inference that each of the six indicators primarily taps the same latent construct. The evidence indicates that business does not systematically perform better or worse at one stage of the legislative process than another. When the composition of the agenda favors business, for example, business also prevails on floor votes and in the legislation enacted into law. If business fares well at one stage, it fares well at all stages.

Even if one were primarily interested in a single stage, from a statistical standpoint it would make the most sense to examine the factor derived from all six indicators because the individual measures probably contain a greater amount of random measurement error. The Enactment Scorecard, in particular, undoubtedly has a lower reliability than the others, owing to its construction from the fewest number of items—an average of only fourteen per year and as few as six. For both conceptual and statistical reasons, investigating all of the legislative

Table 4.2 Principal Components Analysis of Six Policy Indicators

FACTOR	EIGENVALUE	ADDITIONAL VARIANCE EXPLAINED
1	5.03	85%
2	0.43	7%
3	0.27	4%
4	0.15	2%
5	0.08	1%
6	0.04	1%

INDICATOR	COMMUNALITY WITH FIRST FACTOR
Agenda composition	0.79
Out of committee	0.89
Passed one chamber	0.96
Enactment scorecard	0.77
House margins	0.83
Senate margins	0.86

Note: Results are shown for a principal components analysis of six indicators of the favorability of policy making to business as represented through the federal legislative process. The indicators are measured annually from 1953 to 1996.

activity simultaneously provides the clearest window into the questions motivating the book.

Based upon the principal components analysis presented in table 4.2, I extracted a latent dimension from the data. As is normally the case when one derives a factor, the values for each year are measured in units matching the standard normal distribution, here ranging from -1.4 to 2.3. To make the scores easier to interpret, they were rescaled to take the metric of the first indicator, Agenda Composition, through a linear transformation.[16] To calculate the value for each year, the raw scores were multiplied by the standard deviation of Agenda Composition and then added to its mean. The resulting scale can theoretically vary from 0 to 100; it is graphed in figure 4.2.

Figure 4.2 identifies the particular years that were most and least favorable to business. High scores denote times when business was disproportionately prevailing at all kinds of legislative activity, while low scores locate times when policy was often incongruent with business preferences. The data indicate that business fared best in the early 1950s, the early 1980s, and the mid-1990s. The worst years for business were in the mid-1960s, mid-1970s, and early 1990s.

The graph matches common understandings about political eras in America. It comes as no shock that business enjoyed many political victories in the 1950s and during the early Reagan years. Students of American politics would have believed business to be more often on the defensive during the middle parts of the 1960s and 1970s. The peaks and valleys depicted in the figure correspond reasonably closely to the ebb and flow of business-related legislation described by Vogel (1989). Incidentally, the graph's predictable configuration of legislative outcomes provides reassurance that the stands taken by the U.S. Chamber of Commerce reflect views prevalent throughout the business community. If the Chamber's positions were not representative of the business voice, the graph would not show such coherent movement in federal policy from one period to the next.

Understanding and explaining lawmaking on unifying issues requires a broad perspective. Because of difficulties in interpretation, one should exercise caution in selecting any single legislative outcome from the period under study and calling it either a "win" or a "loss." Writing legislation, the German leader Bismarck memorably remarked, is like

16. Because the indicators share nearly the same mean, variance, and movement over time, it does not much matter which one is chosen to provide the reference metric. For the sake of simplicity, the metric of the first indicator is used.

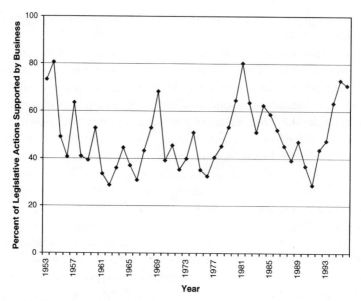

Figure 4.2 The Favorability to Business of Legislative Action on Unifying Issues

making sausage: The process is inherently messy. Coalitions can quickly shift, turning former opponents into allies. The reference point frequently changes as well; what seems to be a victory could be construed as a defeat if an even better development had been expected. Most enacted bills result from bargaining and negotiation where neither side gets everything it wants but both sides could have imagined something worse. In cases of compromise, finding the true winners and losers can sometimes be difficult.

Thus an element of subjectivity would seep into any attempt to characterize each legislative decision in the data set as either a victory or a defeat for business. The decisions need not be analyzed one-at-a-time, though, for they reveal clear patterns when aggregated. Most observers would agree that certain eras have yielded policies considerably more favorable to business than have other eras. No one doubts, for example, that—as figure 4.2 shows—legislative decisions were much closer to business's preferences in 1981 than in 1971. Even though any one decision from either year could be subject to competing interpretations, the overall differences between the two years' records are real. The changes over time depicted in the figure accurately capture the fluctuations in business-related legislation.

The story told by the figure is ultimately incomplete, though, for it says nothing about why changes have arisen in the favorability to business of legislative action on unifying issues. In the next four chapters I seek to provide the necessary explanation, which obviously must address questions of business power. Scholars widely concur that power is a slippery concept, a conclusion reflected most notably in the massive literature attempting to define, describe, and understand it. Given an element of ambiguity in what power really means, it is extremely difficult to prove whether any particular actor has exerted power; the best one can do is to marshal evidence. The approach developed here bears a similarity to Nagel's (1975) admonitions on how power can be empirically studied. Congressional and presidential decisions on unifying issues have already been recorded and measured on an annual basis. The objective is to determine the degree to which those decisions respond to what unified business interests want, to what the public wants, or to what both business and the public jointly want.

Business power could manifest itself in three primary ways, often called the three "faces of power" (Lukes 1974). First, through all kinds of political activity, a unified business community could help determine policies and thereby push them away from the public's preferences. Second, by anticipating what private enterprise needs in order to sustain the economy, officeholders could tilt legislation toward business even without any explicit actions by corporations, trade associations, or peak associations. Third, business could mold what the public wants, creating an indirect means of power over lawmaking.

All three sources of power will be investigated empirically in the chapters that follow. Figure 4.2 cannot directly speak to those sources, for it shows a measure of lawmaking rather than a measure of power. The fluctuations depicted in the graph simply highlight the times when legislative activity was most and least favorable to business. Legislative decisions by themselves cannot reveal the influence of a unified business community or any particular business organization such as the Chamber. The points on the graph cannot recount why policy unfolded in a certain way, nor can they specify the sources or degree of unified business power. Measuring legislative outcomes on unifying issues, as this chapter has done, is only the first step. Assessing the scope of business power requires not only measuring the outcomes, but determining whether business did something, through any of the three faces of power, that actually affected those outcomes.

The mere fact that analysts believe business "won" a certain battle does not necessarily make it powerful, for factors beyond the control of business may have caused the desired legislative result. Similarly, a business "loss" is not synonymous with lacking power, for the outcome may have been worse had business not intervened. Hence it cannot be overemphasized that figure 4.2 presents a measure of legislative action, not a measure of the political power of business or the Chamber. To attribute power to political actors, one must show that their behavior, or at least the expectation among others that such behavior could occur, made a difference in changing outcomes over what otherwise would have resulted. Now that the outcomes have been measured, though, unified business power can be brought into the story in subsequent chapters.

Before analyzing sources of business power, I will first determine the extent to which popular representation transpires on unifying issues. The widespread scholarly assumption that business unity leads to strength gains much of its energy, force, and potency from the corresponding likelihood that the general public would be largely excluded from the political process. Indeed, it is this potential threat to democracy that has caused social scientists to exert so much effort studying whether unity ever arises. To address this motivation, I will cut straight to the heart of the matter. The next chapter assesses for unifying issues the congruence between public preferences and legislative action.

FIVE

Public Opinion, Elections, and Lawmaking

When the Speaker of the House banged his gavel to close the first session of the 85th Congress, business lobbyists were gratified with the year's legislative outcomes. Staff from the U.S. Chamber of Commerce, reflecting upon developments in 1957, catalogued a successful session. During that year business normally played offense and sought to push favorable legislation into law. Some of the business-supported proposals, such as budget cuts that would restrain government spending, eventually became law. Very few bills threatening to the broad business community even reached the congressional agenda, and those that did typically failed to progress beyond hearings. When considered in its entirety, legislative action in 1957 pleased business.

Fifteen years later, the tables had turned; business at large finished 1972 with regret rather than satisfaction. Instead of spending time on offense, business frequently fell into a defensive mode of attempting to block legislation. Congress passed and the president signed business-opposed measures to strengthen federal water pollution controls, create a commission to set standards for product safety, and regulate the wages and fringe benefits paid by government contractors. The initiatives business promoted usually did not advance far in the legislative process. When the dust had settled on Capitol Hill, business fared poorly in 1972 on unifying issues.

The two years thus produced contrasting results. The fact that in both 1957 and 1972 the outcomes spanned diverse policy domains suggests that factors general to the legislative process were at work. Thus any explanation of why business fared worse in the later year requires one to look beyond the individual policy initiatives at stake. The parallelism in outcomes points to causes that simultaneously affected regulatory affairs, social welfare programs, taxation, and other areas. One conceivable explanation is that business conducted a well-organized lobbying effort in 1957 but failed to mobilize as effectively in 1972, a possibility to be examined in chapter 6. The data presented in this chapter, however, lead to a different conclusion. Namely, public opinion and election outcomes were advantageous to business in the earlier year but became unfavorable by the later one.

The outlines of the argument can be stated briefly. In one key factor, public demands for conservative, business-friendly policies were high in 1957. Large segments of the public, showing few signs of holding major corporations responsible for the nation's troubles, felt widespread trust and confidence in business. In addition, the strength of the Republican Party, although falling short of a majority in either the House or the Senate, nevertheless reached a level not to be attained again until Republicans rode the electoral wave of 1980. These forces combined to create conditions propitious for policies desired by business.

The picture looked very different in 1972. Though opinions among the citizenry were changing in the conservative direction, the public wanted a more energetic federal government in some areas. Beyond actual policy preferences, public attitudes had turned sour on business as an institution. Leading corporations were increasingly blamed for problems like pollution, discrimination, and inflation, fueling public support for policies that would place greater regulations on business. The Democratic Party, despite having slipped from early days of the Great Society, easily controlled Congress with an advantage of 256–179 in the House and 54–45 in the Senate. As was the case throughout the 1960s and 1970s, Democratic members often took the lead in promoting expansions of the regulatory and social welfare state. Together these forces produced a legislative climate that often worked against business.

Public opinion and election outcomes, then, appear to have ushered in very different policies on unifying issues in the two years. The remainder of this chapter expands upon this idea and tests it against the available evidence. The specific differences between 1957 and 1972 will be subsumed within a broader model of why business witnesses passage of its desired legislation at some points but not others.

Lawmaking on unifying issues, as described in the previous chapter, will ultimately be the dependent variable. Because of the challenges posed by the need to identify factors with sufficient breadth to affect the entire population of unifying issues, matters of conceptualization and measurement require more than passing attention. Accordingly, I will begin by discussing how I address those challenges. Once indicators have been constructed for the relevant variables, the relationships among them can be systematically assessed. The chapter concludes by conducting and interpreting this empirical analysis. The results, I will show, call into question the notion that the public exerts little influence over the resolution of unifying issues.

PUBLIC SUPPORT FOR LIBERAL AND CONSERVATIVE POLICIES

The tendency for business victories across policy domains to bunch together in one year, and for its defeats to accumulate in another year, hints at the presence of factors operating within the entire set of unifying issues. To explain why the clustering of outcomes occurs, one would naturally search for characteristics that unifying issues hold in common. One such characteristic is their ideological nature. The policies business endorses, such as those that increase managerial discretion and minimize social spending, are commonly labeled as conservative. The policies business opposes usually fall on the liberal end of the ideological spectrum.

The ideological nature of unifying issues has a direct parallel within the mass public. When seeking to explain decisions on issues dividing liberal and conservative belief systems, one might reasonably begin by examining the liberal-conservative dimension of public opinion. In particular, citizen expectations about the proper role of government could be central to determining how business fares in the policy process. We can identify periods when Americans in the aggregate have shifted toward demanding stronger government and other periods when citizens turned toward private over collective solutions to problems (Stimson 1999; Schlesinger 1986). Such changes in public sentiments appear in many different policy areas simultaneously. As the public becomes more liberal on environmental policy, for example, it moves toward liberalism on health care as well (Stimson 1999). Stimson labels the comprehensive facet of public opinion underlying these common changes *public mood*. Understood as fluctuating between liberal and conservative perspectives on the appropriate size and scope of government, public mood possesses the breadth to affect outcomes across the full population of unifying issues.

Swings in public opinion between liberal and conservative orientations could help explain how favorable policies will be to business.

For that explanation to be accurate, elected officials must observe and respond to public mood. As the citizenry becomes more conservative and supportive of private over government action, business should find its positions more likely to prevail in congressional and presidential decision-making. When the mass public changes in a liberal direction and demands greater involvement of government, the positions favored by business should have a reduced chance of winning.

The high salience of unifying issues provides the electoral incentives that encourage officeholders to heed public mood. Because of the publicity surrounding unifying issues, politicians recognize that their behavior could either attract or repel voters during the next election. With their careers at stake, rational officeholders would strive to reduce their odds of defeat at the polls. Elected officials, using available information to interpret public mood, can continually redetermine the positions that best enhance their reelection prospects. Assessing the overall public mood thus can yield information applicable to many different policy areas. Based upon that information, officeholders can alter their behavior to move closer to constituents' preferences. Such a process implies a positive relationship between the liberal-conservative dimension of public opinion and subsequent lawmaking on unifying issues.

PUBLIC ATTITUDES TOWARD CORPORATIONS

Overall preferences on the responsibilities of government in society are not the only kind of public opinion that could affect decisions on unifying issues. Another kind of public opinion, which I will call *public attitudes toward corporations,* also attains a level of generality allowing it to affect policymaking across many unifying issues. When business unifies, firms normally are expressing support for or opposition to the general principles behind legislation. Officeholders are keenly attuned to those same principles. Some of the time, the principles at stake directly implicate the business community. Legislation may reflect the principle that business, through either intended behavior or through negligence, has caused problems such as environmental degradation or unsafe products. In those cases, public attitudes toward corporations could affect the decisions that officeholders reach.

Public attitudes toward corporations are conceived here to represent affective, gut-level perceptions of business. People can hold either positive or negative views about corporations and business in general.

By comparison to times of disapproving attitudes, when business is regarded positively people tend to think corporations are run by competent executives, contribute to the well being of society, and behave ethically. During periods of negative attitudes, the public believes that corporations hold too much power, stifle competition at the expense of their consumers and workers, and frequently ignore ethics in a quest for profits.

Although devoid of explicit policy content, these dispositions could influence lawmaking. In the same way that the public's affective attitudes toward gays, the wealthy, immigrants, the elderly, or blacks might influence policies relating to those groups, perceptions of corporations could help determine congressional and presidential decisions on business-wide issues. Negative attitudes permit politicians to gain electoral advantages by promoting bills that restrict corporations in some way. Legislation forcing businesses to make their products safer could prove popular, for instance, thereby encouraging officeholders to back it. Warmer public sentiments make bills seeking to restrain business, which by definition imply that companies must be doing something counter to society's interests, less likely to be proposed or enacted. As a consequence, the odds that policies reflect business preferences should—all else being equal—decrease as public attitudes toward corporations become more negative.

Later in the chapter, an empirical test attempts to discover whether politicians actually do respond to public attitudes toward corporations. Business leaders have long suspected such a relationship. During the early 1970s, when observers could easily recognize that Americans were becoming more distrustful of business, many corporate executives blamed their contemporary political woes in part on this change in public opinion (Silk and Vogel 1976). In examining a longer time span, Vogel (1989) subsequently argued that the declining attitude climate did indeed facilitate enactment of initiatives that business opposed.

Looking further back in time, some historians and social scientists conclude that negative perceptions of corporations at the beginning of the twentieth century helped stimulate government restrictions on corporate behavior, leading to initiatives such as meat inspection and the banning of child labor (Eisner 1993; Hicks 1961; Galambos 1975). Other scholars, spurred by the seminal work of Kolko (1963), contend instead that reforms enacted during the Populist and Progressive eras were actually shepherded by business elites who would benefit from them. In any event, outside of Vogel's (1989) work, little empirical research has examined whether corporations' standing among the public has affected legislative decisions in modern times.

Such a relationship is most likely for issues manifestly linked to the actions of business. Antitrust policy provides an obvious example. In a climate of broad disapproval of business, which would likely include beliefs that corporations profit by impeding competition, the suitable policy response would block the formation of monopolies or perhaps even restrict the growth of any corporation beyond a certain size. Likewise, in the rest of the regulatory domain, one has little trouble envisioning how elected officials could translate diffuse sentiments about business into concrete legislation. It is only a short step from public perceptions that corporations behave unethically to regulatory policies requiring corporations to clean up their pollution, improve the safety of their workplaces, or give stronger protections to consumers. Similar opinion-policy relationships could appear during taxation or trade debates that raise questions such as whether corporations pay their fair share of taxes or too readily abandon communities to search for cheap labor overseas.

It is apparent, however, that not all decisions on unifying issues can be meaningfully linked to the public's positive or negative perceptions of business. Although American companies have regularly participated in debates over the Social Security program, for example, a bill to raise Social Security benefits or change eligibility requirements is unlikely to arouse public sentiments about business. If Americans hold corporations in low esteem, elected officials might be less inclined to listen to business leaders' arguments on Social Security, but such an effect on officials seems likely to be modest. Thus within the universe of unifying issues—which includes both issues that can and cannot be framed around business—the relationship between public attitudes toward corporations and subsequent lawmaking is probably bounded in size.

The public's global preferences on the size and scope of government are likely to produce a larger effect. The vast majority of unifying issues revolves around ideological questions of government capacity. While public attitudes toward corporations are relevant only some of the time, the liberal-conservative dimension of public opinion applies to a broad swath of issues. The latter kind of public opinion therefore should produce stronger impacts upon lawmaking when the full range of unifying issues is considered. Before this expectation can be examined empirically, though, the essential concepts need to be accurately measured.

MEASURING PUBLIC OPINION OVER TIME

To measure longitudinal changes in public opinion, relevant survey items must be located and somehow combined. Stimson (1991, 1999) presents a procedure to extract the common dimension from a collection of discontinuous time series of public opinion. Stimson in fact developed his algorithm to measure public mood, a vital concept in this study, and I will employ an updated version of the measure constructed with his method and data. I later borrow the same approach to measure public attitudes toward corporations. Given its importance for my analysis, a brief description of the measurement strategy is fitting.

Stimson's (1999) measurement strategy solves conceptual as well as methodological dilemmas. The conceptual motivation stems from the fact that no single survey question so clearly captures public mood that one could confidently consider it the sole indicator. While the concept of public mood is construed broadly, the survey items invariably inquire about specifics. Two of Stimson's questions, for example, ask people whether the government should spend more money on the environment and whether it should guarantee everyone a job. Certainly both questions connect to the broader concept of the proper responsibilities of government, but neither item completely encapsulates it. Each question also probably captures some forces unique to the indicator. For this reason, the first indicator might show a different relationship to the phenomenon being explained, the favorability of lawmaking to business, than would the second indicator. Without theoretical grounds to choose between them, the analysis would face an impasse.

The methodological motivation for Stimson's measurement strategy arises because none of the available survey items have been administered continuously in the period under study. The multiple-indicator measurement models commonly used in the social sciences, which can handle the conceptual conundrum noted above, cannot address this additional complication. The challenge is not merely one of occasional missing data, which can be addressed in principal components models by calculating pairwise covariances based upon common observations. The massive gaps in the available series render such an approach unsuitable because any two series frequently do not share any observations, making it impossible to calculate their covariances.

To overcome this difficulty, Stimson develops an algorithm that begins by converting each component series into a comparable metric. In measuring public mood, the algorithm calculates for each series

the percentage of respondents taking the liberal position at each observation. Ratios can then be constructed that track the within-series
movement over time. If 50 percent of the sample expresses the liberal
position on a question at time t, for example, while only 45 percent
offer the liberal response at an earlier point, the data indicate that
attitudes are more liberal in the current period. Using that series alone
we would estimate that public mood was 45/50, or nine-tenths, as
liberal in the earlier period. With each discrete series converted into a
common metric, it becomes possible to average over all series having
observations for any two periods. Although combining those averages
is somewhat complex, the process yields the primary latent dimension
underlying the data.

Besides the conceptual and methodological problems noted above,
Stimson's approach also addresses the widely recognized tendency for
the answers surveys yield to depend upon the questions they ask. Alter-
ing the wording of a question, even slightly, can induce major changes
in aggregate responses. When studying longitudinal changes in public
opinion, the interpretations that result—that is, the direction public
opinion moves in any given period—may merely reflect the questions
examined. To make matters more complicated, there is often no way
to determine which survey questions capture the truest expression of
public opinion. Investigators may observe questions that promote a
certain interpretation of public opinion, but other questions may point
to different conclusions.

In surmounting these quandaries, Stimson proceeds in the most
catholic manner possible: he incorporates all the questions he could
locate that were asked of the American public more than once and that
tap some aspect of public preferences on government responsibilities.
The problem of question wording effects is controlled by first looking for
trends in aggregate responses to a single survey item and then averaging
across the available items. The danger of the researcher unknowingly
selecting certain items because they tell the story he or she wants to
advance is controlled by including all relevant questions. Stimson's
approach is thus superior to any alternative that would attempt to pick
which questions best measure public mood. The movements uncovered
over time are simply the common patterns detectable in the massive
database of questions Stimson has compiled.

In measuring public mood Stimson's raw inputs are over two thousand marginals—the percentages of the public favoring each response
category—from some 145 survey questions administered more than

once. When applied to those marginals, his estimation technique generates a continuous time series. The resulting measure is interpreted as a left-right scale capturing public preferences on the desirability of government action to solve the nation's problems. If the questions truly tap the intended concept, then one would expect aggregate responses within ostensibly separate policy domains to change in the same direction over time. This is, in fact, exactly what Stimson finds. The constituent items tend to correlate strongly with the latent dimension, demonstrating that ideological shifts within the mass public are simultaneously reflected across multiple policy areas including taxation, environmental protection, health, employment, and welfare. A relatively liberal public exhibits liberal preferences across the sphere of controversies in domestic policy.[1] More conservative views, when they are popular, likewise pervade many different domains.

The majority of the survey questions producing that finding inquire about issues like federal spending, economic policy, and regulation. Business has regularly unified around those matters. A minority of the questions asks about what are often labeled "social" issues—such as abortion, gun control, school prayer, and capital punishment—that do not attract much concern from business and certainly do not stimulate business unity. The measure derived when these items are excluded, though, correlates so highly with the original one (better than .99) as to be indistinguishable from it. Hence I retain the original index of public mood.

Best (1999) contends that Stimson's measure of public mood taps primarily economic, government-spending, and size-of-government issues; changes in public opinion on social and racial issues, according to Best's analysis, follow different tracks. Best argues that Stimson's measure of public mood is inappropriate as an independent variable if social or racial policy forms the dependent variable (see also Sharp 1999). The complexities Best introduces could prove fruitful for some studies but are not relevant here. Policies that unify business clearly belong to the cluster of issues that, if Best is right, define the core of Stimson's measure.

Figure 5.1 shows the values of public mood, calculated annually from 1953 to 1996. The measure follows what Stimson (1999) presents but differs in showing conservative moods rather than liberal ones as the

---

1. Foreign policy questions, which would be expected to follow different patterns, are not included among the survey items.

largest values. High points on the graph indicate desires for weaker government, while low points reflect aggregate public preferences for stronger government. The graph shows movement during the 1950s from conservatism to liberalism that culminates during 1961. The policy initiatives of the early 1960s coincided with the most liberal public over the entire period. Public opinion then steadily becomes more conservative, peaking around 1980. Shortly after President Ronald Reagan took office, the pattern reversed itself. Subsequent movement proceeds in the liberal direction until the early 1990s, when public mood changes again and starts becoming more conservative.

FLUCTUATIONS IN PUBLIC ATTITUDES TOWARD CORPORATIONS

The broad ideological contours of public mood, the evidence suggests, can be accurately gauged through the Stimson measurement strategy, but this is only one of our concepts of interest. Can the same measurement strategy be successfully used for public attitudes toward corporations? Like other data-reduction techniques, the algorithm can be applied to any set of indicators but may or may not yield useful information. If the raw indicators reflect a meaningful facet of public

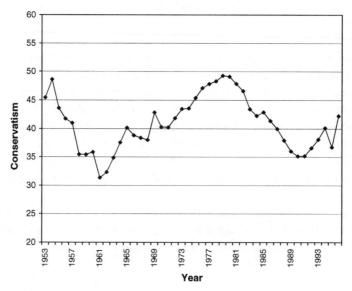

Figure 5.1 Public Preferences on the Size and Scope of Government

opinion, then we should find (1) systematic movement over time in the measure generated by the algorithm, and (2) substantial correlations between the constituent survey items and the extracted latent dimension.

In determining whether these criteria are met for public attitudes toward corporations, I first identified 135 questions related to the desired concept that were asked of the public more than once by the same survey organization.[2] Several sources, most importantly the online database of the Roper Center for Public Opinion Research, were used to collect the survey marginals. I included all items that appeared to tap some aspect of people's attitudes toward corporations.[3] Most of the series are short, as indicated by an average of only five observations for the 135 questions.

With the Stimson algorithm applied to the complete set of available items, the extracted dimension explains 61 percent of the variance.[4] As expected, the items usually correlate positively with the latent factor. These findings provide solid evidence that aggregate responses to the various questions move together over time. The questions, then, primarily measure the same facet of public opinion.

Table 5.1 presents, for each item with ten or more administrations, the question topic and the indicator's correlation with the extracted dimension. The average correlation shown in table 5.1 is .80, documenting that most of the items relate strongly to the latent factor. The questions inquiring about business in its entirety load in similar ways as those asking more specifically about "big business." This finding suggests that when people consider business as an abstract concept, they have in mind the large corporations that dominate the economy. Put differently, attitudes regarding business more generally are probably not separable from attitudes toward large corporations.

2. One needs at least two administrations of any given question to gain leverage upon changes over time. Because of the tendency for different survey organizations to show slightly different aggregate responses owing to variations in methodology and sampling, I treat each organization's questions separately.

3. Questions asking people about individual policy issues—say, a question on whether the minimum wage should be increased—were excluded from the analysis because they appear to tap policy preferences rather than affective attitudes toward corporations. These are, however, precisely the kinds of questions from which Stimson (1999) derives his measure of public mood. Also, I did not include questions asking about only one company or industry rather than business as a whole.

4. The percent of variance explained and the correlations of the constituent items with the latent dimension are interpreted in the same way that they would be in an ordinary principal components analysis.

Table 5.1 Correlations between Constituent Items and Extracted Dimension

QUESTION	NUMBER OF YEARS ASKED	CORRELATION WITH EXTRACTED DIMENSION
"Confidence" in "the people running major companies"	19	.65
"Confidence" in "big business"	18	.07
Agree or disagree that "one or two companies have too much control" in many industries	14	.98
Agree or disagree that "as they grow bigger, companies usually get cold and impersonal"	14	.95
Agree or disagree that "large companies are essential for the nation's growth and prosperity"	14	.79
Agree or disagree that "there's too much power concentrated in the hands of a few large companies"	14	.96
Agree or disagree that "many of our largest companies ought to be broken up into smaller companies"	14	.97
Agree or disagree that "the profits of large companies help make things better for everyone"	13	.97
Agree or disagree that "corporations generally strike a fair balance between making profits and serving the public interest"	13	.96
"Rate the honesty and ethical standards" of "business executives"	13	.59
"Business as a whole is making too much profit, a reasonable profit, or not enough profit"	12	.81
Will "big business, big labor, or big government" be "the biggest threat to the country in the future"?	11	.74
"Feeling thermometer" for "big business"	10	.94
Improve workers' lives "by all workers producing more" or "by workers getting more of the money companies are already making"	10	.75
"Opinion of most big business corporations"	10	.91

Note: The table shows, for each question tapping public attitudes toward corporations that was asked of the public in at least ten years, the correlation of the item with the latent dimension extracted from all the items. The extracted measure is graphed in figure 5.2.

Figure 5.2 shows the resulting measure of public attitudes toward corporations, calculated annually from 1953 to 1996. The higher the score on the graph, the more favorable attitudes are to corporations. At the beginning of the time series in 1953, the American public felt relatively warmly toward corporations. This finding parallels Fisher and Witney's (1951) contemporary depiction of a public largely at ease with big business. Using means such as philanthropy, public relations, and pension and health benefits for employees, business had worked hard to achieve this legitimacy in the public eye (Mitchell 1989).

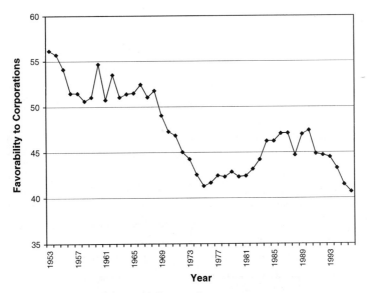

Figure 5.2 Public Attitudes toward Corporations

Though only a seer could have known it at the time, the early 1950s would represent the high-water mark for the American public's sentiment toward business. The data in figure 5.2 indicate that major changes were imminent. Following fluctuations in the 1950s and 1960s, public attitudes toward corporations turned increasingly sour from 1968 to 1976. This finding matches the scholarly and journalistic literatures of the era, which described both the public's growing suspicion of business and also the anxiety this suspicion created among leaders of major corporations.[5] The series moves toward the positive end of the scale during the 1980s before reversing course in 1990. Public attitudes then flow substantially toward unfavorability during the 1990s, falling back to the levels of the 1970s.

Corroborating my expectation that public mood and public attitudes toward corporations represent different facets of public opinion, measures of the concepts actually have a negative correlation of −0.38. Conservative sentiment need not correspond with warm feelings about business; indeed, sometimes the public has simultaneously become more conservative regarding what government should do and less

5. See, for example, Silk and Vogel (1976); "The American Corporation under Fire" in the May 24, 1971, issue of *Newsweek;* and "America's Growing Antibusiness Mood" in the June 17, 1972, issue of *Business Week.*

confident in business as an institution. When considered in the context of populist strains of thought on both the left and right, which have often questioned the integrity, morality, and public-spiritedness of major corporations, the independence of public mood and public attitudes toward corporations should not be surprising. That independence shows up among elite-level political actors as well. Presidential candidates George McGovern and Barry Goldwater, the major-party nominees furthest left and furthest right in the postwar period, shared a deep suspicion of big business even as they disagreed on most everything else.

The broader point is that beliefs about the appropriate scope of government and affective feelings toward business reflect different dimensions of public opinion that should be kept analytically distinct. Blending them together will distort any analysis of how mass preferences affect legislative action. Both public mood and public attitudes toward corporations, if the propositions developed in chapter 2 are accurate, should have a positive relationship with lawmaking on unifying issues. Moments marked by conservative sentiment and relatively favorable attitudes toward corporations should be those that engender legislative actions beneficial for unified business interests. Similarly, public demands for stronger government programs and growth in negative attitudes toward corporations should lead to more legislative losses for business.

PUBLIC OPINION NATIONALLY AND LOCALLY

Because they face voters throughout the country, presidential candidates could gain electoral advantages by monitoring and responding to national public opinion. Congressional candidates are more likely to care about the publics within their districts and states. One would expect, for example, senators from Minnesota to recognize that their state is more liberal than Oklahoma and to behave accordingly. How then could changes over time in national public opinion cause a response from legislators who do not confront a national electorate? Such a result follows if different parts of the country generally change in conjunction with each other.

People in both Minnesota and Oklahoma could easily shift alongside national trends. When the country as a whole grows more conservative, the differences between the two states could be maintained even as both become more conservative. The population center in Minnesota moves in the conservative direction but still appears liberal next to the people of Oklahoma, who also have gravitated toward conservatism.[6] Using national public opinion over time to predict the longitudinal behavior of legislators, then, assumes that changes within districts and states are primarily common rather than relative. For instance, one geographic area does not become more conservative at the same time that another area is becoming more liberal.

Erikson, Wright, and McIver (1993, 31–32; see also Smith 1997, appendix) show that this assumption is justified. Using survey data on liberal-conservative self-identifications aggregated within each state, they show that from 1976 to 1988 the states fluctuate in complete tandem with each other. The distance between any two states on their liberalism scale remains virtually the same over time even as the states collectively become more liberal or conservative. This means that changes within each state perfectly reflect the national changes. National opinion over time, by correlating so strongly with opinion over time in each state,[7] can be used to explain changes in legislators' behavior.

In a similar finding, Page and Shapiro (1992, chap. 7) report that opinions within all kinds of groups—including those based on age, race, education, and region—typically move together. Segments of the population obviously differ from each other on policy preferences, sometimes dramatically, but they each tend to change at the same point by about the same amount. One can reasonably assume, then, that districts and states generally change alongside national opinion. If they did not, then one probably would not find strong effects of national opinion on national policy.

CONCEPTUALIZING AND MEASURING ELECTION OUTCOMES

Assessing the linkage between public opinion and public policy tests a conception of democracy requiring not only that citizens gain influence

6. Similarly, if one marks two dots on a painting and then raises the height of the painting, the distance between the two dots remains constant; the increased distance from the floor applies equally to both dots.

7. Another way to think about this is to recognize that Erikson, Wright, and McIver's (1993) findings demonstrate that each state's time series has a unique mean but shares the same variance as the other states. Hence the correlation over time between any two states is extremely close to 1.0. Under these circumstances, an investigator estimating relationships with a dependent variable could use the opinion time series for Minnesota, or the nation at large, in place of the one for Oklahoma since they all share the same variation.

through their votes during elections, but also that their opinions achieve representation in the period between elections (Pitkin 1967). Without continuous responsiveness by officeholders, public opinion will produce only intermittent impacts. Nevertheless, elections still offer a powerful mechanism for translating public demands into government policy. Any conception of how representation could properly function, connecting citizens to government in a deep and enduring way, must consider the ability of voters to choose among competing candidates and parties through regular elections.

Elections realize their greatest potential to presage new programmatic initiatives when the parties offer the electorate explicit alternatives. On unifying issues, as chapter 4 showed, the parties' stances often differ from each other, meaning that changes in legislative decisions should follow when voters opt for candidates from one party over the other. Given that legislative decisions are what I seek to explain, it is fitting to include as potential determinants the partisan composition— set through elections—of the lawmaking institutions. Consequently I include variables measuring how congressional and presidential elections alter the balance between the parties.

CONGRESSIONAL ELECTIONS

Measuring the partisan composition of Congress resulting from elections is straightforward. The analysis to follow includes a variable for the Republican proportion of the total Democratic and Republican seats,[8] where separate measures for the House and Senate are averaged to construct the final indicator. Figure 5.3 shows the relative balance between the two parties from 1953 to 1996. The high points of Republican strength occur during 1953–1954, 1981–1982, and 1995–1996. The partisan composition of Congress is most advantageous to Democrats during the late 1950s, mid-1960s, and mid-1970s. If partisan turnover leads to policy changes, then the surges in Republican strength should produce legislative gains for business.

PRESIDENTIAL ELECTIONS

In contrast to congressional elections, conceptualizing and measuring the outcomes of elections for president introduces substantial difficulties. Bond and Fleischer (1990), through an exhaustive analysis of inter-

8. Any seat changing hands during a congressional term is counted for the party holding it for the greatest amount of time.

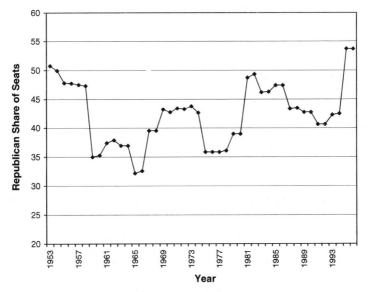

Figure 5.3 Partisan Composition of Congress

actions between Congress and the president over several decades, offer evidence that presidents usually cannot systematically influence how House and Senate members vote.[9] That finding implies that presidential elections typically do not initiate major redirections in legislation, though obviously presidents can use other means, such as executive orders and appointments to the executive branch and judiciary, to achieve their goals. The potential for presidential elections to cause shifts in legislation will be considered here as a conditional phenomenon, one requiring a Congress receptive to presidential pressure for policy change.

A favorable setting of this sort will be called a *presidential leadership opening*. A candidate winning a presidential election does not automatically gain a presidential leadership opening, but such a possibility materializes when partisan turnover in Congress runs in the president's favor. Under these circumstances the president acquires effectiveness through the cooperation of the expanded congressional ranks of his party. In addition, the inexperience of first-year legislators, often a large group when partisan turnover occurs, could make them more susceptible to presidential direction than veteran legislators.

9. See also Edwards (1989), C. Jones (1994), and Peterson (1990).

The independent variable used here therefore connects a presidential leadership opening with its foundation in congressional elections. In keeping with the conditional nature of the posited presidential influence, all presidents without such an opening (i.e., those whose party lost seats in the last congressional election) are considered to be equivalent and scored as zero. For Republican presidents with a leadership opening, the variable is scored as the Republican share of congressional seats at time t minus the Republican share of congressional seats at time $t - 2$. For Democratic presidents with a leadership opening, the variable is correspondingly calculated as (the negative of) the Democratic share of congressional seats at time t minus the Democratic share of congressional seats at time $t - 2$.

The indicator created by this procedure is graphed in figure 5.4. Republican leadership openings have positive numbers while Democratic ones are negative. The graph shows a huge Reagan opening in 1981–1982 and a substantial Johnson opening in 1965–1966. More modest possibilities occurred for Eisenhower in 1953–1954 and for Nixon in 1969–1970. Most of the points are scored as 0, consistent with previous findings that presidential direction of Congress takes place only irregularly.

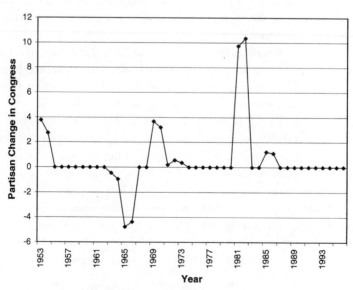

Figure 5.4 The President's Leadership Opening

THE EFFECTS OF PUBLIC OPINION AND ELECTIONS ON POLICY DECISIONS

It may be useful now to step back to review the path taken thus far. This chapter has focused solely on developing appropriate indicators of public opinion and election outcomes, the primary channels through which citizens can affect what government does. Previous chapters have identified instances of business unity and measured the corresponding legislative action. Matters of measurement thus have absorbed considerable attention, and that is entirely appropriate. The conclusions produced by any piece of social science research can only be as strong as the measures upon which they rely. Thinking through the motivation and rationale for measurement choices, particularly when most indicators are being constructed from original information collected specifically for the project, should be time well spent.

With the exigencies of measurement now completed, the data are ready to be analyzed. I will therefore proceed to the substantive concerns propelling the search for proper measures. The central question has been posed and measures have been constructed, so only the answer awaits. Can fluctuations in lawmaking be traced to the preferences and voting patterns of the public?

The dependent variable the analysis attempts to explain, graphed in chapter 4 as figure 4.2, is the dimension extracted from six indicators of the favorability to business of legislative action. The measure's statistical properties render it a fitting dependent variable for a regression analysis. Figure 4.2 reveals that the series crosses its mean many times and appears well behaved. This appearance is confirmed by statistical tests for integration, which show the measure to be clearly not integrated. With an Augmented Dickey-Fuller test statistic of -3.44, the null hypothesis of first-order integration can be rejected at the .05 level. Given a dependent variable lacking a unit root, the potential of spurious relationships resulting from including integrated series on both sides of the equation (Granger and Newbold 1974) will not plague a regression estimation.

If the citizenry determines the broad thrust of legislation on unifying issues, then policy decisions should change according to public mood, public attitudes toward corporations, the partisan composition of Congress, and the president's leadership opening. All four relationships are expected to be positive. For purposes of analysis, public mood and public attitudes toward corporations are measured over the twelve-month period beginning July 1 of the previous year and ending June 30 of the current year. To account for policy decisions made during calendar year 1975, for example, the public opinion indicators range from July 1, 1974, to June 30, 1975. As explained in greater detail in appendix B, staggering the measures this way ensures that the causal ordering of the data matches that of the theoretical claims being tested. Within the data to be analyzed, the public opinion measures temporally precede the lawmaking measure by an average of about six months. The electoral variables, because they reflect what happened in the last election, necessarily lead rather than follow the measure of lawmaking.

The final task consists of determining the statistical procedure that can most effectively determine whether the data support the propositions offered in earlier chapters. Ordinary least squares (OLS) regression, the most common statistical procedure social scientists employ to analyze nonexperimental data, has the twin advantages of being widely understood and yielding easily interpretable results. For these reasons, OLS will be used here to find the linear combination of the four explanatory variables that best predicts legislative action. The impact attributable to each variable will be its unique contribution, independent from the other variables in the equation. Each variable could have a positive, negative, or no relationship at all with legislative action, depending upon what the actual data indicate.

Table 5.2, which depicts the results of the regression analysis, offers evidence for important linkages between citizens and government. The first column lists the unstandardized coefficients, which are the model's best estimates of the independent effects of each variable. Two coefficients are statistically significant at the .01 level and a third crosses the .05 threshold. The only coefficient failing to reach statistical significance corresponds with the presidential leadership opening. That coefficient nevertheless has the right sign, and the presidential leadership opening is retained in the model for its theoretical interest.

The relative importance of the four variables can be gauged by examining the standardized coefficients, shown in the second column of table 5.2. The standardized coefficient on public mood is easily the highest at 0.58, followed by the partisan composition of Congress at 0.47, public attitudes toward corporations at 0.23, and the presidential leadership opening at 0.09. Based upon these findings, one would conclude that public mood is the most important determinant of legislative action on unifying issues.

Table 5.2 Public Opinion, Elections, and Lawmaking on Unifying Issues

VARIABLES	UNSTANDARDIZED COEFFICIENTS	STANDARDIZED COEFFICIENTS	EFFECT ANALYSIS
Constant	−113.08**		
	(30.69)		
Public mood	1.87**	0.58	13
	(0.41)		
Public attitudes toward corporations	0.73*	0.23	6
	(0.36)		
Partisan composition of Congress	1.20**	0.47	11
	(0.27)		
Presidential leadership opening	0.48	0.09	3
	(0.62)		
Diagnostics			
Durbin-Watson statistic	1.81		
N	44		
R^2	0.68		

$*p < .05$ $**p < .01$

Note: The model covers 1953–1996 and has 44 observations. Parameters are estimated with OLS. Standard errors are in parentheses. The dependent variable is the factor extracted from a principal components analysis of six indicators of the favorability of policymaking to business. The effect analysis provides the point change in the dependent variable resulting from increasing each independent variable from the 25th to the 75th percentile, while holding the other independent variables constant at their means.

Because standardized coefficients are measured on an artificial scale, one can gain additional insight into the magnitude of the relationships by performing what is called an "effect analysis." Through this procedure, the predicted change in the dependent variable is calculated as each independent variable is increased from the 25th to the 75th percentile. During the calculations, all other independent variables are held constant at their mean values. The effect analysis, then, describes what happens to the dependent variable when each independent variable moves from the lowest quartile to the highest one.[10]

The third column of table 5.2 summarizes the results of the effect analysis. We can see that in substantive terms, public mood—the measure of global public preferences for stronger or weaker government—constitutes the strongest driving force. If we want to know whether business will be either celebrating legislative victories or absorbing defeats, the best place to look is at demands among the citizenry on the appropriate scope of government action. An increase in public mood

10. For the presidential leadership opening, there is no difference between the 25th and 75th percentiles—both scores are 0. In performing the effect analysis for that variable, the comparison is therefore based upon the difference between the mean of the negative values and the mean of the positive values.

from the 25th percentile to the 75th percentile produces a 13-point change in lawmaking.

Just how big is a change of 13 points? Lawmaking has a potential range from 0 to 100 but fluctuates mostly between 35 and 65. The typical values thus resemble election returns in a two-candidate race. In legislating as in elections, a swing of a few points can make a substantial difference. For example, going from 45 to 58 on the lawmaking scale— a shift of 13 points—represents a critical change in the favorability to business of congressional and presidential decisions. Such a change would represent nearly three-quarters of the difference between 1957, a year falling within an era characterized by many business wins, and 1972, a year in the middle of a run of business losses.

As expected, the effects of public attitudes toward corporations are smaller than those of public mood. An increase from the 25th to the 75th percentile in public attitudes toward corporations, with the other variables held constant at their means, leads to a change in lawmaking of 6 points. Much of this variable's effect stems from the fact that its period of greatest decline, 1968–1976, corresponds to a notable drop in the favorability of legislative action to business. Many of the business losses during that era occurred in the regulatory domain. The late 1960s and early 1970s witnessed numerous initiatives on environmental protection, worker health and safety, consumer protection, and other forms of regulation. The degree of public trust and confidence in the nation's corporations appears to produce notable consequences for policies that directly restrict how private companies operate.

A 25th to 75th percentile increase in the partisan composition of Congress corresponds with a sizable change in lawmaking of 11 points, an impact almost as large as that seen for public mood. Eleven points are large enough for business to go from disproportionately winning, as in 1985, to cleaning up in the legislative process, as in 1996. Thus on unifying issues, congressional elections are important determinants of how well business will fare in the legislative process. Former Alabama governor and presidential candidate George Wallace famously charged that "there's not a dime's worth of difference" between the two major parties, implying that electing members from one party over the other will not change the policies enacted. Similar perceptions persist today in some quarters of scholarly and popular discourse. While the relationships uncovered here afford no global conclusions about parties and elections, with respect to the issues unifying business, Wallace's colorful contention was wrong.

The diagnostics of the model provide information on whether assumptions about the temporal independence of the errors have been violated. The Durbin-Watson statistic of 1.81 indicates that the null hypothesis of no first-order autocorrelation in the residuals cannot be rejected. This finding suggests that changes in the independent variables produce changes in the dependent variable solely within the current period.[11] Most importantly, the relationships presented here gain credibility because the main threat to inference has been avoided.

SIZING UP THE MODEL'S PREDICTIONS

The overall fit of the model is high. The four independent variables jointly explain nearly 70 percent of the variance in lawmaking, and this explanatory power is not inflated through a dynamic term or autocorrelated errors. The dependent variable, it should be remembered, is not integrated, providing confidence that the inferences are not confounded by spurious associations. The model's strong fit can be depicted visually. Figure 5.5 compares the actual values of the lawmaking measure with those predicted by the model.

The graph shows visually that the success of unified business interests tightly tracks the four variables examined here. Numerous victories for business materialize precisely when the model predicts they would, and the defeats for business also closely match expectations. The model's predictions are not perfect, but in no case do they substantially miss the mark. Unified business preferences are most likely to prevail when public opinion is conservative, when the public views corporations relatively warmly, and when the electorate chooses Republican congressional and presidential candidates. Lawmaking becomes least favorable to business when the public demands a stronger government, corporations are held

11. Because the dependent variable is the factor score derived from a principal components estimation of six indicators, I could make more efficient use of the data by estimating measurement and structural parameters simultaneously. Given that the model does not show a dynamic relationship between the independent variables and the dependent variable, the DYMIMIC specification estimated with the Kalman filter (Kellstedt, McAvoy, and Stimson 1995) is not appropriate here. A LISREL setup with multiple indicators on the left side of the equation, though, potentially could provide a more efficient estimator. However, estimating such a model and allowing for nonrandom measurement errors among the dependent indicators do not change the statistical inferences presented in table 5.2. Hence OLS is retained for its transparency and simplicity.

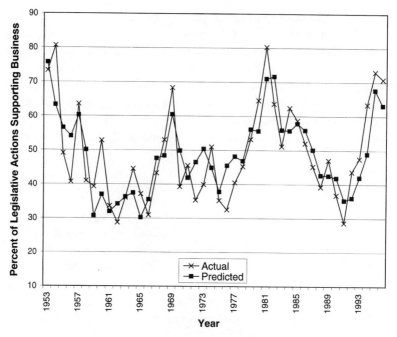

Figure 5.5 Actual vs. Predicted Success of Unified Business Interests

in low esteem, and voters grant Democrats substantial strength in the nation's governing institutions.

One might suspect that the pronounced role of the citizenry that emerges is simply an artifact of the issues chosen to examine. In particular, perhaps the analysis is picking up relatively trivial matters, where the public voice can be channeled without making any real difference in how society is governed. In fact, exactly the opposite is true. As shown in chapter 4, the data set includes a large portion of the most salient and important legislative battles of the postwar era. If the theoretical propositions developed in earlier chapters are accurate, it is largely because these issues are so important that the public voice shines through so starkly.

The empirical results call for a reexamination of current thinking about business unity. Scholars as diverse as pluralists, power elitists, and ruling class theorists have assumed that business unity leads to a politics largely shutting out ordinary citizens. The findings presented here contradict this expectation, for unifying issues incorporate the public's voice into legislative actions in a major way. The results cannot directly speak to questions of business power, which are addressed in the chapters to follow. Business potentially could affect policy decisions independently of the impacts of public preferences and voting choices, and business could shape those public preferences. Multiple causes, with business power undoubtedly among them, probably interact to account for policies on unifying issues. The results are unmistakable, however, in demonstrating that if the citizenry were left out of the explanation, the resulting picture would be severely out of focus.

AN ASSESSMENT OF BUSINESS UNITY AND REPRESENTATIVE DEMOCRACY

By their very nature, theories and the models they inspire seek to address a wide range of phenomena. Practical limitations, though, normally force empirical research to narrow the focus to a manageable level. While often necessary, this practice comes at a price. When a theory is broader than the evidence used to evaluate it, the investigator cannot draw definitive conclusions about the theory's accuracy. The cases studied may fit the theory, but those excluded from the analysis may not. Thus a leap of faith is required to generalize beyond the evidence specifically examined. Indeed, a scholar may unknowingly become interested in the cases selected for analysis precisely because they match the theory's expectations.

To surmount this problem, the current chapter proceeds in the most encompassing manner possible. The analysis includes all legislative decisions on unifying issues over several decades, not just a subset of the decisions. Accordingly, the findings manifest considerable external validity. No leap of faith is necessary to generalize because the full set of unifying issues is included. By incorporating so many issues, the analysis allows, even demands, far-reaching conclusions.

No doubt one could find specific cases that violate the patterns described in this chapter. Given the complexities of the political world, no model will ever explain every phenomenon that falls within its scope. Models must instead be evaluated according to their ability to account for general patterns. If we define a valuable model to be one that yields substantial explanatory power from a small number of moving parts, then the model developed here easily passes the test. With only four independent variables, this parsimonious model explains about 70 percent of the variance in legislative action on unifying issues. Rather than having only marginal impacts on legislative decisions on unifying issues, which the existing literature would predict, public opinion and election outcomes instead are central driving forces.

Democracy does not cease to exist when business unifies. To the contrary, democracy begins to approach its potential during instances of business unity. Policy decisions on unifying issues are highly responsive to the preferences and participation of the citizenry. To provide a convincing explanation of legislative activity on issues marked by business unity, one must account for the impacts of public opinion and elections.

SIX

Overt Sources of Business Power

Although we have now seen evidence demonstrating how public opinion and elections affect lawmaking, important questions remain unanswered as to why business wins or loses in legislation. The possibility remains that a unified business community, either through overt political activity or through economic leverage, could cause policymaking to veer from the trajectory set through public opinion and elections. Notwithstanding the close fit between the theoretical model proposed in earlier chapters and the empirical data analyzed in chapter 5, a small gap—which might reflect the collective influence of business— separates actual and predicted policy choices.

The current chapter assesses the potential for business to wield power through overt means. To provide added context for studying overt business power on unifying issues, I will begin with a concrete case. The labor law reform bill of 1978, described in chapter 1, opens a window into determining the extent to which business influences legislation. Employing all available weapons in its arsenal, the business community fought the legislation as it worked its way through the Senate. A diverse group of companies, prodded by trade associations, peak associations, and temporary lobbying organizations, contacted their senators. Some of this contact was through letters and postcards, but much of it took place face-to-face. Many executives traveled to Washington to personally present their company's position to senators and their staffs. Small business owners, too, lobbied in great numbers, often flying to Washington on jets that major corporations made available for the purpose. The business organizations coordinating the campaign performed extensive public relations work through polling, sending out prepared editorials to newspapers, and commissioning research studies purporting to document the adverse effects the legislation would create (Levitan and Cooper 1984).

Although unions spent considerable time, money, and energy promoting the bill, their efforts were eclipsed by the more extensive opposition mounted by business. On the surface, this case appears to be a clear-cut instance of business dictating the outcome through its political activity. After all, business got what it wanted—the bill was indeed defeated. This correspondence between business demands and the ultimate outcome invites an attribution of overt power to business. There is, in fact, considerable merit to that perspective. Closer scrutiny of the factors surrounding the bill's failure, however, reveals that the decision reflected much more than just a raw demonstration of business power.

A very similar bill had passed the House of Representatives in 1977 with 61 percent of voting members in favor. While seemingly a comfortable victory, the vote margin foreshadowed potential problems—in particular, a filibuster—in the Senate. On legislation that many senators feel strongly about, of which labor-law reform certainly qualifies, the ability to filibuster often means that more than a simple majority is necessary for passage. Breaking a filibuster through a cloture petition requires sixty votes which, if all senators vote, equals 60 percent of the body. Had the percentage of supporting senators exactly matched the percentage of House members voting yea the previous year, the bill would have cleared the necessary supermajority—but barely. As it turns out, no more than fifty-eight senators ever supported the cloture motion. The point is obvious but nevertheless worth mentioning: If the Senate operated under the same rules as the House, where only a majority was needed to pass controversial legislation, labor-law reform probably would have been enacted. From an institutional perspective, the right of senators to filibuster killed the legislation.

But leaving aside the Senate's rules and procedures, why is it that the labor bill could not secure the final two votes to reach the requisite sixty? The extensive direct and grassroots lobbying campaign undertaken by business was certainly one critical reason, but there were others as well. On fundamental questions of whether to side with unions or management, senators elected to office bring preexisting preferences based upon their upbringing, work experiences, and partisan affiliations, and those preferences should be taken into account when explaining the final decision. If two more pro-union senators had won elections for terms that included 1978, history books would likely depict the episode much differently. The behavior of the president, too, is a relevant consideration. After the bill's defeat, some observers believed that the Carter administration could have won two additional votes with a more vigorous campaign to convince senators (Donnelly 1978).

Election outcomes had created conditions auspicious for passage—the Democratic share of congressional seats was 6 percent higher than its average from 1953 to 1996—but public opinion undermined the bill's prospects. The public was growing more conservative toward how deeply the federal government should involve itself in areas like providing support for the poor, expanding the regulatory and social welfare state, and overseeing collective bargaining. In 1978 public mood was 7 percent more conservative than its average over the forty-four years under study and, perhaps as important, was moving further rightward. Votes to extend federal oversight of labor-management relations were less likely to meet public approval than they would have been a few years earlier.

In another pertinent dimension of public opinion, Americans held more positive feelings toward corporations than unions. Around the time of the debate, several polls inquired about relative attitudes toward the competing institutions. The polls asked respondents to state their levels of trust and confidence in corporations and unions and to determine which institution was more responsible for the nation's economic woes. In each case, corporations fared better than unions in the public eye.[1] While business at the time was not well liked by large segments of the public, unions were even less popular. In a bill framed as a battle between companies and unions, the companies had the advantage in the realm of public opinion.

All of these variables contributed to the final decision in the Senate. Which was the deciding factor in the failure of the bill to gain two more votes? Certainly a case could be constructed that the lobbying efforts of business made the difference. If business had opted to stay out of the

1. See Public Opinion Online, Roper Center at the University of Connecticut, question numbers:
   USCBSNYT.041178,R21
   USGALLUP.061178,R6
   USGALLUP.061178,R8
   USGALLUP.77121N,R04A
   USGALLUP.77121N,R04D
   USYANK.78MAP,R11
   USORC.78JAN2,R2
   USORC.78MAR,R01L
   USORC.78MAR,R01N.

conflict, ignoring the bill altogether, it surely would have passed. From that information, one can infer that business killed the bill. The problem with such an inference is that when a bill falls two votes short, every contributing factor is, in a sense, the deciding factor. If the preexisting preferences of senators winning election in the preceding years had been just slightly more supportive, or if the Carter administration had made the bill a top priority, or if public opinion had been more favorable, the bill may well have passed. One can be led astray in attempting to draw grand conclusions from a vote that could have gone either way. A knife-edge decision can be misperceived as inevitable by attaching too much importance to a single causal force.

More generally, any analysis of the labor-law reform bill encounters a problem that frequently plagues scholarly inquiries. We observe only a single outcome, the failure of the bill, and several explanations each tell part of the story. Under these circumstances, it is difficult to pinpoint the precise contribution of each factor because, with more variables than outcomes, the system is what social science methodologists call underidentified. While we can discern business political activity as one critical determinant of the decision, assessing the relative importance of each factor is a tricky enterprise.

In the end, though, assigning a relative weight to each variable in this particular dispute is not the best way to understand business power, for it is the patterns across a range of cases that scholarly debates have focused upon. A theory that explained this bill but no others would be of little use to social scientists; conversely, a theory that accounted for a plethora of legislative decisions would command widespread scholarly attention regardless of whether it accurately depicted the outcome of the labor bill. There is no way to know a priori whether any given case is representative of the population of unifying issues or whether the forces shaping its resolution are idiosyncratic. For this reason, the fullest perspective on business power results not from studying one case but from studying many. That orientation motivates the analyses in this chapter, which address the entire set of unifying issues. I turn first to examining how corporations might wield overt power through their funding of elections.

FUNDRAISING AND CORPORATE PACS

The faces, dates, and locations may change, but all congressional and presidential fundraisers follow a similar template. The guests, most of whom have promised funds for the candidate before the event begins, gather in a gaily decorated ballroom or a well-maintained private residence. Continuous background music and free-flowing alcohol provide the necessary lubrication to keep the mood pleasant and lively. During the unofficial parts of the program, the candidate moves purposefully across the room, shaking hands and making small-talk. Despite having participated in such events many times before, the candidate strives to make the evening seem fresh to the participants.

Some of the contributors attend to represent not themselves but rather their corporations. Since the 1974 amendments to the Federal Election Campaign Act legalized the practice, corporations and business groups have helped finance federal candidates by forming Political Action Committees (PACs). By the mid-1980s, numerous corporations and trade associations had moved to establish their own PAC and begin the process of targeted giving. During the 1997–1998 election cycle, corporate PACs donated a total of about $100 million to congressional candidates, a sum surely shocking to most citizens.

While business can spend money on elections in other ways, most notably through independent expenditures and "soft money"—unlimited amounts given to political parties—PAC contributions are one of the most controversial forms of financial involvement. With a direct transfer of a crucial resource candidates usually need to win elections, the potential for corruption is obvious. The question inevitably arises: What are corporate PACs receiving from politicians in exchange for contributions? There is one commodity that scholars and journalists, plus the congressional candidates and PAC directors actually involved, universally agree is bestowed upon many contributors: access. Access means that during deliberations leading to relevant legislative decisions, corporate PACs, and other PACs for that matter, get a respectful hearing from House and Senate members who have won election with the PAC's help. Corporations giving PAC contributions frequently receive "face time" from members or their staffs and gain a valuable opportunity to present their perspectives. Whether or not the corporation has constructed a winning case for itself, the officeholders will at least listen to their arguments, appeals, and evidence. Thus time, perhaps the rarest of legislators' resources, is allotted to those who open their checkbooks.

The central dilemma is determining when *access* becomes *influence*. Does access—the opportunity to inform and persuade—so consistently lead to influence for corporate PACs that we have a distinction without a difference? For those citizens most cynical about politics, the answer is self-evident. If he who pays the piper gets to call the tune, then corporate PACs must be directing a political orchestra. For the large amounts of cash they contribute, corporate PACs seem certain to receive favorable policies in return, a straightforward quid pro quo. Incumbent politicians from both parties, seeking to attract this funding and prevent it from flowing to their challengers, will logically be more likely to support the probusiness side of all kinds of issues, including unifying ones. On unifying issues, decisions would invariably tilt toward what business wants, making it more difficult for the preferences of the ordinary citizen to be heard above the din of PAC money.

Despite the intuitive appeal and widespread currency of these claims, the reality may be more complicated. The influence of corporate PAC contributions must be demonstrated, not assumed, for there are always many other potential reasons to explain why officeholders behave as they do. Even if corporate PAC contributions do influence elected officials, one should not assume that the influence is constant and applies equally to diverse legislative situations, processes, and issues. The total funding traceable to business is simply the accumulation of myriad contributions on individual races and candidates. If corporate PACs do directly affect legislative decisions, the impacts could be felt on particularistic or conflictual issues rather than unifying ones. A winning candidate who received contributions from a certain company's PAC, for example, could reward the company through a narrow policy benefit irrelevant to the rest of the business community.

No existing research has investigated PAC impacts across the spectrum of cases marked by unity within business. Yet answers to the central questions driving the book will become clear and credible only in light of such an examination. Accordingly I will now undertake a broad empirical study of corporate PAC impacts.

THE IMPACTS OF CORPORATE PAC CONTRIBUTIONS

My objective is to determine whether the volume of corporate PAC money flowing into candidates' coffers bears a systematic relationship, all else being equal, to attendant legislative decisions. Lawmaking on unifying issues has already been measured and used as the dependent variable in the previous chapter. What now remains is to measure the funding given by corporate PACs and estimate its relationship with policy decisions. Corporate PAC funding is defined here as the total corporate PAC contributions to House and Senate candidates as a proportion of all congressional campaign spending. This variable taps the ability of corporations, relative to other interests forming PACs and other sources of campaign revenues, to finance legislative elections.[2]

Conducting the empirical analysis requires specifying the period to be examined. While PACs became legal a few years earlier, the Federal Election Commission did not possess the resources necessary to accurately compile data until the 1977–1978 election cycle. That limitation restricts the analysis to the years 1977–1996.[3] To ensure that the statistical model keeps causality moving in the right direction (i.e., that contributions come before the legislative action they may help explain), corporate PAC funding is measured during the preceding election. To explain the decisions of House and Senate members in 1979 and 1980, for example, corporate PAC funding is measured for the most recent election in 1978. Corporate PAC contributions given for the next election in 1980, in turn, will be used to help explain policy decisions in 1981 and 1982.[4]

Given the relatively short period during which PACs have been legal, the estimation will be based upon only eighteen observations. That restriction will reduce the reliability of all statistical estimates. For a longitudinal inquiry using an annual measure of lawmaking as the dependent variable, the small number of cases has to be accepted as a product of data availability that could only be avoided by waiting until

2. Another potential measure might use the number of corporate PACs in existence as a share of all registered PACs. Such an indicator, though, would have lower face validity than the one used here. Rational candidates care not about the raw number of any given type of PAC, but rather about the extent to which that type of PAC actually funds campaigns. A corporate PAC contributing $100,000 across all candidates, for example, should count for more than a corporate PAC contributing $20,000. As it turns out, when the model uses an indicator defined as the corporate share of all registered PACs, the result is a coefficient considerably less reliable statistically than the one reported below.

3. Most research tracking PAC influences on policy choices is cross-sectional, seeking to assess the covariance of PAC contributions with the behavior, actions, or voting of individual members of Congress. My approach uses longitudinal data at the aggregate level, for which only a few existing studies examine PAC contributions (Williams and Collins 1997; Quinn and Shapiro 1991). Time series analyses using PAC data have the obvious problem of few observations, which probably explains the dearth of empirical studies.

4. Without this kind of lag built into the model, the estimated relationships would make little sense theoretically. PAC contributions for the 1982 election cycle, to continue the example, were contributed right up until the general election in November. If those contributions were used to predict legislative decisions in 1981 and 1982, then much of the independent variable would be transpiring after—rather than before—the dependent variable.

more years pass. As we will see later, though, other kinds of tests that address campaign finance more broadly can overcome this limitation.

The initial analysis builds upon the model originally presented in chapter 5, which includes four variables tapping the ability of citizens, through both their aggregate choices in elections and through office-holders' responsiveness to public opinion on a continuous basis, to affect the course of lawmaking on unifying issues. Because those variables are present in the model, the policies they predict become the implicit standard of reference for the overt power business might wield through corporate PAC contributions. *Overt* business power is defined here as the ability of business to cause lawmaking to deviate from the path established by public opinion and elections. Of course, another kind of power would result if business helps to shape public preferences, a possibility to be addressed in chapter 8.

In a statistical analysis, the definition of overt power has a straight-forward interpretation. In a model controlling for public opinion and elections, business is overtly powerful to the extent that its actions have a systematic effect upon legislative actions. Even though public opinion and elections are critical determinants of policymaking, bringing overt business power into the model could add depth to the explanation.

Table 6.1 presents the results of an ordinary least squares estimation spanning the available years. The coefficient on corporate PAC strength has a positive sign, indicating the existence of overt power. With a magnitude only a bit more than one and a half times its standard error, the coefficient does not clear the conventional .05 level of statistical significance or the more generous .10 level.[5] The data thus cannot tell us with much precision whether corporate PAC contributions produce a noticeable effect on legislative decisions relating to unifying issues.

At the same time, only two of the four variables measuring public opinion and elections retain the correct signs and reach statistical significance at the .05 level. Most of the variation in public attitudes toward corporations occurs before the first observation in the analysis, which probably accounts for the statistical imprecision of its coefficient. With only eighteen cases, the model has difficulty in accurately estimating the impacts of any variables, including corporate PAC contributions. One should be leery of making strong inferences on any of the factors from such a thin evidentiary base. The PAC findings suggest a possible

---

5. With twelve degrees of freedom, the critical values for the .05 and .10 levels of statistical significance, respectively, are 2.18 and 1.78.

Table 6.1 The Impacts of Corporate PAC Contributions

VARIABLES	COEFFICIENTS
Constant	−142.49
	(85.68)
Public mood	3.53**
	(1.17)
Public attitudes toward corporations	−0.58
	(0.80)
Partisan composition of Congress	0.86*
	(0.41)
Presidential leadership opening	−0.72
	(0.68)
Corporate PAC funding	3.45
	(2.11)
Diagnostics	
Durbin-Watson statistic	2.34
N	18
R^2	0.86

*$p < .05$ **$p < .01$
Note: The model is estimated with OLS and covers 1979–1996. Standard errors are in parentheses.

effect, but the low statistical reliability of the estimate means that no definitive inferences can be drawn.

DETERMINING WHEN CORPORATE PACS INFLUENCE
LEGISLATIVE DECISIONS

Although the data presented here cannot resolve the matter decisively, previous research on corporate PAC contributions can aid our understanding. Based upon existing research, there are solid reasons for concluding that while there may be some effect of corporate PAC contributions on the outcomes of unifying issues, the size of that effect is likely to be modest. That is, if the effect could be estimated reliably, it would probably not reach a magnitude sufficient to be called a dominant influence on policy decisions.

Several pieces of evidence point to that conclusion. Most importantly, the behavior of corporations and trade associations with PACs leads us to infer a strategy of seeking benefits primarily on particularistic and conflictual issues rather than unifying ones. One relevant detail is the long-standing tendency for most PACs in the business sector to contribute regularly to incumbents of both political parties. Even in 1992, a year with substantial volatility, open seats, and scandals, corporate PACs gave mostly to incumbents, both Democratic and Republican

(Herrnson and Wilcox 1995). After their party took control of Congress in 1994, Republican incumbents started garnering a larger share of corporate PAC contributions, as one would expect given the enhanced legislative power (particularly in the House) of majority-party members. Yet corporations have continued to contribute to Democratic incumbents. An ideological strategy aimed at furthering the unified interests of business would dictate greater support for Republican challengers, a strategy taken by only a minority of corporate PACs (Eismeier and Pollock 1988).

The pattern of contributing to incumbents implies an overriding intention to gain benefits on the corporation's special concerns, which often can be equally well advanced by congressional members of either party. Such seeking of special benefits is also indicated by the finding that companies who have the most to gain or lose through public policy are most likely to establish and heavily use a PAC. PACs whose parent corporations are government contractors contribute substantially, particularly to members on the committees who make the relevant procurement decisions (Andres 1985; Mitchell, Hansen, and Jepsen 1997). Corporations gaining many of their revenues from government contracts obviously want to keep those revenues flowing, ordinarily a higher priority for them than winning on unifying issues. Similarly, PACs in sectors marked by industry-specific regulation are among the largest contributors; those PACs steer funds especially to incumbent members serving on the committees with jurisdiction over regulation affecting the parent corporations (Grier, Munger, and Roberts 1994; Masters and Keim 1985). A regulatory decision of little or no importance to most of the business community can nevertheless substantially impact the bottom line of a handful of corporations. With their PAC contributions, those corporations hope to influence the narrow decisions that directly affect them.

These modes of behavior are all consistent with a strategy of seeking access and influence with those congressional members exerting the greatest control over legislation of special interest to certain corporations. Hence a member of Congress who votes against business on unifying issues but nonetheless has the advantage of incumbency and service on relevant committees will continue to receive money from corporate PACs. Corporate PAC contributions thus appear to be targeted primarily at shaping policy outcomes on particularistic and conflictual issues rather than unifying ones. Indeed, some scholars (Gray and Lowery 1997) see PAC contributions as a kind of competition among corporations for access and influence on the issues most important to them.

Research that explicitly dissects their impacts on policy finds a pattern of corporate and other PACs producing noticeable effects at some times but not at others. PAC effects appear weakest on issues that are ideological, partisan (Wright 1985; Frendreis and Waterman 1985), and salient (Davis 1993; Jones and Keiser 1987; Neustadtl 1990)—precisely the qualities that best define unifying issues. Sorauf (1992, 170) identifies the scholarly consensus as holding that the influence of PACs is "strongest on the narrower, less visible issues" that lack "the usually dominant influences of party, district, leadership, and mass opinion." If that consensus is correct, then PAC effects should be most pronounced on particularistic issues and weakest on unifying issues.

The prospect of corporations using PACs to gain power on particularistic issues is enhanced by the frequent dearth of voices and financial contributions promoting the other side. While a corporation may contribute in hopes of gaining a special provision in the tax code, normally no interest group is giving specifically to oppose that provision. To be sure, competition on particularistic issues does often emerge, but competition becomes much more likely on unifying issues where money usually flows from all sides of the dispute. When business coalesces, its contributions will be partially offset by those from other interests, especially unions. Unions often care considerably about unifying issues, and their PACs contributed $47 million to congressional races in 1997–1998. The implication is not that there is any one-to-one balancing, for the total number of corporate dollars spent on politics far outstrips what unions can afford. Rather, the point is that while many of the corporate dollars are diverted to affect particularistic matters, union contributions more often focus on broad matters like those that elicit business unity.

Unifying issues are thus far more likely than particularistic ones to see corporate pressure met by at least some mobilization on the other side. A convincing case can be advanced that we should be more concerned about PAC influence when business unity does not exist than in those instances where diverse firms stand together. Some of the strongest critics of the role of business in campaign finance (Clawson, Neustadtl, and Weller 1998, especially chap. 3; Stern 1992) seem to agree, for they emphasize special-interest provisions of legislation as the arena where corporations gain benefits through their PACs.

A recent book carrying forward the notion that corporate money earns benefits unique to the giver, written by Charles Lewis and the staff of The Center for Public Integrity, is aptly titled *The Buying of the Congress*. The book sifts through publicly available records to uncover the movement of money from corporate interests to Congress and the patterns of legislation relevant to those interests. Lewis (1998) identifies instances where food producers successfully fought tighter controls on foodborne bacteria, cable companies won deregulation of rates, agricultural interests benefited from price supports, the airline industry avoided tougher safety requirements, and all kinds of companies and industries received special tax breaks. Lewis concludes that corporate money, most of it filtered through PACs, has caused all of these outcomes.

Regardless of the ultimate veracity of Lewis's account, the relevant point here is that his examples are particularistic and occasionally conflictual issues. Instances where a prima facie case exists for corporate PACs strongly affecting legislation on unifying issues, while they surely exist, are simply much harder to find. That is exactly what we would expect if unifying issues, embodying characteristics that make lawmaking responsive to public opinion and elections, restrict the capacity of corporations to wield overt power successfully. Corporate PAC money probably makes some difference in the eventual outcomes—the contributions certainly can't hurt when decisions are reached on unifying issues—but the effect is likely to be limited in size.

THE BROADER RAMIFICATIONS OF MODERN CAMPAIGN FINANCE

While PAC contributions must be considered a central element, business participation in campaign finance also includes money given to candidates by individual executives and businesspeople, the amounts business groups spend independently of candidates to elect or defeat them, sums allocated to purchase issue-related advertising, and the soft money directed to parties rather than candidates. These avenues of influence could combine to create systematic advantages for business on unifying issues, particularly when one considers innovations during the postwar era that have increased the importance of money in elections.

To test empirically whether the current system of campaign finance creates a distinctive set of outcomes, one must determine when that system actually commenced. As historians and social scientists have long recognized, defining when one era ends and another begins is never easy. When nearly any political, economic, or social phenomenon is studied from a longitudinal perspective, one can always identify continuities that coexist with the changes. That complexity certainly applies to the role of money in American politics. From the earliest moments of the nation's history, hard currency has always found a home in political affairs. Money emerged as a political force even during George Washington's 1757 run for the House of Burgesses in Virginia. Using a method of campaign spending available at the time, Washington purchased liquor to reward his supporters at polling places.

In recent decades, concerns about money in elections have taken a new urgency. While breaks from the past do not resemble night and day, the importance of cash appears to have grown considerably in degree. The contrast remains even if one restricts attention to the postwar years. A reasonable case could be constructed for treating the period from the 1970s to the present as being different from the 1950s and 1960s. Part of this difference stems from the Federal Election Campaign Act (FECA) amendments of 1974, which—along with judicial rulings and minor amendments added later—created the legal framework within which federal campaigns have operated ever since. But even more than the changes wrought by FECA, broader trends in electoral politics separate recent campaigns for Congress and the presidency from those of the early postwar years.[6]

One of the most consequential changes involves the balance of control over campaigns between the parties and the candidates. For most of the twentieth century, it was the parties who ran the campaigns. They recruited the candidates, collected information about voters' concerns, identified issues and crafted themes for campaigns, printed campaign literature and distributed it to voters, and organized their supporters. The parties' control over campaigns also meant that they carried out most of the fundraising. When money was needed, parties usually turned to a small number of wealthy contributors.

On balance, however, money was not as crucial a resource in the 1950s and 1960s as it is today. For starters, the party-run campaigns in earlier days made considerable use of noncash assets. Hordes of volunteers—supplemented, in places where patronage continued to exist, by those who owed favors to the party—would canvass the precincts and wards. The party workers gathered information, maintained contacts in the community, and ensured that voters arrived at the polls.

Reasons beyond the usage of noncash resources also contributed to making money a less pressing requirement than it would be later. In the

6. This section draws heavily from Sorauf 1988, chap. 2.

early postwar years, partisan affiliations in the electorate were solidly entrenched but soon started a fitful yet noticeable decline. At the same time that the proportion of Americans strongly identifying with one of the two major parties fell from 35 percent in 1960 to 26 percent in 1980, the ranks of independents grew from 23 percent to 34 percent.[7] Strong party affiliations restrained the need for campaign spending because many voters would simply vote the party ticket. In a sense, many elections were decided by the distribution of partisan affiliations in the electorate, for normally even massive levels of spending cannot deliver victory to a candidate when partisan identifications among voters strongly favor the opponent. With generally weaker partisan affiliations today, those situations are less common, consequently increasing the need for candidates to control an independent means to attract voters. Frequently lacking the ability to run and win solely on a party label, candidates must offer voters other reasons to elect them. It takes money to identify, build, and maintain a coalition of voters.

The evolution from party-centered to candidate-centered elections, while occurring gradually, had arrived by the 1970s. This transformation featured several new elements. The noncash assets parties formerly commanded diminished; increasingly, campaigns became a cash economy. Everything that candidates needed—from polling to consultants to advertising—could be purchased. The catch was that campaign services, especially those related to advertising through the electronic media, did not come cheaply. The electoral uses of television advertising in the 1960s, the first decade when television ownership was nearly universal among American households, appeared tame and inexpensive compared to what came afterward. The availability of pricey campaign services, combined with the need for candidates to create a personal connection with voters, fueled a firestorm of escalating campaign costs. Campaigns developed aspects of an arms race whereby candidates watching their opponents raise large amounts of money responded in kind.

The increased importance of money in determining who would win elections is crystallized most clearly in data documenting the rising costs of campaigns. In 1960, according to the best estimates, candidates at the federal, state, and local levels spent a combined $175 million. By 1980, that figure had climbed all the way to $1.2 billion, an increase of

---

7. The data come from the American National Election Studies, conducted by the Center for Political Studies at the University of Michigan.

250 percent in inflation-adjusted dollars.[8] To maximize their chances of winning, both actual and prospective officeholders must spend considerable time and effort raising funds. While no systematic data exists, there are good reasons to believe that House and Senate members focused more attention and energy on fundraising in the 1980s and 1990s than did their counterparts in the 1950s and 1960s. That change was a predictable consequence of the shift to candidate-centered elections and the escalating campaign costs that accompanied them. Though money was certainly a relevant factor, one normally did not need large sums of it to run a competitive campaign for Congress in 1960. Two decades later that was no longer true.

Some commentators contend that the rising costs of elections have wreaked havoc upon the American political system. The dependence upon fundraising, many scholars, journalists, and others believe, leaves officeholders more responsive to financial contributors than to constituents (Clawson, Neustadtl, and Weller 1998; Jackson 1988; Stern 1992). Susan Manes (1990, 19), a high-ranking official in Common Cause, writes: "the need to raise large amounts of money to wage a competitive campaign increases candidates' dependence on special interest money." A related contention holds that the money chase biases policy toward the collective interests of business, from which the largest share of contributions arise (Ferguson and Rogers 1986). As a corollary, some observers blame the new system of campaign finance for severing the link between elections and governing. If sufficient funding is necessary for a candidate to mount a viable campaign, then elections may degenerate into a fundraising contest whereby whoever collects the most checks emerges the victor. It does not take a cynic to at least suspect, absent evidence to the contrary, that the needs and voices of the ordinary citizen could be overlooked and unheard as a consequence.

TESTING THE EFFECTS OF CHANGES IN CAMPAIGN FINANCE

We have already seen evidence in chapter 5 that, as far as unifying issues are concerned, these arguments are overstated. Despite the fact that candidates raise substantial amounts of business-related cash, citizen preferences do affect what government does and elections do bear a clear relationship to governing. Just as the necessity for many nonprofit and charitable organizations to find donors need not force them to abandon their founding missions, so too the sums of money candidates collect need not sever the linkage between citizens, elections, and

8. The figures are taken from Alexander (1984).

government. The findings presented in the previous chapter demonstrate that these linkages shine through in a major way.

One could argue, though, that the findings are concealing considerable variation by treating the entire period from the 1950s to the 1990s as a single unit. During that period the pressure on candidates to raise funds intensified. If the current system of campaign finance—roughly demarcated by the passage of FECA—has created a serious divergence between what citizens want and what government does, then some testable implications follow. Perhaps most notably, the model of policymaking developed in chapter 5—which includes only the four variables measuring public opinion and elections—should underpredict the favorability of policies to business during the era of modern campaign finance. If the increased dependence upon business largesse forces both parties toward contributors' positions on unifying issues, then lawmaking in the later period should be more advantageous to business than my model predicts. Relative to earlier decades, the most recent ones should contain a greater proportion of probusiness legislative decisions.

This possibility can be tested by adding to the statistical model a dummy variable taking the value 0 from 1953 to 1974, before FECA and related electoral changes took effect, and 1 from 1975 to 1996. The dummy variable will capture any changes in legislative action between the two periods that cannot be explained by the other independent variables. If campaign finance has realigned the playing field in business's favor, the dummy variable should be positive and statistically significant. Such a finding would indicate that policy decisions in the later period are systematically higher than one would expect based upon public opinion and elections alone.

This test has two advantages over the empirical analysis of corporate PACs earlier in the chapter. By including the entire slate of innovations in campaign finance—everything from the rise of soft money to the growth in issue advocacy to the higher costs of campaigns more generally—the test captures several different methods whereby business funds elections. Any evidence uncovered will not be limited strictly to corporate PACs, though of course their emergence is one of the main changes that could move policy toward unified business interests in the post-FECA era. Adding another advantage over the earlier analysis of corporate PACs, the test can use all forty-four observations upon which the inferences in chapter 5 rested. Because the test will not face the problem of very few observations, the statistical estimates will be more reliable. We can thus have more confidence in them than in the earlier findings on the effects of corporate PAC contributions.

The results of the test appear in the first column of table 6.2. The most important information is the coefficient on the dummy variable denoting the modern era of campaign finance. This coefficient clearly fails to attain statistical significance. Legislative decisions in the post-FECA era do not, all else being equal, become more favorable to business on unifying issues. This finding provides evidence against the claim that the current regime of campaign finance has tilted policies toward business as a whole. Whether certain companies and industries have benefited, of course, is a question that these data cannot address.

An additional test could further illuminate the possible impacts of campaign finance innovations in the 1970s. If business contributions through PACs, individuals, and soft money have undermined the means

Table 6.2 Representation in the Modern Era of Campaign Finance

VARIABLES	COEFFICIENTS	
	(1)	(2)
Constant	−114.35**	−103.12**
	(36.22)	(34.29)
Public mood	1.88**	2.18**
	(0.41)	(0.59)
Public attitudes toward corporations	0.75	1.02*
	(0.51)	(0.50)
Partisan composition of Congress	1.20**	0.32
	(0.27)	(0.45)
Presidential leadership opening	−0.48	1.92
	(0.62)	(1.13)
Dummy for modern era	0.28	
	(4.02)	
Public mood X		−0.38
Dummy for modern era		(0.59)
Public attitudes toward corporations X		−1.03
Dummy for modern era		(0.52)
Partisan composition of Congress X		1.50*
Dummy for modern era		(0.57)
Presidential governing mandate X		−1.94
Dummy for modern era		(1.29)
Diagnostics		
Durbin-Watson statistic	1.82	2.17
N	44	44
R^2	0.68	0.74
F-statistic for interaction terms		1.89

*$p < .05$ **$p < .01$

Note: The models are estimated with OLS and cover 1953–1996. Standard errors are in parentheses. The dummy for modern era takes the value 1 from 1975 to 1996 and 0 from 1953 to 1974.

for citizens to guide lawmaking, then we should find the coefficients on the four variables measuring public opinion and elections to be weaker after FECA was enacted. The variables should have lesser effects upon legislative action, showing that the gap between citizens and government increased as candidates depended more upon contributions from business. Note that this test, which focuses upon the potential weakening of representation, is different from but related to the previous one that sought to determine whether policy became more favorable to business.

To test this additional hypothesis, I again used the dummy variable, taking the value 1 during the period 1975–1996 and 0 during 1953–1974. I then calculated four interaction terms by multiplying the dummy variable by the four variables for public opinion and elections. In a regression estimation, the coefficient on each interaction term gives the change in the relevant coefficient between the two periods. The associated t-statistic determines whether this change is statistically significant. If the modern era of campaign finance subverts representation on unifying issues, the interaction terms should be negative and statistically significant, thus indicating weaker effects of public opinion and elections in the later period.

Column 2 of table 6.2 summarizes the results of the statistical analysis. Because they are based upon all forty-four observations, the estimates should have sufficient statistical reliability to allow sound inferences. The interaction term for public mood has a t-ratio of -0.65, indicating no change in the impacts of public mood between the two periods. The other three interaction terms demand closer inspection. The interaction terms involving public attitudes toward corporations and the presidential leadership opening, while not statistically significant, have reasonably large t-statistics of -1.98 and -1.50, respectively. Both have the signs predicted by observers who contend that the modern system of campaign finance has undercut popular representation. At the same time, the interaction term relating to the partisan composition of Congress is statistically significant in a direction opposite to that predicted by those observers. In recent years congressional elections have become more important, not less, in determining subsequent legislative action. This change probably reflects the growing ideological distance between the two parties that has arisen since World War II (Poole and Rosenthal 1997) and especially since the late 1970s (Abramowitz and Saunders 1998).

The overall findings, then, are mixed. Two channels of representation appear weaker under the contemporary system of campaign finance. Public attitudes toward corporations, in particular, seem to produce few effects upon lawmaking after the enactment of FECA. Distrust of the nation's corporations has grown during the 1990s with little apparent consequence for the outcomes of unifying issues. On the other hand, despite the arguments of some observers that a dependence upon fundraising has rendered the congressional parties virtual clones of each other, the Democratic and Republican parties are now further apart than they were in the early postwar decades. As a consequence, citizens have a greater opportunity to initiate policy redirections by choosing candidates from their preferred party. Given these conflicting findings, the data indicate that the changing face of campaign finance has not brought consistent implications one way or the other for representation on unifying issues.

OTHER MECHANISMS OF OVERT POWER

Though it receives the most attention, financing campaigns is only one potential way for business to exert overt power on unifying issues. Companies can also organize for collective action through membership in trade associations and peak associations, which then represent the views of their members to government. The strength of peak associations, especially the U.S. Chamber of Commerce, could be an important factor in an explanation of legislative action. Because its strategy for influencing legislation emphasizes mobilizing its members to contact policymakers, the Chamber is well situated to stimulate and coordinate the collective political involvement of various factions of business.

Different companies and trade associations, responding to these calls, can bring pressure upon policymakers from across the country. To present their preferences on unifying issues, businesses can use letter-writing, telephone calls, or face-to-face contacts. Multifaceted lobbying from throughout the world of private enterprise could be effective for several reasons. Elected officials could find convincing the substantive arguments advanced, making straightforward persuasion the dominant means of influence. With its access to all kinds of consultants, researchers, and public relations personnel, business will construct the best possible case on the merits, and officeholders may agree that the nation's interests would be furthered by granting business's demands.

Perhaps most likely, political motivations may cause legislators to listen to the firms located in their districts and states and lead presidents to react to the general business preferences in the nation. If a broad array of firms expresses a common position, House and Senate members may accede to mollify the businesses in their constituencies. Owners and managers of companies often stand among opinion leaders in the community. The popularity of politicians among constituents could depend upon whether they have satisfied business leaders, whose lobbying on unifying issues thus becomes a crucial determinant of the eventual legislative outcome.

Competing pressures, though, may mitigate the impacts of business-wide lobbying. As unifying issues tend to be ideological and partisan, politicians bring with them into office preexisting preferences that business may have to overcome. The salience of unifying issues means that officeholders recognize that an action contrary to public opinion could cost them votes in future elections. Unifying issues attract attention and concern from other groups, moreover, so any lobbying conducted by business could be at least partially checked by pressure from the other side. Berry (1999) shows that the citizen groups often opposing business have resources of their own—such as skilled staff, credibility, and access to policymakers and the media—that make them effective players in the policy process. Labor unions, too, can affect legislative decisions, especially through grassroots organizing.

As the foregoing reasoning suggests, the scope of overt business influence on unifying issues is unclear on theoretical grounds alone. Ultimately this question needs empirical investigation to uncover evidence allowing an answer. The effectiveness of the various avenues of business power can be appraised by measuring them and determining their relationship to policy decisions. Identifying and testing concrete mechanisms creates precision in inferences about the means of business power, for social scientists care not only about the degree of power but also about the ways through which it occurs. Some of the empirical analyses to follow, therefore, attempt to propose and test specific means of business power. That kind of approach requires the investigator to correctly isolate and measure the right channels. Considering the many possible mechanisms of influence, this task can be difficult.

An additional and complementary approach is to explore the factors that might lead to business-wide collective action. While leaving the actual mechanisms of influence unspecified, this research strategy potentially could identify the circumstances under which multiple forms of collective action, some of which cannot be measured, might arise. In line with the book's focus on unifying issues, searching for the precursors that stimulate cooperative efforts throughout business could be fruitful. Possible instigating forces include interlocking directorates, family and social ties among business executives, and commercial banks operating as mediators (Mills 1956; Schwartz 1987; Mintz and Schwartz 1985). While those factors are difficult to measure on an annual basis, several empirical studies, including those by Jacobs (1988), Quinn and Shapiro (1991), Hicks (1984), and Devine (1984), have identified a potential precursor to cooperative efforts that can be measured over time: the concentration of production within the largest firms.

Ever since massive corporations emerged at the end of the nineteenth century, many observers have expected greater concentration within the economy to facilitate coordination among firms. An economy dominated by relatively few large corporations might generate more collective action by business than an economy marked by a plethora of smaller ones. Olson (1965) supplies the most detailed reasoning for such an expectation. Within a group having few members, each has a sizable stake in the joint benefit and will likely make some contribution irrespective of the other members' actions. For the contrary case of groups with many small members, incentives for free riding exist because each individual stake is lessened. Thus, one might expect business to undertake more joint actions when economic production is concentrated within a limited number of large corporations. If this expectation is accurate, and if the ensuing political activity influences elected officials, then policies should be most favorable to business when the smallest number of firms dominates the economy.

INDICATORS OF POLITICAL MOBILIZATION

Because of the large variety of ways by which business, when unified, might exert overt power, the best research strategy is to surround the target to the greatest extent possible. The strategy here therefore develops indicators of both specific mechanisms of influence and also the conditions making cooperative efforts more likely. Utilizing both approaches, whose advantages and disadvantages are offsetting, should lead to a better understanding of business power than would be reached through either of them alone. Several measures, each scored on an annual basis, can be constructed to employ the two approaches:

BUSINESS LOBBYING CAPACITY

This indicator is calculated by taking the number of registered lobbyists for business interests as a proportion of all registered lobbyists from business, citizen groups, and unions.[9] The measure captures the capacity for lobbying that business enjoys relative to the groups most frequently opposing it on unifying issues. Business interests include individual corporations, trade associations, peak associations, and other business organizations. The definition of citizen groups follows that of Berry (1999), namely nongovernmental organizations lacking a basis in employment, a profession, or business, and it includes well-known groups like the Sierra Club and the National Association for the Advancement of Colored People plus a litany of smaller ones. Unions are defined as organizations engaging in collective bargaining on behalf of workers.

The availability of data was made possible by The Federal Regulation of Lobbying Act of 1946, as interpreted by the Supreme Court in 1954, which required all groups directly lobbying House and Senate members to register with the clerk of the respective chamber.[10] The statute was replaced by new legislation in 1995 expanded to include lobbying of legislative staff and executive branch officials. This major change in the law limits the span of comparable data to the four decades between the mid-1950s and the mid-1990s.

The measure unfortunately cannot distinguish, for any given lobbyist representing a business interest, his or her allocations of time among particularistic, conflictual, and unifying issues. For this reason, the

9. Most of the data were collected from the regular reports of lobbying registrations in *Congressional Quarterly Almanac* and *Congressional Quarterly Weekly Report*. The data for 1994 were taken from *Congressional Record*. All registrations from after Congress convenes (and thus makes no more policy decisions during that year) are counted with the next year's data. If Congress adjourns on October 16, for example, then the registrations from November and December are included with the following year's data.

10. The 1946 statute never succeeded in identifying all lobbying efforts because it required the registration only of direct contacts with legislators, thus excluding grassroots organizing and contacts with legislative staff or executive branch officials (Hrebenar and Scott 1982). The data necessary to paint a more comprehensive portrait of the lobbying population over the last several decades simply do not exist. My indicator's validity therefore depends upon the degree to which the proportions of registered lobbyists to all lobbyists within business, citizen groups, and unions move together over time. For example, if a given year picks up an increased number of registered business lobbyists relative to the total possible, while the proportion of lobbyists for citizen groups and unions who choose to register remains constant, then the indicator has nonrandom measurement error. It seems plausible, though, that any increases and decreases in registration rates would affect all groups roughly equally, thereby having limited effects upon my measure's validity.

measure of lobbying capacity assumes that each new business lobbyist spends some time on matters for which firms share agreement. That is, business interests, when they have a substantial number of available lobbyists, are assumed to deploy some of this capacity on unifying issues.

CHAMBER MEMBERSHIP

The second indicator is the total membership in the U.S. Chamber of Commerce, including state, local, and regional chambers of commerce, trade associations, and individual firms and businesspeople. This indicator taps one aspect of business-wide collective action, belonging to the organization with the most diverse membership. Because of the Chamber's reliance upon outside lobbying, its effectiveness in winning favorable legislation might depend upon the size of its membership. Greater membership levels both provide additional financial resources to the Chamber and incorporate a wider base that can be organized for political action.[11]

SALES CONCENTRATION

This indicator, measured as the total sales of the Fortune 100 corporations divided by the Gross Domestic Product, captures the degree to which the largest industrial corporations dominate the economy.[12] The data cover the entire period, 1954–1993, during which *Fortune* maintained a consistent requirement for the corporations making its directory.[13]

THE CONSEQUENCES OF BUSINESS-WIDE POLITICAL ACTIVITY

As was done in assessing the role of business in campaign finance, the analysis builds upon the statistical model developed and tested

11. To increase the readability of the results, I rescaled the variable for Chamber membership by dividing it by ten thousand.

12. Alternatively one could measure the concentration of assets instead of sales, a possibility rendered infeasible due to the unavailability of consistent longitudinal data on assets.

13. The indicator is lagged one year based on the assumption that any increases in collective action resulting from changes in industrial concentration need time to develop. *Fortune* first published its directory to cover corporations' fiscal years ending in 1954. From 1954 to 1993, corporations in *Fortune*'s directory of the largest industrials had to derive more than 50 percent of their revenues from manufacturing and/or mining. Beginning with the 1994 data, *Fortune* eliminated this requirement, thereby rendering the new directory noncomparable to the previous ones. Accordingly, the variable I use ranges from 1955 to 1994, covering the lagged data from 1954 to 1993.

in chapter 5. The model to be estimated includes the four variables tapping public opinion and election outcomes plus the new variables on the possible means for business to wield overt power. The statistical analysis, conducted with ordinary least squares, initially considers each indicator of business activity separately. The limitations of data availability dictate that the various models be based upon slightly different time spans. Because the business indicators are coded such that a higher value reflects greater political mobilization, the presence of overt power would be inferred if they show a positive effect upon legislative action.

Table 6.3 displays the empirical results. Paralleling the findings from earlier chapters, the four variables measuring public opinion and elections usually have sizeable and statistically reliable effects. The results presented in Column 1 suggest that business lobbying capacity has no systematic relationship with policy outcomes. The relevant coefficient, .11, has the right sign but is not statistically distinguishable from zero. The number of lobbyists commanded by business interests vis-a-vis their most frequent opponents appears to make little difference for legislative decisions on unifying issues.

Column 2 shows the results of a specification including as an independent variable the total membership in the U.S. Chamber of Commerce. The coefficient on Chamber membership presented in table 6.3 is not statistically significant.[14] The results reported in Column 3 reflect a model including as an independent variable the concentration of sales among the largest corporations. If a greater degree of concentration promotes collective action and therefore increases business influence over policymaking, we would expect a positive relationship between sales concentration and legislative decisions. The coefficient on sales concentration, however, has the wrong sign and is not statistically significant.[15]

The findings listed in Column 4 stem from a model simultaneously incorporating all three indicators of business political activity. The results of this more encompassing specification match those already discussed. None of the coefficients on variables measuring overt political activity reach statistical significance. Overall, the four models estimated here point to public opinion and elections as the most important determinants of whether unified business preferences will be either

14. The same inference results if Chamber membership is differenced.
15. The results reported here are for a variable defined as the first lag of sales concentration. Models using either 0 or 2 lags produce the same inferences.

Table 6.3 Tests of Overt Business Power

VARIABLES	COEFFICIENTS			
	(1)	(2)	(3)	(4)
Constant	−121.86**	−132.17**	−72.80	−94.41**
	(40.70)	(34.29)	(38.84)	(40.91)
Public mood	1.87**	2.08**	2.13**	2.45**
	(0.41)	(0.44)	(0.53)	(0.54)
Public attitudes toward corporations	0.98*	1.08*	0.50	1.05
	(0.43)	(0.45)	(0.45)	(0.53)
Partisan composition of Congress	0.89*	1.00**	0.71*	0.32
	(0.34)	(0.31)	(0.33)	(0.38)
Presidential leadership opening	0.91	0.68	1.19	1.58*
	(0.69)	(0.63)	(0.71)	(0.71)
Business lobbying capacity	0.11			−0.09
	(0.24)			(0.35)
Chamber membership		0.26		0.45
		(0.21)		(0.29)
Sales concentration			−0.66	−0.64
			(0.64)	(0.69)
Diagnostics				
Durbin-Watson statistic	1.89	1.86	1.72	1.96
N	42	44	40	40
R²	0.66	0.69	0.62	0.66

*$p < .05$ **$p < .01$
Note: All four models are estimated with OLS. Due to slightly different periods of data availability, the four models cover 1953–1994, 1953–1996, 1955–1994, and 1955–1994.

upheld or overridden in legislative decisions. Potential avenues for business to wield overt power over policy yield only modest impacts.

The dependent variable used in these analyses subsumes all issues over four decades that were marked by consensus in business preferences. The extensive scope of the data therefore affords a high degree of generalizability in the findings by applying to all of American national politics for a long time span. An investigator might discern an effect of business-wide political activity on a more restricted policy indicator, a conclusion that Griffin, Devine, and Wallace (1982), for example, report for defense expenditures. This chapter's strategy of examining multiple policy domains simultaneously, however, provides the most encompassing tests to date of theoretical claims about how legislative decisions unfold.

OVERT BUSINESS POWER AND LEGISLATIVE DECISIONS

The analyses in this chapter suggest that business, particularly through campaign finance, does exert some overt leverage over the outcomes of unifying issues. It would be hard to imagine otherwise. Yet that leverage appears to be limited in magnitude. The overt power of business cannot explain broad changes in lawmaking on unifying issues. Business normally does not go from winning to losing, or vice versa, because of the effectiveness of its own efforts to influence policy. Instead, public opinion and elections remain the most important forces determining fluctuations in policy even when the analysis considers possibilities for influence by a unified business community. And, it should be remembered, these findings follow not from an inquiry into trivial matters but from examining many of the most important legislative issues from the past few decades.

Many potential mechanisms could provide business with influence on unifying issues. This chapter has studied the most widely discussed route, the funding of campaigns. The lobbying population and membership size of the U.S. Chamber of Commerce have also been explored, as has the concentration of sales among the largest corporations. As a group, these factors appear to produce only minor effects upon long-term swings in policy. If the political activities business undertakes cannot explain why lawmaking changes from being advantageous at one point to being unfavorable at another, then the overt power of unified business interests would seem to be smaller than social scientists have believed.

On certain occasions the leverage a unified business community exerts over lawmaking will be large. The chapter's finding of modest overt power is really an average calculated across all 2,364 unifying issues. That finding, like all averages, probably masks the existence of variation around the central tendency. For some unifying issues, political activity by business likely yields a considerably greater return than is depicted here. And even for the greater number of unifying issues where overt business power is bounded in size, that power sometimes will make a difference in the outcome. If lawmakers are close to evenly split on a decision, which happens on many occasions, the overt pressure business brings could swing the outcome in its favor. Such a process is entirely compatible with the central themes of the book. The finding that business pressure cannot explain large changes in policies over time does not mean that business cannot use its overt power to affect certain legislative decisions.

One should exercise caution in extrapolating the empirical results to means of influence not addressed here. For example, Domhoff (1983), Mills (1956), and Miliband (1969) argue that common social backgrounds among public officials and corporate leaders, such as their attendance at the same prep schools and their intermingling through such institutions as marriage and social clubs, bias policies toward corporate interests. Reflecting the immense difficulties in constructing a longitudinal measure of the convergence in social backgrounds between government and corporate elites, the consequences for legislative action caused by the degree of convergence have not been empirically assessed in my analysis or, for that matter, in any previous research. The data presented in this chapter cannot provide direct evidence either for or against an effect of common social backgrounds upon the outcomes of unifying issues.

Still, because the chapter has addressed several of the most plausible sources of overt business power, the results—even if they do not provide a complete understanding—nevertheless serve to narrow the debate. In any event, there are ample grounds for doubting that incorporating additional means of overt business power would fundamentally alter the conclusions advanced here. Most importantly, the four variables measuring public opinion and elections—as we saw in chapter 5— together explain about 70 percent of the variance in policymaking. Simply put, the strong effects of these factors mean that little is left to be attributed to overt business power.

SEVEN

Structural Sources of Business Power

The previous chapter empirically analyzed the overt avenues through which business attempts to influence legislation, but other forms of power could exist as well. Here I address a prominent and popular school of thought in political economy contending, as its core proposition, that imperatives embedded within democratic market economies lead to policy initiatives serving the interests of capital owners.[1] Within this perspective, policy choices in the United States, and throughout the world, are critically conditioned by the tendency of capitalists to invest only when policies facilitate the earning of profits. The economic imperative is said to force governments to enact initiatives favorable to business even without any organized effort by capital owners and managers. The resulting process undermines political representation by mitigating the impacts of elections and weakening the ability of public officials to respond to the policy desires of their constituents.

Though the central idea in simplified form had been mentioned by Milibrand (1969), Rose (1967), and others, Poulantzas (1969, 1973) was the first scholar to develop this kind of structuralist perspective in detail.[2] According to Poulantzas, business is internally divided because firms protect their own narrow interests rather than those of capital as a whole. Responsibility to take actions for the broader benefit of capital falls to the state, which enjoys autonomy from the pressures

1. The argument and analysis developed in this chapter is a revised version of Smith (1999).

2. I follow tradition here and outline a set of claims commonly known as "structuralist" or "structural" even though those labels are somewhat ambiguous. Their precise meaning should be apparent shortly.

brought by factions of business. In maintaining a long-run orientation the state arbitrates between sectors, accomplishing for capital what capital cannot do for itself.

While substantially refining these ideas, Poulantzas' theoretical discussion was ultimately limited by his lack of attention to the mechanisms forcing the state to reproduce the conditions for capitalist accumulation. Lindblom (1977) and Block (1977) correct this oversight by stressing the importance of economic performance to the electoral prospects of incumbent politicians. As Lindblom (1982, 329) states: "When a decline in prosperity and employment is brought about by decisions of corporate and other business executives, it is not they but government officials who consequently are retired from their offices." With their electoral survival depending upon private capital owners' willingness to invest, officeholders are highly motivated to maintain a favorable business climate. This motivation shapes their perceptions of the actions necessary to establish and sustain that climate, thereby constraining their policy decisions.[3]

THE LOGIC UNDERLYING THE STRUCTURAL POWER THESIS

Lindblom (1977) and Block (1977) wrote early statements of what is alternatively called the privileged position of business, the structural source of business power, or the structural dependence of the state on capital. The main ideas have been restated by Bowles and Gintis (1986), Cohen and Rogers (1983), Dryzek (1996), Elkin (1985), and Mitchell (1997). Based upon this line of research, one can identify the set of assumptions and implications defining the structuralist position. The discussion and analysis are grounded here within the American political system, but the central claims in principle apply to all governments that regularly face elections and operate within a market system of exchange.

The theory begins with the assumption that incumbent politicians of all kinds—at the federal level in the United States, this means the president, House members, and senators—expect their odds of reelection to rise under a strong economy and fall under a weak one (Mitchell 1997, 61–62). Given the abundance of evidence indicating that economic

3. Block (1977) and Offe (1984) add another potential mechanism by which state officials must cater to the needs of business, namely the state's dependence upon a strong economy to provide the revenues necessary to finance public programs. To the extent that such a mechanism exists, it would complement the electoral incentives described here.

performance actually does affect American election outcomes,[4] it is easily understandable that politicians perceive such a relationship.

Structuralist theory makes no explicit allowance for voters to reward politicians who have followed constituent preferences on substantive policy issues beyond simply the demand for prosperity. Indeed, as will be developed in greater detail later in the chapter, the theory downplays the possibility that politicians can respond to any public desires other than the preference for a robust economy. Achieving a healthy economy, in turn, requires adequate domestic investment. Thus, the argument continues, decisions by private business owners to curtail investment would jeopardize the nation's future affluence just as increases in investment would stimulate prosperity for the years to come (Lindblom 1982, 328–29).

Perhaps the most important assumption underlying the theory is that elected officials generally agree that certain policies would hurt the American business climate. Politicians believe that efforts in particular policy directions—such as labor laws favorable to unions, strong restrictions on pollution, or high taxes to fund social programs—would hinder investment and precipitate an economic slowdown. Through capital owners' decisions to invest in new and existing enterprises at a lower rate, or decisions to disinvest by laying off workers or shifting productive capacity overseas, the United States would suffer declines in total investment and economic growth. By harming the economy, such an outcome would threaten politicians' electoral careers by making them more vulnerable to successful challengers during the next election. Perceptions that a given policy would weaken the business climate therefore make politicians less likely to enact it in the first place (Dryzek 1996, 80–82; Block 1977, 16–17).

In addition to avoiding harmful policies, incumbent politicians are motivated to pursue initiatives believed to promote investment, such as cutting taxes or weakening regulatory programs. Actions of this sort attract investment from both domestic sources, whereby some individuals reallocate resources from consumption into investment in expectation of sufficient returns, and from internationally mobile capital seeking the most favorable location (Lindblom 1977, 173–75). These incentives to avoid decreases and seek increases in investment restrict the responsiveness of elected officials to their constituents' preferences on

4. For entry points into research focusing upon the United States, see Erikson (1990), Fiorina (1981), and Holbrook (1994).

substantive issues, thus subverting popular representation (Elkin 1985, 187–96). The economic imperative also severely reduces the capacity for elections bringing new parties to power to initiate a systematic change in the policies enacted. The incentives apply equally to elected officials "of the right or the left" (Mitchell 1997, 67), in practice eliciting "substantial convergence among governments of different partisanship" (Dryzek 1996, 79). One can think of these pressures as arising either from the individual investors who provide capital or from the businesses that decide whether or not additional investment would create the necessary returns. The outcome is identical in either case.[5]

In another important assumption, the structural power thesis does not require any overt action by corporations. Policymaking and elections within a market-based economy dictate that officeholders serve the needs of business even without lobbying, campaign contributions, common social origins of business and government leaders, interlocking directorates, or any other direct means of business influence (Lindblom 1977, 175; Block 1977, 19). The ultimate result, while not dictating that business always wins, does create a built-in advantage for business preferences.

Within the structuralist perspective, capitalists who fail to invest under unfavorable policy regimes are not intentionally punishing incumbent politicians. Nor do capital owners who augment their portfolios because of beneficial policies consciously establish a reward system for current officeholders. Instead, investors simply attempt to maximize their profits (Dryzek 1996, 25–26). They respond to adverse policies in a rational way, namely by investing less or disinvesting, and they increase their holdings if policy initiatives enhance the likelihood of profits (Bowles and Gintis 1986, 88–90). Yet these decisions at the individual level combine to affect the legislative policies considered and enacted. By anticipating the reactions of capital owners, elected officials avoid policies expected to diminish investment and adopt policies perceived to encourage investment.

5. Block (1977, 24–5) argues that the incentives giving capitalists structural power fade during depressions and all-encompassing wars. Under these conditions, governments exert substantial direct control over investment, rely upon military spending to stimulate the economy, and enjoy a heightened capacity to ignore the implicit threats of firms to disinvest. The structural power thesis, then, seeks to explain policymaking during "normal" times. Accordingly, the statistical tests developed later in the chapter stay within the theory's intended scope and do not include any periods of depressions or major wars.

Such a process implies a certain kind of popular sovereignty. If voters desire economic prosperity and reward incumbents who deliver it, then one dimension of citizen preferences is being satisfied. By holding shared demands for a sound economy, citizens and private companies jointly benefit when the goal is reached. With the preferences of the general public and the business sector nearly synonymous, it becomes easy for politicians to make decisions that benefit everyone.

But the public surely desires more from government than simply collective prosperity. Majority opinion often coalesces on the various principles underlying specific policy questions. In addition to having preferences over ends—of which prosperity is one, but not the only, example—people often hold preferences over the means and instruments of policy. These means and instruments are designed to achieve ends including but not limited to strong economic performance. Several recent studies have canvassed abundant survey evidence in order to portray public opinion on the tools defining the welfare state, regulation, economic policy, and social issues (Page and Shapiro 1992; Mayer 1992) and on the proper size of government more generally (Stimson 1999). In a nation purporting to be democratic, government policies should represent the policy preferences of the citizenry. The structuralist argument, though, contends that this kind of popular sovereignty is undermined by the inevitable linkage between the economy and elections.

STRUCTURAL POWER AND REPRESENTATION

The structural power thesis contains two critical arguments about the workings of political representation that motivate the analysis to follow. First, the necessity for politicians to sustain the economy is said to restrict policy choices. In shaping the resolution of issues important to corporations, the incentives prevent officeholders from fully considering the preferences of their constituents (Elkin 1985, 187–96). Public opinion on concrete policy decisions need not necessarily diverge from what business wants, in which case both can be satisfied simultaneously, but when conflicts arise politicians must follow the preferences of business. Dryzek (1996, 72) summarizes this problem in arguing that "the first priority of policymakers must be to attract investment and prevent capital flight. Popular control of policy cannot be allowed to interfere with this imperative."

The second argument about representation is just as important as the first. According to the structuralist thesis, policy changes that otherwise might result from elections disappear because the economic imperative affects officeholders from all political parties. By impinging upon elected officials "irrespective of their ideological views or party affiliations" (Mitchell 1997, 5; see also Mitchell 1997, 67–68) the powerful incentives "reduce the effective latitude for state action" (Bowles and Gintis 1986, 189; see also Dryzek 1996, 79–80). Within the United States, Democrats and Republicans alike must constantly cater to investors and thus behave similarly. With policy distinctions between Democrats and Republicans blurred, citizens unknowingly forfeit the ability to redirect policymaking by electing representatives from their preferred party. Instead of serving as an important channel for citizen control of government, elections lose much or all of their potential to transform government decisions. This implication, if true, is profound. Common expectations that citizens can instigate new policy directions through elections would become a mirage.

The structuralist theory, then, claims that economic incentives undermine government responsiveness to public opinion and also thwart the capacity for elections to spark systemic policy change. When stated in the strongest possible form, the theory holds that the imperatives inherent within democratic market economies completely eliminate the potential for ordinary citizens to affect policy decisions in any major way. That is, economic imperatives are so dominant that neither citizens' policy preferences nor their choices through elections have a meaningful effect upon policymaking. Based upon the results from chapter 5, the strongest statement of the theory's implications for representation can be rejected. Through a longitudinal analysis of 2,364 policy issues marked by business unity, public opinion and election outcomes were shown to be critical determinants of whether congressional members and presidents either embrace or avoid unified business preferences.

Although its strongest version cannot be squared with the evidence, the structural power theory undoubtedly shares good company in this respect. Expecting social science theories to provide convincing explanations in their boldest form imposes a standard rarely achievable. The findings from chapter 5 do not imply that a more restricted version of the structuralist argument is unsustainable. Most scholars embracing the theory probably subscribe to a milder version contending that the structural power of capital significantly weakens, but does not eviscerate, citizen control of government. If the logic underpinning the milder version is accurate, popular representation ought to be weakest during economic downturns, for it is at those moments when politicians depend the most upon stimulating the economy to further their own electoral futures. This more restricted proposition forms the focus of the remainder of the chapter.

EXISTING EMPIRICAL RESEARCH ON THE STRUCTURAL POWER THESIS

The structuralist thesis purports to explain both why certain issues never reach the government agenda and why government officials make particular decisions on the issues actively considered. Because of the obvious challenges to identifying options that never rose to the agenda and therefore left no observable record, the former component of the theory is difficult to test. Though nondecisions are important in their own right (Bachrach and Baratz 1963), one cannot easily develop concrete evidence to determine whether the failure to consider a hypothetical option reflects the structural power of business or whether some other explanation more convincingly accounts for the outcome. The first part of the thesis is, therefore, difficult to falsify (but see Crenson 1971). Discussion later in the chapter will return to this theme of keeping items off the agenda.

However, the second component of the thesis—its implications for the policies actually discussed and enacted—is testable, and the theory can be evaluated on that basis. Indeed, theorists writing in the structuralist tradition frequently invoke real laws and programs when describing the insights the theory may contribute. For example, both Lindblom (1977, 173–75, 178, 188, 347) and Block (1977, 13, 17) attempt to show how the structuralist perspective might explain the mix of policies implemented by governments. Given that proponents of the theory include concrete laws and programs within its explanatory scope, a corresponding empirical analysis of actual policies is appropriate. A test based upon government decisions can establish the theory's boundaries, though of course any findings cannot speak directly to the matter of nondecisions.

Several researchers have suggested that if politicians face an electoral imperative to maintain a healthy business climate, then policies should be most beneficial to business under sluggish economies and least favorable during robust times. A simple test of the theory follows as a result, requiring one to determine whether the incidence of pro-business policies changes according to the prevailing level of economic performance.

The evidence is inconclusive on whether the expected relationship exists. Among the null findings, Jacobs (1988) offers evidence that U.S. corporate taxes do not vary systematically with the state of the economy, seemingly undermining the structuralist theory. The pooled time series and cross-sectional model of Swank (1992), when estimated with statistical techniques that accurately assess sampling error (Beck and Katz 1996), also find the economy to be statistically unrelated to policy. In an analysis of corporate and individual taxes, Quinn and Shapiro (1991) report that declines in investment are actually associated with increasing rather than decreasing tax rates.

Campbell and Allen (1994), however, present apparently contradictory evidence that corporate tax rates fall when unemployment rises. Similarly, Allen and Campbell (1994) provide support for the structural power theory in establishing a relationship between tax progressivity in the United States and the unemployment rate. Quinn (1988), in a five-country study of investment tax initiatives, discovers that they fluctuate according to the state of the economy, particularly during economic downturns. Based upon a cross-national analysis of welfare spending, Hicks and Swank (1984) report that expenditures change as investment rises and falls.

Thus while some scholars have failed to find the prevalence of probusiness policies to rise under weak economic performance, other research uncovers the expected relationship. Some of the inconsistency in the findings surely reflects the studies' usage of differing dependent variables, independent variables, countries, and time periods. Despite these differences, though, the studies all seek to evaluate the structuralist argument in the same way. Does assessing the covariation of probusiness policies with the state of the economy—the approach taken by these studies—yield a valid test of the structural power thesis? Existing research begins on the right track by identifying times of the strongest and weakest economic pressure on policymakers. If incumbent politicians seek to enhance their own electoral prospects by promoting a favorable business climate, then the strength of this incentive cannot be constant over time. The urgency of the posited motivation necessarily depends upon the current level of economic prosperity. This point will later prove critical in finding the best way to test the theory's implications.

Consider economic performance sufficiently poor to be called a recession. Incumbent politicians quite reasonably believe a stagnant economy of this sort threatens their chances of reelection. Sensing the possibility that their careers could be terminated, officeholders should become especially focused upon achieving collective prosperity. Other potential influences upon policy decisions lose much of their impact, for incumbent politicians face heightened incentives to reject policies deemed threatening for investment and to advocate policies thought to encourage investment.

The studies mentioned earlier typically motivate their analyses by making this kind of argument. For example, Jacobs (1988, 860) notes: "According to the Block-Lindblom model, when confidence is reduced and investment is declining, political officials should enact economic measures that enhance returns to investment." However, this statement's flip side—that during robust economic times elected officials implement policies presumed to hinder investment—is definitely not a structuralist prediction. Structuralist theories do not imply that the economy will affect policy decisions in a linear fashion, whereby a poor economy induces policies benefiting investors while a strong economy instigates policies harming investors. The regression models used by previous researchers, though, assume this kind of linear effect. The theory instead describes economic performance as a *constraint* upon policymakers' behavior that becomes most pressing during a sluggish economy. That is, the impetus that supposedly overrides other influences upon politicians becomes most compelling when the economy is weak.

Under a booming economy, by contrast, politicians need not single-mindedly channel their energies toward encouraging investment. In times of solid economic performance, officeholders who look upon the horizon see that the level of prosperity bolsters their odds for reelection. Incumbent politicians can expect to benefit electorally even without a further rise in investment. They cannot completely ignore the needs of capital owners, the theory would suggest, but in comparison to periods of declining prosperity the economic motivation weakens. Officeholders therefore gain some freedom to follow other rationales for policy, such as their party's collective goals or the preferences of their constituents. If the theory is accurate, policymakers do not necessarily respond by adopting policies expected to cause investment to decline. With the constraint posed by economic incentives reduced, different forces will influence policy decisions. Depending upon the direction these other forces point, the resulting policies may or may not be those believed to adversely affect the business climate.

Expressed in the language of quantitative analysis, a one-unit change in a particular independent variable produces not a constant effect but rather one that increases according to the state of the economy.

For example, the partisan composition of government can have little impact upon policy choices during economic downturns, when elected officials of all partisan stripes most vigorously attempt to induce private investment. Under times of prosperity, investment needs are not as urgent and officeholders' partisanship can influence their behavior. Thus regression models assuming a linear relationship between economic performance and policy outcomes cannot determine whether structural power mitigates the impacts of forces like partisan turnover in governing institutions.

DEVELOPING AN APPROPRIATE TEST

There is a straightforward method available for evaluating theories positing conditional relationships. Interaction terms within a regression equation capture a parameter's dependence upon the level of another variable.[6]

Consider first a simple model of policymaking where the explanatory variables are the partisanship of government and the state of the economy, leaving aside for the moment the channel of representation that arises when officeholders respond directly to public opinion in the period between elections:

$$\text{Policy}_t = \beta_0 + \beta_1 \text{Government Partisanship}_t + \beta_2 \text{Economy}_t + \varepsilon_t \quad (1)$$

For equation (1), the effects of Government Partisanship$_t$ are (by assumption) constant across all levels of Economy$_t$. In this model economic incentives do not limit the ability of citizens to redirect policy by voting new parties into office; instead the economy has a simple linear effect upon policymaking. A specification taking the form of equation (1) cannot test the structuralist argument's implications for representation. The theory instead implies a model such as:

$$\text{Policy}_t = \beta_0 + \beta_1 \text{Government Partisanship} \\ + \beta_2 (\text{Government Partisanship}_t \times \text{Economy}_t) + \varepsilon_t \quad (2)$$

Within this model, the effects of a one-unit change in Government Partisanship$_t$ are not constant, but rather they vary across the levels of Economy$_t$.[7] The structuralist thesis expects β_2 to be positive, meaning

6. Friedrich (1982) provides a cogent description of this method.
7. The structural power thesis predicts that the effects of government partisanship are conditional upon the state of the economy, but it does not imply the reverse. That

that Government Partisanship has its largest effects under a strong economy and loses its impact on policy as the economy weakens.[8] The model easily generalizes to the multivariate case where multiple interaction terms each capture the dependence upon the economy of one independent variable's impacts. To test the structuralist theory, the chapter later develops and estimates a multivariate version of equation (2).

Theorists writing in the structuralist tradition have intended that their ideas explain government decisions across many policy areas. For example, in addition to the tax code, Block (1977, 13) mentions specific spending programs and labor laws unfavorable to unions as the kinds of policies resulting from the structural power of business. Within Lindblom's (1977, 173–75, 188) description of the policies governments pursue because of their need to facilitate investment, he references "enterprise autonomy" (presumably as little regulation as possible), patent laws, restraints on competition, and government subsidies of transportation systems. As for the initiatives difficult to implement because of structural power, Block (1977, 17) refers to policies designed to increase employment, redistributive programs, and social welfare programs more generally. While Lindblom (1977) usually highlights the probusiness policies enacted rather than the antibusiness policies produced in insufficient amounts, he suggests that his analysis also applies to policymaking in the environmental, energy, and education domains (Lindblom 1977, 347).

Scholars advancing the structuralist argument have offered a general explanation of decision-making not restricted to any single policy domain. The most encompassing test of the theory's implications should therefore examine many different kinds of policies. Yet it would be unfair to require the theory to explain every government action affecting some private capital owner. For instance, a particularistic policy decision having impacts upon only a small number of firms probably falls outside the theory's purview. By affecting so few firms, such a policy choice

---

is, the impacts of the economy are not expected to be constrained by government partisanship. Adding to equation (2) a variable for the economy itself, not subsumed in an interaction term, would inappropriately assume two-way dependence. This distinction makes no difference for the empirical estimations to follow, which yield identical inferences in either case; nevertheless, I proceed with the specification that conforms closest to the structuralist theory.

8. I refer here to the mild version of the theory. As noted earlier, the strong version of the theory claims that elected officials are so constrained by economic imperatives that partisan preferences never have much impact upon their decisions.

normally has little impact upon overall economic performance and consequently cannot be expected to motivate politicians seeking to promote prosperity. In like manner, the notion of structural power is unlikely to provide an accurate explanatory lens for conflictual issues characterized by discord within the business community. When business internally divides on a policy question, government officials cannot easily determine which course of action will actually facilitate investment.

The theory should apply, however, to issues that attract interest from a broad spectrum of business enterprises and create a rough consensus in the firms' positions. Policies of this sort affect a multitude of firms in similar ways either positively or negatively. To exhibit the behavior the theory predicts, government officials need large numbers of firms to express a united sentiment that a certain policy will either boost or retard economic performance. If a united sentiment prevails across different segments of business, then politicians can surmise that the policy would affect a diverse array of private investment decisions. Incumbent politicians catering to investment needs in ways predicted by the theory probably concentrate on unifying issues that, through their similar impact upon a variety of firms, could make a noticeable difference in the economy as a whole.

Incorporating the complete population of unifying issues allows an empirical test close in generality to the theory's breadth. Accordingly, the sections to follow analyze all legislative debates, identified in chapter 3 through the positions of the U.S. Chamber of Commerce, that are characterized by a high degree of business unity.

MEASUREMENT AND MODEL SPECIFICATION

To test the predictions of the structural power theory, the state of the economy must be measured over time. Theorists writing in the structuralist vein are not entirely clear about how to measure the economy, and my description of the economy earlier in the chapter is equally imprecise. Scholars use a plethora of terms to describe what politicians are supposed to be keenly sensitive to: "the level of economic activity," "investment," "business confidence," "employment," the "growth rate," and about a half-dozen others (Block 1977, 15–16; Bowles and Gintis 1986, 88–90; Lindblom 1977, 173–83; Lindblom 1982, 328–29; Offe 1984, 244).

These terms are obviously interrelated, reducing the potential problems for inference. Using a single economic indicator to test the structuralist theory, however, still runs some risk of making inferences appropriate for that measure but inappropriate for the underlying concept of interest. Therefore, I use a variety of indicators in different specifications and evaluate the theory according to the preponderance of the evidence. By estimating several equations, I hope to minimize the possibility that substantive inferences hinge upon measurement choices.

After reviewing the scholarship expounding the structuralist argument, I have identified four of the most plausible measures of the economy:

1. *Rate of growth in GDP.* The rate of growth in real Gross Domestic Product.[9]
2. *Employment rate.* The proportion of civilian job-seekers who are currently employed, calculated by subtracting the unemployment rate from 100.
3. *Rate of growth in investment.* The rate of growth in real nonresidential fixed private investment.
4. *Change in the index of leading indicators.* The yearly change in the index of leading economic indicators. Intended to predict the performance of the economy in the near future, the index is derived from eleven different series measuring such factors as manufacturers' orders, contracts for new plants and equipment, stock prices, consumer expectations, and new building permits. Annual changes are used because the raw index, like many of its constituent items, trends upward over time.

Economic growth and the employment rate can be interpreted as measures of current prosperity, while investment growth—because the returns to investment will be felt in the future—and the change in the index of leading indicators predict future prosperity. If elected officials turn first and primarily to contemporary information, they might look toward the former indicators. If officeholders instead seek to promote affluence in the future—say during the next election—they might concentrate on information that explicitly forecasts the future. Hence incorporating contemporaneous as well as forward-looking economic indicators into the analysis addresses both possibilities.

9. I centered each economic indicator by subtracting the mean from each observation, which ensures that the value zero is within the range of observed experience. Given these transformations, the models yield substantively meaningful estimates of conditional coefficients at the point where each economic indicator takes the value zero. In addition, the transformations ease comparisons across the different specifications because in each case the zero point for the economic indicator falls at the mean.

According to the structural power thesis, popular sovereignty should be undermined when politicians face the strongest need to stimulate the economy. Chapter 5 explicitly developed and tested a model of popular sovereignty, a model that includes variables for public mood, public attitudes toward corporations, the partisan composition of Congress, and the president's leadership opening. This model is extended here to encompass the structuralist argument, which claims that any effects on lawmaking of public opinion and election outcomes should shrink as the economy gets worse.

If accurate, those expectations demand urgent consideration, for they would recast our understandings of popular representation. Representation would be shown to be, in effect, a luxury that can be bought only when prosperity allows it. The linkage between citizens and government on unifying issues would change from appearing robust and ubiquitous, as chapter 5 indicated, to appearing shallow and conditional.

PUBLIC OPINION, ELECTIONS, AND THE ECONOMY

To test the mild version of the theory, I develop, estimate, and interpret a multivariate version of equation (2) as presented earlier in the chapter. Each variable measuring public opinion and elections is entered separately and also multiplied by an economic indicator. The t-ratio for each interaction term provides the test statistic for determining whether the data support the existence of a conditional coefficient. An F-statistic, calculated using the sums of squared residuals from the unrestricted model and from a model with all coefficients on interaction terms constrained to be zero, can be used to assess the joint significance of the interaction terms. The structural power thesis would be supported if the coefficients on the interaction terms are *positive and statistically significant as a group*.[10] The coefficients for the interaction terms, then, provide the critical information to evaluate the mild version of the theory. If those coefficients are positive and statistically reliable, that would indicate that representation becomes weaker during poor economic times.

10. Because four interaction terms within each specification are all partially based upon the same economic indicator, they will exhibit multicollinearity. This makes it all the more important to focus upon the F-test for their joint significance. While multicollinearity causes each individual interaction term to be estimated less precisely, it does not affect the statistical significance of the group as a whole (Kennedy 1985, chap. 10).

The models have the same dependent variable as chapters 5 and 6, the scale measuring the favorability to business of legislative action. Ordinary least squares regression is again employed to analyze the data. I estimated four specifications, one each for the alternative measures of the economy; table 7.1 summarizes the results. The columns are labeled according to the economic indicator used for that specification.

For the first column of table 7.1, the state of the economy is measured by the rate of growth in real Gross Domestic Product (GDP). The coefficients for the interaction terms supply the essential information for the

Table 7.1 A Test of the Structural Power Thesis

VARIABLES	SPECIFICATIONS BASED ON ALTERNATIVE MEASURES OF THE STATE OF THE ECONOMY			
	RATE OF GROWTH IN GDP	EMPLOYMENT RATE	RATE OF GROWTH IN INVESTMENT	CHANGE IN INDEX OF LEADING INDICATORS
Constant	−115.12**	−100.62**	−105.54	−100.29**
	(31.53)	(33.11)	(41.11)	(33.48)
Public mood	1.92**	1.70**	2.00**	1.74**
	(0.41)	(0.45)	(0.52)	(0.44)
Public attitudes toward corporations	0.75*	0.61	0.58	0.70
	(0.37)	(0.39)	(0.52)	(0.40)
Partisan composition of Congress	1.18**	1.22**	1.09*	1.06**
	(0.28)	(0.32)	(0.30)	(0.30)
Presidential leadership opening	0.63	0.70	0.98	1.11
	(0.76)	(0.69)	(0.79)	(0.81)
State of the economy	16.21	6.11	9.14	16.37
	(13.89)	(5.55)	(22.52)	(15.27)
Public mood X State of the economy	−0.29	−0.11	0.24	−0.29
	(0.19)	(0.08)	(0.38)	(0.21)
Public attitudes toward corporations X State of the economy	0.00	−0.03	−0.13	−0.08
	(0.19)	(0.07)	(0.31)	(0.19)
Partisan composition of Congress X State of the economy	−0.12	−0.01	−0.29	−0.03
	(0.14)	(0.05)	(0.24)	(0.13)
Presidential leadership opening X State of the economy	0.43	0.10	0.23	0.58
	(0.25)	(0.12)	(0.41)	(0.41)
Diagnostics				
R^2	0.73	0.71	0.71	0.71
Durbin-Watson statistic	1.87	1.80	1.88	1.76
F-statistic for interaction terms	1.44	0.54	0.69	1.07

$*p < .05$ $**p < .01$

Note: The columns are labeled according to the economic indicator used within that specification to measure the state of the economy. The models in columns 1–3 are estimated with OLS, cover 1953–1996, and have 44 observations. Column 4 covers 1953–1995 and has 43 observations. Standard errors are in parentheses.

structuralist implications. The theory's predictions receive no support in this specification. Two of the four coefficients on the interaction terms are positive and two are negative, but none of them are statistically significant. Most importantly, the F-statistic of 1.44 shows that the set is not statistically significant.[11]

Columns 2–4 of table 7.1 present results substantively similar to those from column 1. In each case, the interaction terms are jointly insignificant, as indicated by F-statistics of 0.54, 0.69, and 1.07. No matter how the economy is measured, the null hypothesis of constant parameters for the indicators of public opinion and elections cannot be rejected.[12] The overall pattern of results, with as many incorrect signs on the interaction terms as signs in the direction the structuralist theory predicts, offers no support for its expectation of coefficients conditional upon the state of the economy. Because the issues used to test the theory clearly fall within its scope and also afford the generality necessary to yield confidence in the resulting inferences, the findings are particularly compelling.

One potential modification to the specification merits further scrutiny. When included in the model as independent variables in a specification without interaction terms, none of the four measures of the economy generate coefficients anywhere near statistical significance. As argued earlier in the chapter, such a finding has no bearing upon the accuracy of the structuralist implications. Potentially, though, one might devise other reasons to test whether the state of the economy exerts a direct impact upon legislative action. As it turns out, the data do not indicate the presence of any such impact.[13]

The technical details of all these analyses, while necessary to establish systematic evidence, should not overshadow the ultimate payoff. The findings open a new window into understanding business power and

11. Under the null hypothesis, the F-statistic is distributed as $F(4,35)$. The .05 critical value for $F(4,35)$ is 2.65.

12. Specifications based upon other economic indicators, such as first differences in the measures used here or factor scores derived from a linear combination of some or all of them, lead to identical inferences.

13. This finding does not imply that the economy is irrelevant but simply indicates that it has no direct effects upon lawmaking. The economy likely has indirect effects on lawmaking, though, that work through the other variables. Vogel (1989) contends that public support for policies imposing costs on business rises during robust times and falls during a slack economy, an argument for which Durr (1993) adds further evidence. Most importantly for my purposes, this process does not undermine the representation of public preferences or reduce the policy impacts of election outcomes.

public control of policy. The data presented here show that popular representation occurs throughout the period under study, not just some of the time. Responsiveness by members of Congress and presidents to public opinion does not happen only when prosperity allows it; responsiveness is a continuing process, persisting through good and bad economic times. Elections, too, strongly affect what government does regardless of the degree of pressure on officeholders to stimulate investment. The central structuralist claim, that representation will suffer when politicians face the strongest need to attract capital, receives no support from the data.

STRUCTURAL POWER AND AGENDA CONTROL

Some observers may note that the set of issues reaching the government agenda is far smaller than the set of all potential issues. Perhaps the structural power of business can explain why many potential issues never gained active consideration. Lindblom (1977), for example, motivates his theoretical discussion by observing that no democratic nation has ever chosen to eliminate private control of production and replace it with central planning. Within the United States, no bills to establish central planning have even reached the legislative agenda.

Can invoking the potential issues that were not considered shore up the structuralist case? Presumably the theory might help explain the nonconsideration of policies that business opposed rather than the nonconsideration of initiatives that business favored. For any potential issue, though, a myriad of plausible theories could explain why it never reached the agenda. Multiple explanations for the same phenomenon are, of course, endemic to social science inquiry; investigators create knowledge by developing evidence to evaluate the contending explanations. The problem is that within the realm of the purely hypothetical, one theoretical perspective cannot be shown through qualitative or quantitative evidence to be superior to another. When examining potential issues that failed to gain active consideration by elected officials, it is difficult to find evidence that could corroborate one explanation and disprove the others.

Yet even if an especially enterprising social scientist could execute such a study, shifting the debate from existing, tangible issues to hypothetical ones would concede a considerable amount of intellectual terrain. Theorists writing in the structuralist vein seek to understand policymaking on actual disputes, not just the nonconsideration of potential issues. Lindblom (1977) and Block (1977) argue that their theoretical perspectives can explain concrete policy decisions in the regulatory, social welfare, taxation, and labor domains. The boundaries of the structuralist thesis would become circumscribed if, as suggested by the findings presented earlier, its capacity to illuminate concrete issues remains in doubt.

Conceivably one might argue that the issues that do reach the agenda and hence enter into my analysis are unimportant, meaning that the strong representation occurring on them is beside the point. Such an argument would be difficult to sustain. The data in chapter 4 show that a high proportion of the most salient and controversial issues from the 1950s to the 1990s were marked by business unity. The issues include such milestones as the Reagan tax cuts, the establishment of business-wide worker health and safety regulation, multiple defeats of the balanced budget amendment, the failure of tort reform, and the Clean Air Act. To contend that the policy initiatives considered in American politics are fundamentally insignificant, one would have to express indifference to the outcomes of those issues. If the issues reaching the agenda are inconsequential, there would be no need to criticize or praise any particular legislative decisions during the period under study. After all, one's time and energy would be better spent doing virtually anything else than in finding fault or merit in policy matters that are ultimately trivial. Likewise, one could awake on the mornings following decisive elections in 1964, 1980, and 1994 and, assured that any resulting legislative changes would be minor, greet the results with disinterest.

Not many observers can maintain such distance from what actually happens in politics. While clearly more limited than the range of all possible alternatives, those that have appeared on the agenda for consideration are vital in and of themselves. Judging by the amount of resources corporations and trade associations have spent to affect decisions on these issues, business obviously cares deeply about actual policy disputes. If the structural power thesis cannot explain decision-making during the most important legislative debates from the last few decades, it will become less useful to social scientists.

FLAWS IN THE NOTION OF STRUCTURAL POWER

The historical record of lawmaking from 1953 to 1996 provides little support for the strong or mild versions of the structuralist implications for representation. Why would central predictions of a theory that appears plausible fail to survive empirical scrutiny? A large part of the answer lies not in what the structuralist perspective sees or accomplishes but in what that perspective excludes from its purview. The following sections identify and explain the importance of several key points that, I believe, have been overlooked by scholars expounding arguments about structural power.

THE IMPACTS OF PUBLIC OPINION AND ELECTION OUTCOMES

Mechanisms for citizen influence upon officeholders' decisions, arising from both politicians' responsiveness to public opinion and voters' choices during elections, are plentiful and forceful. One could imagine situations in which electoral incentives for politicians to respond to constituent opinions clash with the incentives to stimulate investment. Elected officials might be torn, for example, between promoting a policy because of its public popularity and avoiding the policy because it could hinder economic growth. To the extent that these tensions arise, the former incentives—despite the arguments of the structuralist theory—can be sturdy enough to override the latter. When any two forces meet, one of them can render the other inert, as illustrated by houses with solid foundations that cannot be toppled by even the fiercest gale. Because public opinion and elections form such a stable bedrock, their influence upon policymaking can withstand the leverage business otherwise would gain through its investment decisions.

The structural power thesis ends up caught on the horns of a dilemma. Any pressure upon legislative choices that is exerted by capital mobility should be felt on unifying issues. If politicians are concerned about investment, as the theory assumes, then they are unlikely to spend their time on particularistic and conflictual issues that involve too few firms or create results too inconsistent to affect the economy as a whole. Instead they would expend their efforts on policies that could induce large-scale changes in the economy, changes normally possible only when a policy produces parallel consequences across a broad spectrum of firms and industries. Yet issues jointly affecting business at large are the same ones where the voice of the public has the greatest impact upon legislative decisions. This catch-22 leaves the structuralist theory without a category of issues to explain.

THE WEAKNESS OF THE POSITED INCENTIVE STRUCTURE

In the end, any structural power business might hold could only arise through a set of incentives. When explaining the behavior of elected officials, one can reasonably begin by examining electoral incentives (Mayhew 1974); correspondingly, scholars advancing the structuralist theory have emphasized that reelection needs provide the mechanism that leads to policies desired by business. While potentially important to presidents, whose reelection prospects and public support depend heavily upon current prosperity and expectations about the future (Hibbs 1987; MacKuen, Erikson, and Stimson 1992), the electoral incentives to facilitate investment may not apply to members of Congress, especially those from the opposition party.

Studies of who wins congressional elections stress such factors as party affiliations, incumbency, and the previous experience of the candidates, with the economy playing a generally modest role (Herrnson 1998; Jacobson 1997). While the structuralist thesis purports to address all kinds of elected officials, it might better explain presidential than congressional behavior. The inability of the theory to account for the passage or rejection of bills may result from the fact that the two branches must interact during the legislative process. In the same vein, the theory might better apply to fusion-of-powers systems in which the head of government is drawn from the parliament.

DISAGREEMENTS AMONG ELECTED OFFICIALS ABOUT POLICIES' EFFECTS

The structural power theory also runs astray by relying upon an unrealistic depiction of elected officials. Recall that the theory, in order to generate coherent predictions, needs politicians generally to agree upon the expected effects of a given policy upon the economy. Elected officials supposedly pass legislation they perceive to help the economy while sidestepping policies they think will harm the economy. Like ordinary citizens, journalists, scholars, and others, however, politicians frequently disagree on their forecasts of the consequences of various initiatives.

There is no doubt that business elites *claim* that the policies they oppose would impair economic growth while the ones they favor would lead to greater prosperity. Elected officials, though, need not believe these assertions. Indeed, the essence of politics involves disagreeing not only about which policies are most desirable but also about their consequences. During legislative debates over increasing the minimum wage, for example, business groups always assert that an increase would lead to unemployment by pricing some workers out of the market. Many members of Congress dispute this argument, reasoning instead that the minimum wage could be raised without eliminating jobs.[14] Even if the electoral incentives inducing politicians to facilitate investment were intense enough to dictate their behavior, that would not necessarily lead to policies favorable to business. By disagreeing with the arguments of business leaders regarding the policies that would either foster or retard prosperity, many politicians advocate a very different mix of policies.

In a twist of irony, theorists stressing the structural power of capital play directly into the hands of spokespersons for business enterprises. By failing to counter arguments about the consequences of certain policies, these theorists could unknowingly undercut the prospects for government programs they may personally support. Business groups and their allies in government would like nothing more than to acquire a monopoly over beliefs about how various policies would affect the economy. In many countries during the 1980s and 1990s, conservative political leaders pressed the claim that constraints of capital mobility required deregulation, cutbacks in social programs, and a shrinking of the public sector. Those claims did not go unchallenged, though, as some intellectuals, journalists, politicians, interest groups, and others countered by arguing that policies envisioning a greater role for government were necessary to revitalize the economy and create a workforce that would be productive in the future (see, e.g., Aschauer 1990; Reich 1992).

Ideas are important in politics, as Martin's (1991) analysis of changes in tax legislation demonstrates. In the struggle to define how to achieve economic growth, other segments of society vie with unified business interests, and factions of business frequently disagree with each other. The resulting multiple-sided debate mitigates the threat of structural power.

THE RESPONSIVENESS OF FIRMS TO POLICY DECISIONS

Part of the reason why elected officials need not take the arguments of business at face value is that capital does not react to policy decisions in the manner the structuralist theory assumes. It is often said that capital spans the globe searching for the most favorable returns, implying that firms will desert a country if it does not deliver the policies firms desire. The notion that firms base their location decisions largely or even significantly on different countries' policies, however, is at minimum a major exaggeration. Certainly owners of financial assets—stocks,

14. There is, of course, an answer to questions like this. Both sides cannot be right. Whatever the actual reality of the situation, though, it is the range of perceptions held by politicians that most strongly affects their decisions.

bonds, and other securities—can shift them from place to place if they sense that government policies make one location more appealing than another. Yet when it comes to productive capital—the actual companies and their equipment, machinery, and personnel that financial capital supports—mobility is not nearly as seamless (Frieden 1991). This point is important because mobility is a prerequisite to firms being able to change their locations in reaction to favorable or unfavorable policies.

The unlikelihood that policy differences among nations will attract or repel large numbers of firms is most apparent in the areas of services, utilities, and natural resource extraction. Low-end services like haircuts and restaurant meals cannot be imported, and that principle largely applies as well to high-wage service providers like lawyers, doctors, and consultants. Hence politicians need not worry about those segments of the economy responding negatively to policies and setting up shop elsewhere. As services continue to increase their share of GDP in the economically developed nations, the relative immobility of that sector weakens the threat of structural power. The same logic applies to utilities, for which transmission costs normally dictate being close to customers, and mining and drilling operations, which obviously must operate at the site of the natural resources. Because those industries cannot easily move their production from one country to another, they do not wield the predicted kind of structural power.

Even in the manufacturing sector, mobility is not necessarily highly responsive to policy decisions. Recent research has challenged the contention that manufacturing firms readily abandon high-regulation countries in favor of those with little regulation in such areas as pollution and worker safety (OECD 1996; Vogel 1995). The reason is that beyond variables set through public policy, profits also depend upon other factors that policymakers cannot directly control. Economics research on industrial location decisions has long emphasized as dominant predictors the proximity to markets, the productivity of the workforce, agglomeration effects induced by existing firms, and the costs of transportation, labor, and energy (Chapman and Walker 1991). A firm operating at a site that is otherwise highly profitable is not going to relocate simply to save money on taxes or regulatory costs.

The structural power of business is probably a greater constraint for developing countries desperate for capital than for wealthier nations. Within the United States, structural power is likely to show greater impacts on state and local governments than on the federal government. Subnational governments are more vulnerable to structural power because they cannot control their currencies or establish their own immigration policies. Moreover, there is reason to believe that many subnational jurisdictions are relatively close substitutes for each other on a large number of the factors that firms consider in determining where to locate. For numerous companies, for example, average worker productivity and transportation costs could be similar in Kansas and Pennsylvania. That equivalence means that variables controlled through public policy, such as tax rates and regulatory burdens, become more likely to make the difference in determining which state a firm will choose. That is, if different jurisdictions are roughly similar on an array of nonpolicy characteristics a company deems important, then variations in policy may attract or repel manufacturing firms.

One should not overstate the case; states and localities do indeed differ on nonpolicy characteristics. Those differences, though, are probably less than what we find between nations. When summed across the spectrum of variables that affect location decisions, Kansas and Pennsylvania are probably more alike than are the United States and Germany. For this reason, location decisions should be more responsive to policy at the subnational level than at the national level.

One kind of business enterprise provides what may be the limiting case in practice for how firms react to public policy: sports teams. For professional sports franchises, many different cities are close substitutes. All that teams need is a major metropolitan area that contains ticket-buyers and a stadium or arena in which to play. Because so many localities fit those specifications, sports franchises can demand and attain substantial government subsidies. The package of subsidies available will often be the deciding factor in determining which city a team chooses. If firms across the entire economy were to become as responsive to policy decisions as are sports franchises, then politicians would become much more constrained in what they could do. Popular representation would suffer as a result.

For reasons described earlier, such as the relative immobility of the service sector, that outcome has not occurred and probably never will. Recent years have seen some convergence across the industrialized nations in the areas of macroeconomic policy (Andrews 1994; Motermans 1993) and taxation (Steinmo 1993). The mobility of certain segments of capital, in particular their responsiveness to policy differences among nations, probably contributed to those convergences. Yet the nation-state continues to exist, and the differences between countries in such areas as regulation and social welfare programs remain substantial

(Garrett 1998). Plenty of different policy regimes around the world have brought forth economic growth and prosperity (Freeman 1989, chap. 1). A country's unique history, culture, and institutions still cause it to differ in important policy areas from other countries. Despite the claims of some advocates of the notion of structural power, governments do have real choices to make.

EIGHT

The Role of Business in Shaping Public Opinion

Previous chapters have shown that on unifying issues, the public exercises sizable control over the boundaries of congressional and presidential legislative decisions. At the same time, lawmaking responds only modestly to structural and overt forms of business power. The workings of the legislative process, however, do not imply that the best way for business to achieve its aims is simply to sit back idly and watch policymaking unfold. Even though a unified business community ordinarily cannot cause decisions to deviate substantially from public desires, it could affect policy indirectly by instigating favorable changes in public opinion and election outcomes.

In the statistical results from chapter 5, public mood—aggregate opinions on the size and scope of government—emerges as the strongest single determinant of whether business sees its preferences approved or rejected in legislation. A unified business community therefore would gain the greatest returns by successfully influencing public mood.[1] Policies desired by business would then become a byproduct of the strong linkages between the opinions of citizens and the behavior of elected officials. If business as a collective can marshal public opinion to its side, beneficial policies subsequently become more likely. But can business mold public opinion, and if so through what means?

Lukes (1974) provides the most compelling statement that social scientists studying power must examine the origins of people's most

1. A given corporation or industry might best advance its interests by investing its political resources elsewhere and seeking direct influence on particularistic or conflictual issues. For business as a whole on unifying issues, though, the most effective strategy appears to be shaping public mood.

fundamental beliefs. In his words, "*A* may exercise power over *B* by getting him to do what he does not want to do, but he also exercises power over him by influencing, shaping, or determining his very wants" (1974, 23). In applying this conception to the relationship between business and the mass public, an appropriate starting point resides in the writings of Gramsci (1971). Gramsci argues that widely shared principles, such as the desirability of private property, sustain capitalism, and it is capitalists who promote those principles and create the conditions for workers to accept them. Power elite (Mills 1956; Dye 1978, 1995) and ruling class (Domhoff 1978, 1983) theories also contend that business enterprises influence the beliefs held by ordinary citizens.

Reagan (1963), Engler (1961), and other scholars point to paid advertising and ownership of the mass media as critical means through which corporations and business groups promote viewpoints later embraced by the general public. Lindblom (1977) and Miliband (1969) mention distributing free enterprise materials to schools and colleges, while Fones-Wolf (1994) discusses seminars and workshops directed at workers. As for other means by which business transmits ideas about what government should and should not do, Dye (1978, 1995) and Domhoff (1978, 1983) stress the financing of policy research institutes, commonly known as think tanks. Other scholars (Mitchell 1997, chap. 3; Peschek 1987) also raise this possibility as a source of business influence.

Despite offering ways of thinking about the capacity of business to condition public opinion, the current body of knowledge needs further development both theoretically and empirically. Gramsci (1971) devotes only limited attention to demonstrating how capitalists initiate a society's fundamental principles; other scholars identify possible mechanisms, such as purchasing policy-oriented advertising or funding a probusiness think tank, but do not develop the argument in detail because their central aims are largely unrelated to business influence upon public opinion. Although causal relationships are proposed and potential intervening mechanisms specified, the literature does not complete its undertaking by deriving and testing specific hypotheses. We could profit from a more thorough examination of *how* and *why* business might successfully shape public opinion. And on the empirical side, we need more systematic evidence before concluding whether the posited relationship does or does not exist.

This chapter seeks progress on both the theoretical and empirical fronts, focusing upon think tanks as one important means through which business can disseminate its perspective on public policy. I begin with a descriptive overview of think tanks, devoting particular attention to the growth in corporate financing of those intellectual incubators whose studies frequently manifest probusiness positions and implications. I turn next to examining the coverage think tanks attract in the mass media, the likely avenue through which their research, advocacy, and commentary reaches the broad public. The remainder of the chapter seeks to discover the ultimate effects on public mood.

THINK TANKS AND THEIR NEED FOR FUNDING

Durst and Thurber (1989) define think tanks as private nonprofit organizations engaged primarily in investigating questions relevant to public policy. These organizations originate, develop, evaluate, and publicize ideas about the policy directions the nation should pursue. By emphasizing research as their primary activity, they differ from ordinary interest groups. Many interest groups also conduct and cite policy-relevant research to bolster their positions, but for them research is only one of many means to political influence.

The conventional connotation of the term "think tank" includes both institutes that normally advance a specific point of view and others that maintain no official allegiance to any predetermined convictions. While each type of organization may be said to perform "research," in the former case many conclusions are effectively prescribed before any investigation begins. Although this chapter follows convention in referring to both kinds of institutes as "think tanks," the empirical analysis makes the necessary distinctions between them.

Contributing to like-minded think tanks offers business at least two potential routes to eventually changing public policy. First, the institutes' studies may influence politicians, their staffs, and civil servants. By creating new policy proposals and evaluating existing ones, they express positions that enter and occasionally redirect the discourse prevailing within policymaking circles. This straightforward linkage represents the most obvious payoff to business contributions. Business contributions could also yield returns through a second channel, which I focus upon here, that works in a more subtle manner. Think tanks could shift public opinion toward the preferences of business, which through the process of political representation will later bring policy decisions into closer alignment with what business collectively wants. Such a result could emerge even if not all the corporations and trade associations making contributions explicitly intend such an effect. In this chapter I examine how think tanks attempt to harness and direct the political potency of public opinion.

These organizations possess a crucial quality enhancing their ability to shape public preferences: Their staff specializes in marshalling arguments and evidence to support propositions about policies' desirability and consequences. Reflecting extensive training and expertise, analysts at think tanks can argue persuasively for a particular course of action. This likely makes them more convincing advocates than corporate officials whose background lies in the realm of business rather than politics. By knowing how best to structure and defend an argument, the analysts articulate viewpoints that could appeal to the general public.

Researchers employed by think tanks, moreover, maintain an air of detachment and impartiality unavailable to corporate leaders or officials of business-related interest groups. Business representatives advocating a policy position are typically perceived to be pursuing their own ends, but think tank analysts can expound an idea without having it interpreted as a mere foil for self-interest. The institutes' ostensible credibility increases the persuasiveness of their messages. Social psychologists long ago confirmed the common-sense notion that people are more likely to respond favorably to a message when they see the source as a neutral expert (McGuire 1969).

Because think tanks possess the potential to sway public opinion, business would benefit by enhancing their ability to conduct policy-relevant research and promote its conclusions and implications. The most obvious assistance business can provide is money. In addition to the direct giving from their corporations, executives serving on foundations' boards of directors can affect those organizations' decisions to contribute to think tanks. Think tanks require monetary resources to publish reports, host conferences, and gain access to policymakers. They also need financial backing to perform the activities with the highest likelihood of influencing the broader public, namely building relationships with journalists and placing analysis, advocacy, and commentary in the mass media. Like other political actors (Kernell 1997; Kollman 1998), think tanks can seek changes in policy by first appealing to the general public.

The mass media represent an essential intermediary in this process of persuasion. Understanding how the media can function as a conduit between think tanks and ordinary citizens requires looking no further than the sources journalists rely upon for policy-relevant stories. Zaller (1992) and Bennett (1990) note that the media report arguments and perspectives that fall within the range held among policy experts and government officials. When shifts occur in the beliefs prevailing within networks of private and public specialists working in a policy area, the media alter their coverage of the matter and convey new viewpoints to the public (Baumgartner and Jones 1993). Ordinary citizens, in turn, use available information in the news media, particularly from experts, ideological elites, and partisan elites, to formulate their own issue preferences (Zaller 1992). This several-step process makes it important for social scientists to study the composition of expert communities. By funding institutes who inject individuals with favorable points of view into the population of experts, corporations and business groups initiate a rhetorical process that ultimately may change public opinion.

THE ROLE OF BUSINESS IN THE THINK TANK EXPLOSION

While existing in some form since early in the twentieth century, think tanks only recently became conspicuous political actors in Washington (Ricci 1993). Figure 8.1, which tracks their participation over time in congressional hearings, illustrates the growth in their collective prominence. The graph depicts the total number of annual appearances by a sample of these institutions.[2] I counted an appearance if a representative from a think tank either testified or submitted a statement, a reply to questions, a reprint of a publication, or any other insertion into the official written record.[3] It is readily apparent from figure 8.1 that the high visibility of think tanks, as measured by their appearances in congressional hearings, is a relatively recent phenomenon. Total yearly appearances fluctuate only slightly above zero from 1953 to 1969. The graph shows rapid growth in the 1970s that levels off by the 1980s.[4]

Business helped cause the striking growth of think tanks during the 1970s. At the time, business faced considerable challenges on both the economic and political fronts. On the economic side, the post–

2. The sample includes all the organizations used in the empirical analyses later in the chapter.

3. The information was obtained through online searches of the Congressional Research Service's indices of congressional documents and hearings.

4. Because committees typically hold many hearings early in a two-year congressional term, first sessions usually record more think tank appearances than second sessions. Some of the growth in appearances over time probably reflects an expansion in Congress's ability to hold multiple hearings simultaneously. This change cannot be a complete explanation, however, of the dramatic increases in think tank appearances.

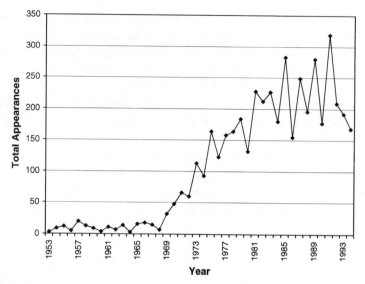

Figure 8.1 Think Tank Appearances in Congressional Hearings

World War II prosperity appeared to be fading as the economy entered a period of low growth and high inflation. Private enterprise fared no better politically, with new social welfare programs and multi-industry regulation contributing to a siege mentality in many parts of the business community. Reacting to these economic and political pressures, corporations actively entered politics to a degree unprecedented in American history (Vogel 1989; Harris 1989).

For the purposes of this chapter, the most intriguing business response arose in the realm of ideas. The owners and managers of the nation's corporations widely believed that their values were being undermined by political elites in academia and the media, creating a political system incapable of appreciating the virtues of free markets and limited government. Many business leaders urged their colleagues to counter what they saw as a liberal bias among academics and journalists by funding research whose policy implications would be more favorable (Silk and Vogel 1976). William Simon, the treasury secretary in the Nixon administration, stated this approach candidly in his book *A Time for Truth*. After strongly criticizing the policy directions of the preceding two decades, Simon called upon corporations and foundations to subsidize scholarly efforts that would prove beneficial to business. In throwing down the gauntlet, Simon wrote: "I know of nothing more crucial than to come to the aid of the intellectuals and writers who are fighting on my side" (Simon 1978, 233).

A financial campaign to articulate and publicize probusiness principles and policies was already under way when Simon penned his exhortations and it continued to expand thereafter. Thanks to funding from many corporations, trade associations, and foundations, the number and reach of conservative think tanks mushroomed.[5] For example, the American Enterprise Institute for Public Policy Research (AEI), originally created as the American Enterprise Association in 1943, enjoyed little political impact and was virtually ignored by the media until grants from corporations and foundations multiplied its budget ten-fold during the 1970s. In addition to its higher overall budgets, AEI saw the corporate share of its funding increase from 25 percent to 40 percent during the late 1970s (Stone 1981). The Heritage Foundation—probably the best known of the conservative institutes—opened its doors in 1973 with financial assistance from Colorado brewer Joseph Coors. Other conservative think tanks founded or greatly expanded during the 1970s and 1980s included the Cato Institute, Competitive Enterprise Institute, Manhattan Institute, and Hudson Institute. Some of them openly acknowledge that their policy positions generally benefit the business community. After noting contributions from eighty-seven of the corporations making the Fortune 500 list, Heritage Foundation president Edwin Fuelner remarked: "From the standpoint of the business community, there's no reason why that shouldn't be 487." (Kondracke 1980, 12).

This correspondence of preferences does not imply, however, that the think tanks receiving business largesse become nothing more than corporate mouthpieces. Giving money to a research institute is quite different than hiring a trial lawyer trained to develop arguments suited to each particular client. Analysts working at think tanks partially funded by business strongly believe in the principles they espouse, and they probably would uphold similar principles if they were employed somewhere else. It also must be noted that while the conservative institutes tend to advocate policies favorable to corporations, this overlap is

---

5. Some liberal policy institutes were expanding at the same time. Corporate donations, however, flowed disproportionately to think tanks on the right. The Olin, Bradley, Smith Richardson, and Scaiffe Family Foundations also were particularly active in funneling money to conservative think tanks. Think tanks typically promoting ideas to the left of center benefited, although in considerably smaller dollar amounts, from the contributions of a different set of foundations.

less than total. Government subsidies flowing to certain industries, for example, have often come under attack from think tanks on the right.

Still, when it comes to the directions for national policy, American corporations and conservative think tanks agree far more often than they disagree. It is precisely for this reason that business has directed the vast majority of its contributions toward ideologically conservative institutes. While not every company would see its interest furthered if the recommendations of an organization like the Heritage Foundation were implemented, business as a whole would profit on issues that unify disparate firms and industries. As its most important consequence, corporate funding allows sentiments beneficial to business as a collective, but which simultaneously are held by many people lacking a self-interested motivation, to be disseminated more widely than they otherwise would be.

Scholars and journalists have extensively documented the increasing business contributions to conservative think tanks during and after the 1970s (Vogel 1989; Himmelstein 1990; Blumenthal 1986; Edsall 1984; Salama 1984). What remains unclear is not the existence of the contributions but rather their effects. This chapter seeks to determine whether the studies and advocacy of the think tanks have caused the American public to become more conservative than otherwise would have been the case. If so, then channels of popular representation have eventually led to policies on unifying issues more favorable to business, making public mood an instrument of business power.

In order for business to possess this indirect source of power on unifying issues, the positions promoted by think tanks need to somehow reach the broader public. Any specification of the intervening process must recognize that few citizens possess first-hand knowledge of various think tanks' investigations of and support for policy initiatives. Given the generally low levels of political information among the public (Delli Carpini and Keeter 1996), it is reasonable to assume that most ordinary citizens do not closely follow the activities of organizations like the American Enterprise Institute. For people to be influenced by the studies conducted and promoted by think tanks, the news media must amplify the primary themes. Those themes could help citizens determine their issue opinions. Media coverage, then, represents the vital link between think tanks and public opinion. A single news story normally will produce no observable impacts upon public opinion, but when combined a collection of stories could have a cumulative effect over time.

Gatekeepers in the media choose to quote institutes' analysts for identifiable reasons flowing from the norms, demands, and constraints of the journalistic enterprise. A journalist or editor may regard the statements and studies issued by think tanks as newsworthy because they fit within the broader context of a news story, because they offer seemingly learned viewpoints on contemporary events or policy debates, or more simply because they express perspectives of interest to readers, viewers, and listeners. In a related motivation, reporters may choose their expert sources based upon who meshes most clearly with current policy discourses. Supply-side factors also surely help determine how much media coverage various think tanks receive. Many of these organizations work hard to make their analysts and studies available to reporters, and greater financial resources multiply opportunities to appear in news stories (Soley 1992).

Reflecting my driving interest in business power, I focus in the rest of the chapter upon the consequences rather than the origins of media coverage of think tanks. Taking the composition of news stories as my starting point, I return to the question of whether that composition helps shape public opinion. We know that journalists often quote or reference analysts from think tanks; we also know that financial contributions from business have helped build many of those institutes. For my purposes, the critical question is whether the patterns of media coverage affect public opinion in a way that could later induce policy changes on unifying issues.

CLASSIFYING THINK TANKS ACCORDING TO THEIR IDEOLOGIES

While many aspects of think tanks' transmission of viewpoints through the news media merit scrutiny, perhaps the most important component is the messages' overall ideological thrust. Given the importance of public mood—the liberal-conservative dimension of public opinion—in determining policy decisions on unifying issues, think tanks should be examined at the same level of generality. That is, the specificity of the institutes' viewpoints should match the specificity at which public preferences show the greatest impact on lawmaking. In seeking to assess impacts upon public opinion, it would make little sense to focus the investigation of think tanks at a level where mass preferences do not crystallize. To keep both sides of the equation at a matching degree of specificity, the inquiry requires classifying the institutes according to their ideological predispositions. In so doing I will employ the categories of liberal, conservative, and centrist/nonideological.

Of course, much of the output of even the most predictable think tanks cannot be neatly placed into one of those three categories. The classification scheme is a simplification designed to capture general ideological tendencies. It is these general tendencies that have the greatest potential, when reiterated by the news media, to affect the liberal-conservative dimension of public opinion. A study targeting a more narrow aspect of public opinion would naturally develop more finely grained categories to classify various think tanks.

I began by consulting a wide variety of scholarly and journalistic sources, plus the World Wide Web, to identify the think tanks in existence over the last two decades (Smith 1991; Burris 1992; Abelson 1996; Allen 1992; Himmelstein 1990; Easterbrook 1986; Blumenthal 1986; Salama 1984; Kuttner 1985; Moore 1992; Jacobson 1995; Morgan 1981; McGann 1992). Research centers directly connected to colleges and universities are not included. Midway though the study, I corresponded with Andrew Rich, who was conducting a broader study of think tanks (Rich 1999). Using some alternative sources including Hellebust's (1996) *Think Tank Directory*, he had uncovered a number of organizations not on my original list. The final compilation includes these additional institutes.

After identifying the relevant organizations, I gathered information that could allow me to classify each as primarily liberal, conservative, or centrist/nonideological. Many think tanks openly declare their guiding philosophy, rendering them easily amenable to classification. Organizations fitting this description embrace a coherent ideology from the top-down, and individual studies and analysts do not deviate very far from it.[6] The Cato Institute, for example, "flatly states that it will not release any study that calls for a government program" (Easterbrook 1986, 78). Coding choices for openly ideological think tanks are obvious and straightforward.

Some social scientists may question whether any think tank analyst can minimize the impacts of preexisting conceptions and interpretations of the problem to be studied. Others will maintain that starting

6. The point is not that all information produced by this kind of think tank follows from the same template, but rather that the range of views offered is narrow by comparison to the spectrum typically discussed and debated in American politics. Some of these organizations claim to operate without any motivating ideology, but scrutiny of their studies indicates otherwise.

with expectations and a guiding framework does not prevent investigators at a think tank or elsewhere from using careful research methods to assemble convincing evidence for an argument. The distinction I draw here operates at the level of the organization rather than at the level of any one investigator. The institutes I classify as either liberal or conservative produce studies and perspectives that demonstrate ideological consistency, an organizational parallel to Converse's (1964) notion of ideological constraint in individuals. Think tanks lacking ideological consistency will be noted as such.

My classification strategy involved determining, for each organization, the general interpretation of its ideology among the scholars and journalists used to identify the think tank population. I also incorporated information from the mission statements, on-line research reports, and links to similar organizations available at many think tanks' World Wide Web sites. Based upon all of these sources, I have coded as centrist/nonideological the Rand Corporation, Council on Foreign Relations, National Bureau of Economic Research, Resources for the Future, and several lesser-known organizations. When examined in its totality, their research and rhetoric do not maintain ideological consistency and therefore cannot be expected to systematically push public opinion in either a liberal or conservative direction. For this reason, they are omitted from the empirical analysis.

For a handful of think tanks—the Brookings Institution, Carnegie Endowment for International Peace, Institute for International Economics, Twentieth Century Fund, Russell Sage Foundation, Center for Strategic and International Studies, and Committee for Economic Development—the literature does not clearly identify their ideological positioning. These organizations require that their research meet the standards of logic and evidence normally demanded of social science. Individual scholars within the institutes may publish a study or advocate a position that can be placed on a left-right scale, but the ideological openness of the organizations allows their analysts to offer a diversity of viewpoints. Yet these organizations are often perceived to be, on average, closer to one ideological pole than the other.[7] When cumulated, their studies and advocacy may push in one ideological direction even though the organization does not prescribe positions at the outset.

Coding decisions for these kinds of think tanks necessarily entail a

7. The qualification "on average" is crucial here, for while the studies by some think tanks display considerable variation, for my analysis the most important feature is their central tendency.

subjective component. To overcome this challenge, I attempt to ensure that no substantive conclusion hinges upon coding choices lacking clear-cut answers. For the purposes of the empirical analysis, I will examine the consequences of two potential classification decisions. First, I will consider the think tanks in question to be either "liberal-leaning" or "conservative-leaning" and group them with the openly ideological think tanks. Second, I will reclassify them as "centrist/nonideological," meaning that they will be excluded from analysis.

Table 8.1 provides a full listing of my coding decisions. A few dozen ideological think tanks that are not very visible—those generating between one and fifteen observations on the measure of media attention to be developed below—are incorporated into the analysis but not listed in the table. Hordes of others would have been included had they attracted any mentions in news stories. The libertarian think tanks, of which the Cato Institute is the best known, are coded as conservative because their positions on issues important to business— such as regulation, taxation, and government spending—are similar to those of the traditionally conservative policy institutes.[8]

MEASURING MEDIA COVERAGE

To assess whether think tanks can influence public opinion through the content of news stories, I first inspect some of the relevant media coverage. My strategy involves collecting and analyzing citations to think tanks in the *Washington Post*. Using the *Post* to construct an indicator of media coverage has two main advantages. First, the *Post* is widely respected as a preeminent source of national political news. Other media outlets might follow its lead in assembling their own stories. Second, the full text of the *Post* is available in electronic form from January 1, 1977, to the present, a longer time span than for any other newspaper.[9]

For a longitudinal study of the kind I am conducting, the choice of news organization probably will not greatly affect the results because different media outlets usually cover either the same or highly similar

8. My coding results are highly similar, though not identical, to what Rich (1999) has provided. The primary difference is that for part of my analysis, I classify as "leaning" in one direction some of the think tanks he codes as "centrist/no identifiable ideology."

9. Another possible leader on matters of national politics, the *New York Times*, is unavailable in electronic form until June 1, 1980.

Table 8.1 Classification of Major American Think Tanks

Liberal	Conservative
Urban Institute	American Enterprise Institute
Institute for Policy Studies	Heritage Foundation
Joint Center for Political and Economic Studies	Hoover Institution
World Resources Institute	Cato Institute
Center on Budget and Policy Priorities	Free Congress Research and Education Foundation
Center for National Policy	Hudson Institute
Economic Policy Institute	Ethics and Public Policy Center
Overseas Development Council	Family Research Council
Worldwatch Institute	Freedom House
Center for Defense Information	Tax Foundation
Environmental Policy Institute	Foundation on Economic Trends
Corporation for Enterprise Development	Ripon Society
Center for Reproductive Law and Policy	Competitive Enterprise Institute
Center for the Study of Responsive Law	American Council for Capital Formation
Center for Women Policy Studies	Manhattan Institute
Commonwealth Fund	Citizens for a Sound Economy
World Policy Institute	Council for Basic Education
Center for Policy Alternatives	Empower America
Institute for Women's Policy Research	American Legislative Exchange Council
Center for Urban Policy Research	Foreign Policy Research Institute
National Center for Economic and Security Alternatives	Institute for Contemporary Studies
Institute for Socioeconomic Studies	Institute for Foreign Policy Analysis
	Institute on Religion and Democracy
	Rutherford Institute
	Institute for American Values

Centrist/Nonideological or Liberal-Leaning

Liberal	Conservative
Brookings Institution	National Legal Center for the Public Interest
Carnegie Endowment for International Peace	Center for the New West
Institute for International Economics	Center for the Study of American Business
Progressive Policy Institute	National Strategy Information Center
Twentieth Century Fund	National Center for Public Policy Research
	Media Research Center
	Committee for the Free World

Centrist/Nonideological or Conservative-Leaning
Center for Strategic and International Studies
Committee for Economic Development

Note: Think tanks generating fifteen or fewer citations are included in the analysis but are not listed in the table.

stories. Content analyses regularly find the coverage within different news organizations to be highly correlated (Graber 1989, chap. 3; Fan 1988). While I claim that Americans respond to messages in the news media—either directly or through second-hand interactions with other citizens previously exposed to media stimuli—I do not assume that large numbers of Americans actually read the *Washington Post*. Instead, I assume that longitudinal changes in the *Post*'s coverage correlate strongly with changes in other media outlets. It is this shared variation over time that will determine the empirical results.

More specifically, my usage of the *Post* rests upon two assumptions that are plausible, though less than certain. First, I assume that any "overciting" of think tanks resulting from the *Post*'s need to serve its audience in Washington, D.C. is roughly constant over the eighteen-year span of my data. The *Washington Post* surely quotes think tanks more often than does the *St. Louis Post-Dispatch*, for example. Yet there is no reason to believe that this difference between the two publications changes over time. While a measure of citations derived from the *Washington Post* undoubtedly would show a higher mean than one constructed from the *St. Louis Post-Dispatch*, the two measures probably would have similar variances. Within a statistical analysis employing a media indicator as an independent variable, means are irrelevant because any relationship with the dependent variable will be determined by covariation.[10] Second, I assume that any ideological biases of the *Washington Post* stay roughly constant from the late 1970s to the mid-1990s. The *Post* probably gives enhanced coverage to left-of-center think tanks, for example, while the *Wall Street Journal* more frequently cites conservative ones. These differences between the two publications, however, are likely maintained over time. Hence the two media outlets probably share similar longitudinal movement. Although the means will differ, time series measures from the two media outlets will likely be highly correlated because they will show the same peaks and valleys.

I gathered the *Washington Post*'s coverage from the Lexis-Nexis full-

10. In other words, for each time period the number of citations in the *Washington Post* is roughly equal to the number in the *St. Louis Post Dispatch* + x, where x is a constant. The statistical precision of the estimated relationship between an independent and a dependent variable does not change if either variable undergoes a linear scale transformation. Increasing the mean of the independent variable by adding x to each observation, for example, cannot alter the information a regression analysis yields. So long as the extent to which the *Washington Post* overcites think tanks remains constant over time, that bias will not affect the results.

text database of news stories, searching from January 1, 1977, through the first half of 1994.[11] A total of over ten thousand stories was identified by recording, for each think tank, all stories that cited it. Over 70 percent of the observations were from only eight organizations, indicating that the think tank community is extremely top-heavy.

THE CONTENT OF MEDIA COVERAGE

Using the citations as data presumes that they capture advocacy of policies or principles rather than simple references to an institute abstracted from any relevant context. For the measures to have validity, the news media must cover the policy-related positions expounded by think tanks. Are the citations valid as indicators of this channel of influence? To answer this question, I performed a content analysis of a sample of two hundred stories, selected randomly from over ten thousand stories for which citations were obtained. I classified into one of several mutually exclusive categories the part of each story citing a think tank. The results of this analysis are shown in table 8.2.

The category with the largest number of stories contains citations in which an analyst, or occasionally the think tank itself, promotes a policy position on issues such as social programs, the budget, or government regulation. Each of these stories includes instances of explicit policy-related arguments or claims. Stories referencing a study contending that a cut in capital gains taxes would spur economic growth, for example, fall into this category. The advocacy stories comprise 44 percent of the total and directly tap the ability of the institutes to openly promote a point of view through the news media. The bulk of these policy endorsements occur within the context of quotes that researchers provide to reporters, although some of the advocacy comes within references to studies published by a think tank or within articles (primarily op-ed pieces) written by one of their researchers.

The 44 percent of the stories consisting of direct policy advocacy are obvious instances of think tanks' ability to disseminate viewpoints. The remaining citations, however, require closer examination. Consider the second largest category, descriptive information about a think tank, whose stories comprise 27 percent of the total. The sub-category labeled "activities" includes institutes' conducting of conferences, their hosting

11. The closing date was chosen to correspond with the periods of data availability for the other independent variables to be described later.

Table 8.2 Content Analysis of News Stories Citing a Think Tank

CATEGORY	SUBCATEGORY	PERCENTAGE	CATEGORY PERCENTAGE TOTALS
Policy advocacy by a think tank analyst	within a quote	28%	
	within a referenced study	9.5%	
	story is written by a think tank analyst	6.5%	
			44%
Descriptive information about a think tank	activities of a think tank	20%	
	reference to study (without policy advocacy)	3.5%	
	new hire	3.5%	
			27%
Information about a person affiliated with a think tank	general	3.5%	
	mention of a person's former association at a think tank	4%	
	person from think tank considered/ already in presidential appt.	2%	
	obituary	2.5%	
			12%
Commentary by analyst from a think tank (without policy advocacy)	politics	4%	
	economy	3.5%	
	current events	1.5%	
	social, political, and economic trends	5.5%	
	history	0.5%	
	story is written by think tank analyst (without policy advocacy)	1.5%	
			16.5%
Other	comment about economics profession	0.5%	
			0.5%
Totals		100%	100%

Note: The data reflect a content analysis of a random sample of 200 from over 10,000 *Washington Post* stories that cite a think tank. The part of each story containing the reference to a think tank was classified into one of the mutually exclusive categories and subcategories.

of speeches by a politician, mentions of their presumed influence, and other information about their operations. While these stories contain no explicit policy endorsements, a citation within this format serves as a reasonable proxy for the likelihood that politicians and other political actors are echoing the arguments and policy programs favored by the institute. Politicians typically do not deliver a speech at the headquarters of a think tank, for example, unless they respect its positions and advocate similar positions themselves.

Similarly, journalists are unlikely to consider a think tank's conferences—which are a constant occurrence—to be newsworthy unless important policymakers are also publicizing the same kinds of ideas as the referenced organization. This line of reasoning about journalists' motivations also suggests that the other stories either covering institutes' activities or offering descriptive information have face validity as indicators of politicians' likelihood to reiterate think tanks' arguments. The same logic also applies, albeit to a more limited degree, to the two remaining categories of stories: those mentioning information about a person affiliated with a think tank (12 percent) and generic commentary on politics, the economy, current events, and the like (16.5 percent). When people affiliated with think tanks are seen as important enough to merit media attention, the sentiments they (and their organizations) support might be reiterated by elected and appointed officials, interest groups, and other policy experts.

Citation counts, then, are reasonably valid indicators of the extent to which think tanks and their allies are promoting policies through the news media. The citation counts capture two different ways through which the viewpoints expressed can affect public opinion. In the first route, think tanks and their analysts make policy-relevant claims through the news media. Via the second route, supporting arguments or evidence are filtered through their political allies, who then become the opinion-shaping agents.[12]

CONSERVATIVE AND LIBERAL THINK TANKS IN THE MEDIA

Some news stories contain ideas and information from think tanks that extol liberal views while others publicize the products of conservative ones. Messages from both sides of the ideological spectrum find their way into the mass media, but the quantity of messages from each side shifts over time. The analysis in the remainder of the chapter attempts to determine whether these shifts help cause movements in public mood. A greater quantity of coverage granted to either liberal or conservative think tanks could lead to a corresponding change in public mood.

12. To the extent that the citations without explicit implications for policy are noise rather than proxies for sentiments expressed by these other political actors, that would make it more difficult to find a relationship between the measures of media coverage and public opinion.

Given that competing perspectives are aired through the news media, the appropriate focal point is the overall ideological balance of the coverage. It would be illogical to examine only the attention given to the conservative think tanks.

To measure the overall balance on a quarterly interval, I used the full population of over ten thousand stories and counted the number of citations to each of the liberal and conservative institutes. The indicator constructed, to be called the *conservative think tank advantage*, is defined as the sum of the conservative citations minus the sum of the liberal ones. I calculated two different variables based upon (1) only the overtly ideological think tanks, and (2) the openly ideological think tanks *and* the eclectic ones whose studies nevertheless on average lean toward one side of the ideological spectrum.

Figures 8.2 and 8.3 graph the conservative advantage, as measured in these two ways, over time from 1977 through the first half of 1994. Points greater than zero signify that the conservative institutes more effectively publicize their messages while observations less than zero indicate a net advantage for the liberal side. Figure 8.2, which includes only the manifestly ideological think tanks, shows that the conservative

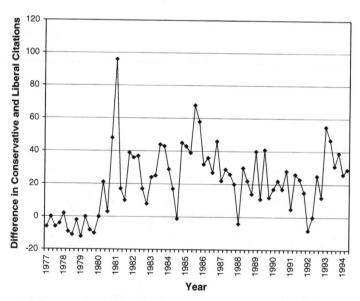

Figure 8.2 Conservative Advantage among Ideological Think Tank Only

ones have been more effective over time than their liberal counterparts in generating publicity for their views. Only during scattered moments in the late 1970s and early 1990s has the balance favored the left side of the ideological spectrum. The conservative advantage was greatest in the early 1980s but fell during the rest of the decade. Figure 8.3 tells a somewhat different story. When the data include conservative-learning or liberal-leaning think tanks, the playing field becomes more level. While the conservative and conservative-leaning institutes generate more publicity than their liberal counterparts at certain times, the advantage frequently switches to the other side.

The differences between the two figures document an important characteristic of think tanks' role in the American policy process. Among those that exhibit clear points of view as organizations, the conservative institutes dominate their liberal competitors. The vastly greater financial resources available to those on the right have surely contributed to their success in publicizing their messages. With business helping to fund their operations, their influence on public opinion would constitute an indirect source of business power. The organizations supported by business are countered to some extent by liberal institutes, but

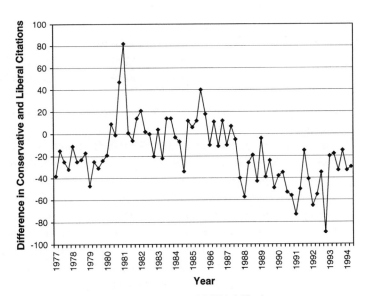

Figure 8.3 Conservative Advantage among All Think Tanks

the two sides are usually not equally matched.[13] Balance emerges only if we include the institutes open to multiple perspectives that nevertheless lean in either the liberal or conservative direction.

It should be noted that while figures 8.2 and 8.3 display different raw numbers (i.e., the means are different), the two graphs' peaks and valleys correspond closely to each other. When estimating the impacts of each series on public mood, the differences in the means cannot affect the statistical precision of the estimated relationships. In both graphs the height of conservative advantage is in the late 1970s and early 1980s, while the nadir occurs about a decade later. The two series have a high product-moment correlation of 0.75, suggesting that statistical inferences on the impacts of the conservative think tank advantage upon public mood might not depend upon which indicator is used.

DEPENDENT AND INDEPENDENT VARIABLES

The dependent variable in the analysis to follow is public mood, Stimson's (1999) measure of support for either stronger or weaker government. Elsewhere in the book I use this variable computed on an annual basis to correspond to the standard interval over which lawmaking unfolds. Because each survey item from which public mood is derived has a date attached to it, the measure also can be calculated quarterly. The quarterly data are used in this chapter, allowing the analysis to assess fully the consequences of quarter-by-quarter variation in the media coverage of think tanks. I have scored the observations of public mood such that large values denote preferences for conservative policy positions, thereby making the measure's polarity the exact reverse of Stimson's original index. The measure of media coverage should have a positive relationship with it.

To estimate the relationship accurately, the specification must control for alternative influences upon public mood that might be correlated with the independent variable of interest. A small but growing literature has sought to explain changes over time in public opinion, and the work of Page, Shapiro, and Dempsey (1987) and Durr (1993) is especially relevant to the argument developed here. Page and colleagues chart the impacts on public opinion of a wide range of media stimuli and find especially strong effects for news commentators and experts. They also discover that interest groups actually have effects opposite in sign (but

13. See Danielian and Page (1994) for related evidence on the prominence in the news media of voices explicitly representing business.

not quite statistically significant) from the intended effects—probably reflecting public perceptions of interest groups as selfish and biased.

The Herculean data collection undertaken by Page, Shapiro, and Dempsey (1987) cannot be replicated within the confines of this chapter. Nevertheless, it is important to include some kind of control for media cues other than the attention given to think tanks. Any findings of a positive effect for policy research institutes would be spurious if they truly have no influence upon public opinion but the indicators developed here correlate with media variables that do have influence. For example, if journalists tend to quote analysts from conservative think tanks at the same time that other sources espouse right-of-center ideas, and the former cannot affect public opinion but the latter produce considerable persuasive impacts, then any estimated positive effect of think tanks would be spurious.

To address this problem, I include a control for antigovernment arguments conveyed by alternative sources through the news media.[14] The variable is derived through a computer-based content analysis, using the methodology developed by Fan (1988), of all stories from the "National Affairs" section of *Newsweek*. As used here, the measure is a quarterly count of the number of paragraphs containing antigovernment themes, such as references to inefficient government programs, approval of cutting spending, or negative discussion of the federal bureaucracy or the welfare state. The measure therefore captures a summary of the claims made by all kinds of political actors. While less than an ideal solution, including the measure will mitigate the possibility of spurious findings on the think tank measures. The degree of antigovernment rhetoric in the media should have a positive association with public opinion. Based upon preliminary analysis suggesting that the effects of this variable do not unfold contemporaneously, it is lagged one period.

Following the finding of Page, Shapiro, and Dempsey (1987) that explicit argumentation by interest groups tends to push public opinion in the opposite direction, I include a variable for the interest group population. The indicator, employed earlier in chapter 6, is calculated as the number of registered lobbyists for business interests as a share of all registered lobbyists from business, citizen groups, and unions. The measure taps the lobbying capacity of business relative to the groups that most frequently oppose it. As such it is not a direct measure of interest groups' advocacy via news stories, but the resources business devotes to

14. Jim Stimson constructed the variable, and I thank him for providing it.

lobbying probably correlate with those it devotes to explicitly promoting policies through the news media. If the public sees interest groups as self-serving and not credible, this variable could have a negative effect upon public mood. An interest group system more biased toward business, that is, might lead public opinion to react negatively and become more favorable to positions traditionally opposed by business.

The specification also borrows from Durr (1993), who argues that when people feel confident about their own economic futures, they turn their attention to the collective needs of society that require government solutions. Economic optimism therefore begets liberal policy positions, while pessimism brings forward conservative preferences. Durr's empirical analysis supports this proposition; it also backs his argument that the public reacts negatively to actual policy enactments, in that consistently conservative policies induce the public to become more liberal and vice versa.

The model specification to follow therefore includes controls for people's economic expectations for the future and for federal policy outcomes. Economic expectations are measured by a question from the University of Michigan's Index of Consumer Sentiment that asks people to assess the likelihood of prosperous economic times for the country over the next five years. If more favorable economic expectations translate into support for more liberal policies, then the coefficient on economic expectations should be negative. Policy outcomes are an updated measure of Durr's (1993) yearly index derived by averaging the share of state and local budgets financed from federal grants-in-aid, the mean tax rate on incomes exceeding one million dollars, and the percentage of all federal expenditures devoted to human resources and defense, respectively.[15] The index reaches its peaks under conservative federal efforts in several important policy domains, including federal-state relations, taxation, social policy, and defense. Because public opinion is coded such that large values indicate conservative sentiment, the posited reactive effect means that the coefficient on federal policy enactments should be negative.

The statistical model to be estimated thus controls for antigovernment references in the media, the composition of the interest group

15. The scores for the annual index are assigned to each quarter falling within a given year. The polarity of the components for grants-in-aid, taxes, and human resources are reversed so that higher values indicate more conservative policies. The overall index, then, has a polarity opposite to that used by Durr (1993).

population, people's economic expectations, and current federal policies. The effects of these variables on public mood, while ancillary to the questions this chapter seeks to answer, nevertheless must be assessed for the analysis to achieve internal validity. Only by controlling for these alternative influences upon public mood can accurate inferences be drawn for the central independent variable under investigation, the amount of media coverage given to competing think tanks.

THINK TANKS AND PUBLIC OPINION: A CAUSAL RELATIONSHIP?

It is important first to determine the directionality of any causal relationship between media coverage of think tanks and the opinions of the citizenry. While the theoretical sketch offered earlier implies that the former causes the latter, a story of reverse causation is certainly plausible. That alternative scenario requires that when conservative principles are already popular, the news media provide extra coverage to think tanks on the right. Similarly, journalists could react to the relative popularity of more liberal sentiments by granting left-of-center institutes greater attention. Because audience sizes help determine the profitability of media outlets, journalists might act in this manner to stay closely aligned with their readers or viewers and thus to capture market shares. Public mood would be determining which think tanks appear in the mass media, meaning that news stories citing think tanks would be a consequence rather than a cause of public mood. Such a process has very different implications for the political power of business in America than does the causal linkage proposed here.

Statistical techniques can help researchers choose between competing causal possibilities. Granger causality tests are commonly used to resolve questions about the direction of causality when the data consist of time series (Freeman 1983). A Granger analysis attempts to determine whether the movements in one variable temporally precede or temporally follow the movements in another variable, or whether the evidence supports both or neither causal linkages. If media coverage changes first and then public mood shifts in the same direction, the causal direction outlined in this chapter would be supported. By contrast, if public mood moves first and then media coverage follows, the alternative possibility would be corroborated.

I conducted direct Granger tests on the variables at hand, and bivariate analysis containing four lags on all variables support the causal ordering proposed in this chapter. With public opinion as the endogenous variable, the past lags of the conservative think tank advantage are statistically significant at the .05 level for both think tank measures. The data do not provide evidence, however, for the reverse causal possibility. When either think tank measure is the endogenous variable, the hypothesis that public mood does not Granger-cause coverage of think tanks cannot be rejected. Given p-values from these tests of .78 and .31, the notion that the media change which think tanks they cover according to public mood does not receive empirical support.

Based upon these findings, I proceed to a traditional econometric specification with evidence that potential problems engendered by simultaneity—namely, a biased and inconsistent coefficient on the key independent variable—will not plague a time series regression. That is, because the data do not indicate that the media's coverage of think tanks is endogenous to public mood, public mood can safely be treated as the dependent variable in a single-equation specification. The specification to be estimated will model public mood as a function

Table 8.3 The Effects of Think Tank Advocacy on Public Opinion

VARIABLES	COEFFICIENTS	
Constant	28.45**	36.41**
	(6.67)	(7.73)
Lagged dependent variable	0.86**	0.78**
	(0.06)	(0.06)
Interest group population	−0.25**	−0.23**
	(0.10)	(0.09)
Antigovernment references	0.06*	0.06*
	(0.03)	(0.03)
Federal policy enactments	−0.04	−0.14
	(0.14)	(0.14)
Economic expectations	−0.00	−0.00
	(0.01)	(0.01)
Conservative think tank advantage (overtly ideological think tanks only)	2.12** (0.85)	
Conservative think tank advantage (including leaners)		1.83** (0.69)
N	70	70
Adjusted R^2	0.92	0.92
Breusch-Godfrey LM statistic	0.55	0.32

*$p < .10$ **$p < .05$

Note: Cell entries are unstandardized regression coefficients. Standard errors are in parentheses and hypothesis tests are one-tailed.

of the current and past values of the independent variables. Given an assumption of weights on the lags that decline geometrically with the passage of each time period, the familiar Koyck transformation yields a specification including as regressors the lagged dependent variable and only current values of the independent variables. For the data at hand, this specification also addresses the potential problem of nonstationarity in the dependent variable by producing stationary residuals.

The regression results for the multivariate specification are summarized in table 8.3.[16] The first column reflects a specification where the indicator for the conservative think tank advantage includes only openly ideological organizations. In the second column, the indicator also incorporates the institutes that tend to lean in either the conservative or liberal direction. The coefficients on the lagged dependent variable are fairly large at 0.86 and 0.78 for the two models, indicating that changes in the independent variables produce effects spread over many periods.[17]

The composition of the interest group population, with coefficients of -0.25 and -0.23 for the two models, has the expected negative effect and both coefficients achieve statistical significance at the .05 level. Similarly, coefficients for the degree of antigovernment rhetoric in the media are correctly signed and reach statistical significance at the .10 level. The inclusion of these two measures gives us greater confidence that the findings on the think tank indicators do not stem from their relationships with an omitted variable.

Federal policy enactments have the expected negative effects, but the respective coefficients are not statistically significant. Likewise, the coefficients on economic expectations cannot be statistically distinguished from zero. This divergence from the findings of Durr (1993) could reflect a difference in periods of analysis (1968–1988 for Durr vs. 1977–1994 here) or from Durr's use of the cointegration methodology to estimate his relationships. Because I have no theoretical reason to expect the

16. The Breusch-Godfrey LM statistic, often used to test for residual autocorrelation in lagged dependent variable specifications, indicates that autocorrelation of the first order is not a problem. Tests for up to fourth-order autocorrelation produced the same inference.

17. The coefficient on the lagged dependent variable captures the effects of past values of the other independent variables. Within a lagged dependent variable specification, the total cumulated effect of a one-unit change in an independent variable is $\beta_k / (1 - \phi)$, where ϕ is the coefficient for the lagged dependent variable. Given the estimates of ϕ presented in table 8.3, the total effect is $\beta_k / (1 - 0.86)$ and $\beta_k / (1 - 0.78)$, or $7.14 * \beta_k$ and $4.55 * \beta_k$, respectively, for the two columns.

central variable of my analysis, the conservative think tank advantage, to have a cointegrating relationship with public mood, I retain the lagged dependent variable specification. The measures for federal policy enactments and economic expectations are included here merely as controls to ensure that the relationship of interest can be estimated accurately; I draw no definitive inferences about their potential effects upon public mood.

The most important findings relate to the variables tapping the conservative think tank advantage.[18] Coding decisions for the avowedly neutral institutes that tend toward either the liberal or conservative side have only minimal impacts upon the inferences drawn from the analysis. Parallel results are obtained regardless of whether or not the analysis includes the organizations leaning in one direction. The coefficients for the variables based upon the two different measurement choices are fairly similar at 2.12 and 1.83, and each of them reaches statistical significance at the .05 level.

In substantive terms, both coefficients point to moderate but noticeable effects. For the first indicator of the conservative think tank advantage, a movement of .15 points—the average quarter-to-quarter change—would lead to shifts in public mood of .32 points in the current period and 2.27 total points over time. Public mood has an average fluctuation between quarters of 1.08 units and a standard deviation of 4.42. An average change in the think tank variable eventually produces a fluctuation in the dependent variable that is about half the size of its standard deviation. The potential swings in public mood resulting from changes in the second think tank indicator, which has a mean quarter-to-quarter change of .20 points, are about two-thirds of this magnitude.

BUSINESS POWER GAINED BY SHAPING PUBLIC OPINION

Analysts at think tanks are likely to enjoy credibility among the public as neutral experts. This credibility becomes more apparent when we consider, by way of comparison, Americans' skepticism of the self-interested pressure groups and vote-seeking politicians who constitute many of the voices advancing policy arguments through the news media (Lipset and Schneider 1983). Of all the people and organizations with

18. To make the regression results more readable, the two indicators for the conservative think tank advantage were rescaled by dividing the original values by 100.

access to the news media, researchers at think tanks stand among those with the highest potential to persuade because of their stature as experts. The finding of an association between their advocacy and public opinion squares cleanly with what we know about how credibility affects a source's persuasive impacts (Petty and Cacioppo 1981; Smith and Squire 1990).

The empirical results build upon those from Page, Shapiro, and Dempsey's (1987) more encompassing study of the influence of media stimuli upon public opinion. In their analysis, "experts" of all kinds produce impacts surpassed only by those of television news commentators. Experts achieve considerable credibility from their knowledge and apparent nonpartisan status, making their policy-relevant statements— as transmitted by the news media—a potent influence upon public opinion. Researchers at think tanks, who ordinarily lack a self-interested motive for promoting a particular point of view, are one important kind of expert called upon by journalists. Because of their independence, these analysts are likely more persuasive advocates of probusiness policies than are spokespersons who explicitly represent corporations, trade associations, or peak associations.

In fact, Page, Shapiro, and Dempsey (1987) find that advocacy through the media by interest groups, a large portion of which represent business, actually has an impact upon public opinion opposite from their intended effect. As they point out, the credibility among the public of interest groups, including those in the business sector, is likely to be very low. The analysis developed here turns up a similar result in that the degree to which the interest group system tilts toward business leads to a public opinion more unfavorable to business. Business elites therefore might more effectively shape public opinion by funneling money into like-minded think tanks than by advocating positions themselves.

If the inferences described earlier are accurate, such a business strategy may have yielded dividends over the last two decades. Under the straightforward assumption that conservative think tanks could not have publicized their messages as loudly without extensive corporate funding, the linkage uncovered between think tank advocacy and subsequent movements in public mood reveal a critical source of business power. A more conservative public does not benefit all corporations and industries in every instance, of course. Such an outcome does, however, confer advantages on business as a collective for the kinds of regulatory, spending, and taxation policies upon which diverse firms can agree. This compatibility of conservative policies with the overall desires of the business community has in fact led business to steer its financial contributions primarily toward conservative think tanks instead of liberal ones. The contributions appear to have helped, in a small but observable way, bring the American public into closer alignment with conservative principles.

This avenue of influence is probably historically contingent because of the evolution of think tanks as prominent Washington actors. Before the 1970s, when the relatively few institutes in existence were underfunded and not very active in policy circles, it seems unlikely that business indirectly shaped public opinion through its financial contributions to them. As think tanks grew in prominence and corporations directed their contributions toward overtly conservative ones, however, business added a new weapon to its arsenal. Without the extensive mobilization among business leaders and foundation heads to support conservative think tanks during and after the 1970s, it is doubtful that the policy institutes on the right would possess the financial backing to promote their ideas as effectively. Part of the impact of these think tanks, then, stems from the ability of business to fund organizations tending to advocate probusiness policies.

QUALIFICATIONS AND IMPLICATIONS

Although this empirical study suggests that think tanks can cause public mood to change, the analysis cannot support any notion that they are the sole or even primary determinant. Such a claim would be far-fetched. The estimation summarized in table 8.3 identifies other plausible causes yet cannot measure all of them. Ideally one would control for the full range of voices who might affect public mood through the news media, beyond just the measure of antigovernment media references used here, but the scope of the necessary data collection renders that approach infeasible. Similarly, other analyses undoubtedly would uncover a stronger causal role for economic and social conditions.

Given that my specification cannot incorporate all possible shapers of public mood, the prominence of think tanks in the media should be considered only one of several causes. Still, the data do indicate that recognizable—if not overwhelming—changes in public mood arise from shifts in the ideological balance among the think tanks that are represented in the media. Because the results from chapter 5 demonstrate that public mood has marked impacts on the outcomes of unifying issues, anything that can change it has to be taken seriously.

The actual process by which think tanks affect public mood is surely more complicated than is depicted here. While my empirical specification tests for a direct effect of think tanks, their influence on public mood may be partly or even primarily indirect. The research and advocacy of think tanks may shape the course of ideas debated and discussed by politicians, bureaucrats, academics, and interest groups. These other political actors may restate the arguments or incorporate them into policy proposals, thus giving the ideas further amplification. Through processes often difficult to model empirically in a comprehensive manner, elite-level debates can lead public opinion in a certain direction. When a widely discussed attack on the welfare state such as Charles Murray's *Losing Ground*—a book written while Murray was a fellow at a think tank—reshapes a policy debate, there are myriad ways public opinion could change as a result. The statistical model presented in this chapter should be seen as a simplification of a much more complicated process.

Though it simplifies reality in order to proceed, the analysis herein suggests that there is now a relationship between the sentiments advanced by think tanks and the opinions held by the citizenry. As a consequence, the ability of business as a collective to embed its interests in government policy appears to change according to the relative effectiveness of competing think tanks in publicizing their messages. The business-funded think tanks are certainly not the only game in town. They have competitors more likely to advocate regulatory, taxation, and social welfare policies that business opposes. The measure of think tank citations in the news media, in fact, takes into account both sides of the ideological spectrum. For that reason, the findings reveal the importance of the overall composition of the population of policy institutes. With their stronger funding, the conservative think tanks enjoy more opportunities to move their ideas into broader circulation. Their liberal counterparts are effective when they attract attention from the news media, but their lower budgets frequently make that harder to achieve.

If the results presented in the current and preceding chapters are accurate, then a unified business community most effectively gains influence over policy not by working against citizen control of government but rather by working through it. Because swimming against the current of public opinion on unifying issues is usually ineffective, redirecting the river constitutes a more productive strategy. If business can shape public opinion, especially people's broad preferences on the proper role of government in society, then gaining favorable legislation from elected officials becomes much easier. The evidence from this chapter suggests that since the 1970s, business may have discovered a means of executing such a plan: providing financial backing to conservative think tanks.

NINE

The Compatibility of Business Unity
and Popular Sovereignty

Can profit-seeking corporations and strong democratic institutions peacefully coexist, or must they necessarily be adversaries? Can the interests of ordinary citizens ever receive fair consideration in an arena where business alliances brandish the awesome resources of money, organization, connections, and control over jobs? In seeking to answer these questions, many scholars rest their thinking and research on an untested central assumption: If diverse firms, industries, and business groups enter politics as a unified bloc, they become a formidable force. The business community wields substantial political power and subverts government responsiveness to the citizenry, the reasoning goes, by establishing solidarity in politics. This assumption and its attendant implications have directed myriad scholarly studies and discussion about the political power of business.

Making assumptions is an integral part of the scholarly enterprise. Social scientists must begin with premises about how the world works in order to determine what lines of inquiry can safely be ignored, what questions remain unanswered, and what evidence must be collected to advance the state of knowledge. Serious problems can arise, however, when assumptions are not examined from multiple theoretical perspectives and when neither assumptions nor their implications are tested against empirical realities. A premise not subjected to logical or empirical scrutiny can do considerable harm if it turns out inconsistent with the facts it ought to explain. The stakes are not only academic, for established propositions and the scholarship that flows from them can and do inspire commitments, affect public policy, and ultimately forge our beliefs and drive our behavior. Our understandings of the world determine what we see and do and, perhaps more importantly, delimit what we do not see and do not do. The beliefs underlying scholarly research tell us not only about the polity and society that is, but they allow us to form visions of the future from our perceptions of the present.

The intellectual world is replete with beliefs, many of far greater import than the one examined here, that have been toppled through theoretical and empirical investigation. Human behaviors like the propensity to commit suicide were once seen largely from the perspective of the individual, but Durkheim showed the importance of broader social forces like religion and the family. Pendulum swings from booms to busts were once seen as inevitable, but Keynes showed that countercyclical government spending could smooth the economic cycle. People were once thought to form political groups naturally, but Olson showed that self-interested individuals refrain from contributing to collective action. Social science can create new knowledge by making implicit assumptions explicit, thinking through the logic accompanying them, and determining their validity. Sometimes an intuitive, common-sense assumption turns out to be wrong, a product of moving too quickly through the chain of reasoning leading from beginning to end. What seems obvious from one perspective often becomes problematic when we change lenses. The debate over unity, built upon a shared assumption about what happens if businesses coalesce around common political aspirations, provides an apt illustration. When we refocus attention from considering the consequences business unity would bring to contemplating the kinds of issues that would encourage disparate firms to unify, previously hidden insights emerge.

Unifying issues stand among those that most clearly define broad-based political conflict in America. Specifically, unifying issues tend to be highly ideological, partisan, and salient. By being ideological, unifying issues permit politicians to use information about the general ideological sentiment in their constituencies to estimate majority preferences on the specific matter at hand. By being partisan, unifying issues divide Democrats from Republicans and make elections a choice between contrasting policy programs. By being salient, unifying issues elicit considerable attention from the mass media and allow ordinary citizens to gain the information necessary to formulate preferences and hold their representatives accountable. The ideological, partisan, and salient character of unifying issues also stimulates groups opposing business to organize for political action. Recognizing that unifying issues possess these attributes leads to a fundamental recasting of the scholarly debate over unity. Rather than deteriorating because of business unity, representative democracy actually becomes most responsive to citizen preferences and least vulnerable to dominance by business when firms share agreement on their desired policies. On unifying issues the public at large exerts substantial control over elected officials' policy decisions. While the public's role on unifying issues does not extend so far as to make political leaders nothing more than rubber stamps—automatons who translate majority preferences into policy in a one-to-one fashion— the public sets the broad parameters under which legislative action unfolds. At the same time, it is difficult for unified business interests to use their direct leverage to push policy directions away from those preferred by the public.

This new vantage point from which to understand business, citizens, and government will be useful to social scientists only to the extent that its predictions conform to evidence collected from the realm of politics. Judged by such a criterion, the perspective advanced here performs well. Earlier chapters have identified the issues marked by the highest degree of business unity and measured legislative decisions on those issues. Unified business interests tended to win, the evidence demonstrated, when public opinion and election outcomes were favorable. When those factors did not hold, business often found itself on the losing end of legislative battles. The actions business undertook to directly affect decisions, meanwhile, produced only modest impacts.

In a large-scale representative democracy such as the United States, public guidance for policymaking does not occur automatically. Government responsiveness to the public customarily requires that citizens form meaningful policy preferences and that candidates offer voters differentiated policy packages. In addition, responsiveness normally means that electorates employ policy-relevant criteria at the voting booth and that incumbent officeholders face electoral incentives to consider constituent preferences. While never met completely, these conditions are approximated far more closely on unifying issues than on particularistic or conflictual ones. On particularistic and conflictual matters—which either affect only a narrow slice of business or pit different factions of business against each other—a different pattern arises. In general these kinds of questions do not possess the characteristics of unifying issues that encourage a close connection between citizens and government. Unifying issues are also distinctive in attracting significant attention from other organized interests, such as unions or environmental groups, whose countermobilization offsets some of the pressure brought by business. Although truly equal pressure from opposing groups would be rare if not inconceivable, neither does business enjoy the advantages of a one-sided mobilization. Business unity, then, coincides with forces that weaken direct forms of business power, heighten the importance of elections in sparking new policy directions, and induce officeholders to listen to constituents' preferences. For these reasons, the nation paradoxically approaches the democratic ideal to a much greater degree when business is unified than when it is not.

The political processes on unifying issues do not mean that the public triumphs over business, for frequently no tension exists between the two. Instead, this book has advanced a more complicated argument: The policy preferences and voting choices of the citizenry determine whether business, when unified, will celebrate victories or absorb defeats. Public opinion and election outcomes sometimes instigate policies very favorable to business but at other times lead to policies business opposes. For this reason, unity does not breed ineffectiveness for business or impose barriers to the passage of legislation business wants. Instead, unity corresponds with a political dynamic that may or may not result in policies desired by business. Similarly, it would be incorrect to interpret the evidence as implying that a congealing of preferences within business actually *causes* democracy to function better, for it is the factors associated with unity—rather than unity itself—that make legislative action responsive to public preferences.

The strong voice of the public that registers on unifying issues coexists with direct forms of business power. Through its political activities and control over economic performance, business often does wield power over legislative action. That is, a claim that business power on unifying issues is nil would stretch the book's logic beyond plausibility. Instead, when business unifies we should think of direct means of power as being noticeable but still weaker than social scientists have routinely assumed. While sometimes bearing fruit, political mobilization by business cannot explain broad changes over time in legislative policies.

THE MISPLACED CONCERNS ABOUT UNITY

The long-standing debates over unity among pluralists, elite theorists, and ruling class theorists have focused our attention in the wrong place. Widespread scholarly concerns about business unity are misplaced, for unifying issues are marked by the highest, rather than the lowest, degree of democratic control by the citizenry. It is the conflictual and particularistic issues that need closer scrutiny.

In terms of their prospects for business power, conflictual issues are not overly troublesome. After all, every time a segment of business wins on a conflictual issue, another segment must lose. The pluralist notion of counterbalancing forces holds some merit here because frequently both or all sides of a conflict within business will possess resources with which to advance their causes. When making the ultimate decisions on conflictual issues, elected officials often will simultaneously alienate one sector while winning praise from another. When construction companies square off against military contractors in a battle over whether transportation or defense will increase its share of the budgetary pie, for example, the conflict has zero-sum aspects for which one side's gain represents a loss for the other. Such a situation is, in a sense, liberating for officeholders. As Wilson (1980) notes, when elected officials feel pressure from many sides and cannot satisfy all claimants, they gain discretion and independence from organized interests. If all issues were conflictual, concerns about business power would be substantially mitigated.

Particularistic issues, however, pose considerably greater threats. By definition, any competition that exists must come from outside of business. When considering the sweep of postwar policymaking in the United States, one can point to some positive trends regarding outside competition. Scholars writing in the 1950s and 1960s, such as Maass (1951), Cater (1964), McConnell (1966), and Lowi (1969), were especially worried about particularistic issues that attracted no opposition at all. That kind of situation appears considerably rarer today. Gais, Peterson, and Walker (1984) found that interest groups faced much more competition within the policy domains they operated than would have been predicted by views of closed policy subsystems. In a more comprehensive study, Heinz et al. (1993) discovered that issues where lobbyists reported no competition from other groups were uncommon.[1]

Much of the competition business interests face on particularistic issues comes from citizen groups that did not exist a few decades ago. Whereas a corporation may once have been able to propose policies that would create monopolistic or oligopolistic advantages without worrying that organizations representing consumers would rise in opposition, now consumer groups do intervene in these kinds of issues. While not possessing the money of the corporations and trade associations, citizen

1. See also Heclo (1978), Browne (1988), and Jenkins-Smith, St. Clair, and Woods (1991).

groups hold other resources like credibility and access to the mass media that make them important players in national politics (Berry 1999).

Baumgartner and Jones (1993) have shown that the success of industries on particularistic issues is far from inevitable. The nuclear power and pesticide industries, for example, enjoyed protection for decades only to see their privileged status eventually erode through revised understandings of the issues, the entrance of previously uninvolved interest groups, a change in the government institutions holding jurisdiction over decisions, and increased attention from the mass public. These cases illustrate the continuing relevance of the solutions Schattschneider (1960) proposed to curtailing special interest policies. Defeating narrow factions of business often requires raising the salience of the issue, which brings new government and nongovernment participants into decision-making, or making the issue one for which the parties stake out positions. Those outcomes have occurred with greater regularity since Schattschneider wrote, leaving particularistic issues as a group less threatening than they once were.

Yet the prospects for citizen participation and influence on particularistic issues, while brighter than social scientists formerly believed, remain far from ideal. Narrow benefits flowing to corporations and industries continue to persist, especially via regulatory protections, subsidies, and tax breaks. Every major tax bill passed by Congress contains particularistic provisions benefiting some slice of capital. Particularistic issues present major problems for democratic control, for in the typical case—though clearly not all cases—broad publics possess little knowledge of the questions at stake or the decisions being made. Under these conditions, policy choices can only occasionally respond to public values and preferences.

THE INTERMIXING OF BUSINESS PREFERENCES AND PUBLIC PREFERENCES

My interpretation of particularistic and conflictual issues has been based upon previous studies rather than additional cases and data collected specifically for this project. Given that new evidence is always welcome, ideally the statistical models estimated in chapters 5–7 would have incorporated these kinds of issues as well as unifying ones. Unifying issues formed the centerpiece of my empirical analysis, however, for good reason: They are the category where I break from existing research and schools of thought. On conflictual issues, it is widely acknowledged that some segments of business win while others lose. On particularistic issues, no one doubts that, at least some of the time, the public has minimal control over policy but narrow business interests can gain favorable benefits. For my purposes, there is little need for additional scrutiny of the political processes surrounding those kinds of issues. It is on the unifying ones where my theoretical framework challenges prevailing perspectives, and so the research design presented in earlier chapters gave extensive attention to uncovering the evidence necessary to substantiate my claims.

In collecting the evidence, I have drawn upon the entire scope of federal legislative politics over four decades. Legislative decisions do not result only from the handiwork of Congress, for the president's veto power and his ability to set the agenda leave his imprint upon the bills that fail and that pass. Both appointed and permanent officials in the executive branch also play central roles in uncovering problems and drafting legislative proposals. When bills become laws, policymaking continues as executive agencies develop the rules, regulations, and procedures that will implement them on a daily basis. Many of these administrative actions produce clear impacts on the management, strategic planning, and ultimately the profits of certain corporations and industries. The Federal Communications Commission, to take one example, decides which broadcast stations will be granted licenses. The Department of Health and Human Services pays hospitals and clinics for services provided to Medicare patients. The Food and Drug Administration establishes scientific and medical criteria that pharmaceuticals must meet before they can be legally marketed.

These sorts of decisions, just like legislative ones, are momentous for various business sectors. As they apply to this study, the administrative decisions share another crucial characteristic: They are usually particularistic or conflictual in orientation. Business at large does not involve itself in choices over whether a television station will retain its license, whether the rate of reimbursement for a given medical procedure will increase, or whether a new drug will be approved. In each of these instances, the decisions strongly impact certain corporations or industries, which naturally appeal to bureaucratic officials in seeking the best possible outcomes. The much larger segments of business not affected by the decisions, however, stay out of the conflicts, preserving their resources for other matters actually relevant to them.

Thus, while unifying issues are rare within the domain of legislative politics, they are even rarer within executive politics. This difference results from a contrast between the purposes and methods of the two processes of policymaking. Legislation is normally broad, creating or revising programs and establishing their guidelines and goals. To carry out their wishes, turning the blueprint for a program into a working operation, Congress and the president must grant money and authority to an implementing agency. The agency's subsequent decisions in administering the program will necessarily be more specific and targeted than the authorizing legislation; for that reason, individual decisions are highly unlikely to draw a unified position from business. As earlier chapters have noted, business more frequently unifies on the general principles that define a course of action than on the specific details necessary to implement it. By comparison to legislative decisions, those made in the executive branch deal with a greater proportion of details, making business unity less likely to arise. Even when business unifies for or against the legislation authorizing a program, the implementation stage quickly uncovers differences of interest among competing companies and sectors.

This reality greatly affects the behavior of business organizations. Associations with large and diverse memberships, including not only the U.S. Chamber of Commerce but also the Business Roundtable, National Association of Manufacturers, and National Federation of Independent Business, spend the vast majority of their resources on the legislative side of government. In so doing, these associations obviously work with officials from the executive branch, but the context of the interactions surrounds primarily legislative policy development rather than the implementing decisions of departments, agencies, and commissions. Because of their missions and their financial constraints to promote all elements of their constituencies, broadly based associations turn their attention to where members can unify—which, when it occurs, is normally on the legislative side where overarching principles come into play.

The narrower the scope of the organization, the higher the proportion of resources it expends on the administrative aspects of government. Trade associations representing individual industries, for example, participate in the proceedings of the bureaucracy at a higher rate than do peak associations. Legislative decisions naturally attract attention from trade associations as well, but legislation does not form their dominant emphasis as it does for peak associations. The smallest grouping within business, a single corporation, is most likely of all to spend its time, money, and energy trying to influence implementation decisions in the executive branch. This all follows from the fact that the details of implementation often have marked impacts upon narrow slices of business but rarely unify the entire business community.

An important implication for research design follows from the differences in the configurations of companies involved in passing laws versus implementing laws. Just as analyzing ethnic conflict would lead one to center the investigation upon multicultural rather than homogenous societies, so too the study of unifying issues inevitably focuses upon legislative rather than administrative processes. Scholarly debates over the consequences of unity can only be resolved by delving into actual cases marked by businesswide consensus, and those cases are predominantly legislative. The actions of departments, agencies, and commissions are nevertheless important to business; narrow economic interests often, though certainly not always, benefit from policymaking in the bureaucracy (Bernstein 1955; Lowi 1969).

This provides another reason for emphasizing the threat to popular sovereignty posed not by unifying issues but instead by particularistic and, occasionally, conflictual ones. Unifying issues are uncommon, but their appearances usually occur within a legislative setting where their ideological, partisan, and salient character keeps decisions within the boundaries prescribed by public preferences. Particularistic and conflictual issues commonly arise in both legislative and executive politics; within either arena, broad publics have difficulty affecting the ultimate decisions but narrow business groups can often make their voices heard. If importance can be defined in terms of the impacts upon ordinary citizens, the average unifying issue is undoubtedly more important than the average particularistic or conflictual one. Collectively, however, the latter kinds of issues may be more important because of their far greater abundance.

By accepting the assumption that business unity leads to strength, many scholars have been led astray in examining the means through which power arises. If business gains strength through solidarity, demonstrating the results should be straightforward. This motivation has encouraged scholars to study the most transparent forms of power, the leverage over lawmaking business gains from explicit political activity and from its control over investment. These forms of power, however, normally are not especially effective at determining legislative decisions on unifying issues. The findings from previous chapters indicate instead that a unified business community wields its most important source of power through indirect means. Surmising that public opinion affects legislative action on unifying issues, business can attempt to win public support for probusiness values and policies. Potential channels for such a strategy include policy-related advertising, public relations campaigns, ownership of the mass media and influence upon its content, distribution of favorable material to schools and colleges, and funding think tanks that promote viewpoints favorable to business through the mass media.

Despite the importance of the topic, the empirical literature assessing the ability of business to influence public opinion is sparse and underdeveloped. The possibility of this source of influence has been recognized for some time, garnering attention in classic works like those by Crawford (1939) and Truman (1951). Yet little systematic research has been undertaken to assess its potency by observing the opinion-shaping efforts of business, documenting any changes in mass sentiment, and ruling out alternative explanations for those changes. Thus our knowledge of the scope, magnitude, and dynamics of business influence upon public opinion remains incomplete and far from precise.

We do have a number of descriptive studies that chronicle the endeavors of various corporations and trade associations to orchestrate favorable attitudes among Americans. For example, Fones-Wolf (1994) describes how, in the two decades following World War II, business attempted to mold public opinion and the nation's political culture through shop-floor seminars in factories and economic education programs directed at schools. Tedlow (1979; see also Kelley 1956) recounts the rise of public relations offices in corporations and trade associations, offices which eventually sought not only to increase sales but also to fashion more favorable images of corporations, industries, and the free enterprise system. Sethi (1977), Loomis and Sexton (1995), and West and Loomis (1998) explore how business uses advocacy advertising, which embodies similar goals as public relations. Mitchell (1989) traces the efforts of corporations in the early part of the twentieth century to gain public legitimacy, while Vogel (1989) addresses their more recent attempts to work through the media and intellectuals to change public attitudes.

With the exceptions of Mitchell (1989) and Vogel (1989), these studies are more concerned with describing the efforts of business than in assessing any actual effects on public beliefs, attitudes, and values. As a result, we lack a body of rigorously conducted empirical evaluations of the linkage between business and public opinion. Five decades ago Stephen Bailey (1950), in his interpretation of the failure of the Full

Employment Bill of 1945, argued that the most important source of business's power was its ability to influence cultural values regarding free enterprise and government authority. Very few subsequent studies have followed up on his insights; a better understanding of the relationship between business and public opinion deserves high prominence on the scholarly agenda. Recent studies of outside or grassroots lobbying by all kinds of interest groups (Goldstein 1999; Kollman 1998) may help illuminate this relationship. Interest groups sometimes go beyond mobilizing their own members and supporters by using advertising, mass mailings, or public relations to seek favorable opinions among the general population. Further research on how effectively business employs outside lobbying could bring sizeable payoffs.

Perhaps a belief among students of politics that the topic is not worth studying helps explain why so little research has systematically assessed the influence of business upon public opinion. When investigating policymaking on issues business cares about, many scholars assume that public opinion is unimportant and that all the central action occurs at the elite level. Such an assumption is especially justified, according to prevailing theories, if business achieves internal unity. Hence the lion's share of research on the role of business in politics focuses on power gained either through overt efforts to influence policies or through officeholders' electoral dependence upon a strong economy.

The evidence presented herein, however, squarely contradicts the view that the mass public cannot affect the course of policymaking when business maintains a unified position. Because the outcomes of unifying issues reveal the impacts of public attitudes, beliefs, values, and preferences, understanding the ability of business to cause changes in public opinion becomes all the more important. That is, given the findings that decision-making on unifying issues is highly responsive to public opinion, we now need to shift attention to earlier links in the causal chain and look for the upstream factors—particularly those stemming from the efforts of business—that affect what the public wants.

IS THE PUBLIC'S ROLE ULTIMATELY HOLLOW?

While its primary contribution lies in challenging the premise that business unity begets business power and undermines democracy, this book also has pursued a secondary line of inquiry. Namely, the vantage point developed here indicates that business, when unified, gains its greatest return on political activities aimed at shaping public opinion. Chapter 8 has attempted to advance our understanding of the effectiveness of such a strategy; the analysis suggests that by funding think tanks, business may have successfully altered public expectations about the proper size and scope of government. Does this conclusion mean that the strong responsiveness of legislative action to public opinion ultimately rings hollow? Is the popular representation that we observe on unifying issues meaningless because representation is merely a conveyor belt for business power? These questions must be addressed before we can fully interpret the book's primary finding that the public provides substantial guidance for lawmaking on unifying issues.

For the popular representation documented in earlier chapters to be ultimately hollow, two conditions must be met. First, business-instigated changes in public opinion must lead citizens to uphold principles and policies that work against their own interests. If business pushes citizens toward beliefs that actually benefit them, then no tension arises. Second, the effects of business on public opinion must reach a magnitude sufficient for us to conclude that business dominates public opinion. If business is but one of many coexisting factors that affect public opinion, then clearly expressed citizen preferences are not simply a cover for business preferences.

Both conditions must be met to support a conclusion that the workings of democracy on unifying issues are a sham. Business has to dictate rather than merely influence public opinion and do so in a way that leads to outcomes making citizens worse off. The primary findings of the book should be considered in light of an assessment of the interactions among business, public opinion, and the interests of the citizenry.

THE PUBLIC'S OBJECTIVE INTERESTS

The first condition requires that public opinion be manipulated and distorted to support policies working against the interests of the people. Page and Shapiro (1992, chap. 9), echoing other scholars, define authentic or genuine public opinion as that which would emerge if citizens possessed all relevant information. As Page and Shapiro note, this standard is very difficult to apply in practice. Is the federal government's oversight and regulation of business practices too extensive or not extensive enough? Should the federal government be streamlined with more functions delegated to the private sector, or would a stronger government best advance the needs and interests of the polity? Some observers contend that we need a more expansive federal government to provide a social safety net, to help citizens acquire the skills necessary to navigate today's economic waters, and to create the kind of society in which most people desire to live. If that course of action best defines what a majority of Americans would prefer if they could investigate the matter thoroughly, then business's efforts to protect its autonomy lead the public astray, away from its true interests. Other observers, however, argue that Americans would be better off with a smaller federal government that left more authority in the hands of private institutions such as business enterprises. Shrinking the reach of government, in this view, would promote the well-being of most Americans, meaning that opinion-shaping efforts by business simply push citizens in the direction they would naturally move in the presence of adequate information and time for reflection.

The main problem in reaching a resolution to this quandary is that debates over the size of government are heavily infused with personal values and experiences. Any objective answer to what responsibilities government should undertake depends at least partly on an independent assessment untainted by one's own predispositions and biases. Achieving such an assessment is extremely difficult, perhaps even impossible. One potential solution would introduce comparisons to other political systems. Take, as an especially prominent example, the scope of social welfare programs. Relative to other industrialized nations, the American welfare state is considerably more limited, particularly in the areas of labor market intervention, health care, unemployment benefits, and support of the poor (Weir, Orloff, and Skocpol 1988; Heidenheimer et al. 1990). At the same time, overall tax rates are lower in the United States. One could pose the question this way: Are Americans well-served by their restricted government programs and lesser tax burden, or would they be better off under a more generous welfare state? Answering that question might help us determine whether the ability of business to shape citizen expectations about the responsibilities of government would be best construed as educative, manipulative, or indeterminate.

Many analysts would agree that, at least in terms of personal and material well-being, the wealthiest and best-educated citizens prosper under the American system, while the poorest and least-educated citizens would fare better in Western Europe, Northern Europe, Canada, or Oceania. For the "median" citizen, however, disagreement will likely arise. The United States offers greater opportunities for a very high standard of living but lower insurance against falling on hard times. In the end, it remains difficult to offer an objective answer to the question of whether the average American would be better off with an expansive and energetic government or a limited and constrained one.

We cannot escape the fact that arguing, debating, and deliberating over such matters as the appropriate role of government in American society is integral to what democratic politics is all about. Unless one is willing to invite charges of hubris by claiming knowledge of a universal answer, uncertainty over such matters will remain. Either we recognize that reasonable people can disagree, or else we must characterize as unreasonable all the citizens, government officials, journalists, policy specialists, and scholars on the other side. My intention in raising these points is not to claim that citizens actually benefit from business indoctrination. Instead, I simply want to highlight the difficulty of determining whether a majority is led closer to or further away from its true interests if business helps to shape public opinion.

THE MAGNITUDE OF BUSINESS EFFECTS ON PUBLIC OPINION

If we had to evaluate, on the basis of the first condition alone, whether the government's responsiveness to the citizenry on unifying issues rings hollow, we would face an impasse. It would be unclear exactly how to interpret the responsiveness earlier chapters have uncovered. Fortunately, social scientists can more effectively assess the second condition, which involves determining whether public opinion in its totality reflects and reiterates business preferences. We possess the concepts and tools to answer the question: Does business dominate public opinion? This inquiry would still be difficult, but for very different reasons than our inability to assess the first condition. The main limitation to a conclusive answer is our lack of extensive empirical evidence on how, whether, and to what degree business has shaped public opinion. I have examined one potential mechanism through which business could accomplish that aim, but many other means exist as well. One would have to examine and evaluate the effectiveness of all potential mechanisms before venturing a definitive conclusion. Because that effort has not been undertaken here or elsewhere, my interpretation will necessarily be tentative.

The most plausible reading of the available evidence, however, leads to the conclusion that the most pervasive values and attitudes held by American citizens reflect much more than just the influence of business. Perhaps most importantly in suggesting that conclusion, public opinion has often turned against business. During certain periods the public has supported more vigorous government efforts to address the nation's

problems and, as we have seen, those attitudes contributed to the enactment of initiatives business opposed. Business also suffered, particularly
in the late 1960s and early 1970s, from a steep decline in people's affective feelings toward the nation's corporations. That decline encouraged
political leaders to design new programs opposed by business, programs
that regulated corporate behavior in such matters as pollution, workers'
health and safety, hiring practices, and product safety.

If business were controlling public opinion, the public would never
change in directions that work against business. After all, it is hardly
conducive to business getting what it wants from legislation for the public to develop unfavorable attitudes and policy preferences. In practice
we observe that public opinion in some periods benefits business but at
other times elicits policies contrary to what business wants. From such
a pattern, one can infer the impacts upon public opinion of something
other than business.

Indeed, explaining the origins of public opinion has engaged a
plethora of political scientists, social psychologists, communication
scholars, sociologists, and historians. While the sheer volume of the
relevant research prohibits a thorough review here, a brief overview
will suffice. A fair inference from the published research indicates
that a wide variety of factors, many of which cannot be controlled
by business, contribute to the formation and maintenance of public
opinion. For starters, people's opinions on political matters form in part
from their experiences in families, communities, and social networks
(Jennings and Niemi 1974; Huckfeldt and Sprague 1995) and from
reactions to existing government policies (Schlesinger 1986; Wlezien
1995). Individuals also frequently differ in their opinions according to
the groups to which they identify or belong, especially those separating
citizens according to race, income, religion, age, and gender (Knoke
1979; Guth et al. 1995). When we consider the public as a whole,
collective opinion in the twentieth century has evolved in response to the
nation's fluctuating economic fortunes, increased educational levels and
the entry of women into the workforce, the rise first of industrialization
and then of white-collar service jobs, and changing societal conditions
such as crime and poverty (Page and Shapiro 1992; Mayer 1992). The
existence of these determinants of public opinion strongly implies that
business cannot be the only or even primary cause of what citizens want
from government.

Some aspects of public opinion also have deep historical roots. Take,
for example, the penchant for limited government, which often has

probusiness implications. We have seen that this sentiment changes over time, and those changes have important consequences for policy, but in comparison with other industrialized nations Americans have consistently expressed greater support for limited government (Smith 1987; Lipset 1996). Traveling in the United States in the 1830s, Tocqueville recognized the pervasiveness of these cultural expectations; he was struck by the tendency for Americans to vest authority in the private institutions of civil society rather than the public institutions of government. Even before the nation was founded, its political culture was characterized by a belief in constraining the powers of government. By imposing checks and balances and granting the federal government only enumerated powers while reserving the rest for the states, the Constitution both reflected and preserved the notion of limited government. The original causes of that belief included the fears of settlers escaping feudal and religious authority, perceptions of available economic opportunities that contributed to individualistic values, and diversity among the colonies (Hartz 1955; Morone 1998). In any event, a belief that the federal government's powers should be limited predates the Industrial Revolution and the subsequent rise of large corporations. For this reason, corporate interests could not have created that belief, though certainly in later periods they may have refined and augmented it.

The analysis presented in chapter 8 suggests that we are in the middle of a period where business affects core public preferences. Even here, though, the evidence indicates that business does not possess a unilateral ability to shape public opinion on the proper role of government. The conservative think tanks partially funded by corporate interests have competitors deriving funding from other sources, such as foundations, individuals, and unions. These other segments of society, by funding and otherwise supporting think tanks that frequently promote policies opposed by business, counter some of the opinion-shaping power held by conservative think tanks.

In addition, many other voices speak through the news media. Page, Shapiro, and Dempsey (1987) find that besides the pool of "experts" that includes business-funded analysts at think tanks, commentary by news anchors and guest commentators and the urging of presidents can sway public opinion. Ideological and partisan elites, the centerpiece of Zaller's (1992) analysis, provide cues through the mass media that citizens combine with preexisting values to formulate issue preferences. Bennett (1990) notes that the content of the mass media reflects the

prevailing perspectives among elected and unelected government officials. Business undoubtedly has previously influenced some of the voices
appearing in the news, but it would be implausible to assert that all or
even most of them—particularly those who have promoted policies
business opposed—are nothing more than corporate spokespersons.

Given so many forces shaping public opinion, it would certainly be
difficult and more likely impossible for business to determine the public's
core values and policy preferences. For this reason, the impacts of
business upon public opinion are probably better described as influence
than as domination. This point distinguishes my argument from Lukes's
(1974) claim that hegemonic groups dictate how others conceive their
interests. My primary difference with him concerns the magnitude of
the relationship. Lukes (1974) might claim an effect of business on public
opinion considerably greater than what I have found and described. If
business influences but does not dominate public opinion, then much of
what the public believes and supports represents an authentic response
to competing political ideas, prevailing conditions and circumstances,
and historical changes in the economy, society, and polity.

CONCLUDING THOUGHTS

The reasoning and evidence presented in this book show that business
unity is not something to be feared. Instead, democracy actually most
closely approaches its potential when business is unified. The premise
that unity leads to strength, which has guided so many scholarly studies,
needs to be seriously modified. That assumption should no longer serve
as the starting point for analyses of the role of business in politics. Future
research on unifying issues could instead profit from considering the
importance of public opinion and understanding how business might
have affected it.

From the standpoint of democratic theory, legislative responsiveness
to the citizenry on unifying issues is neither completely specious nor
entirely satisfying. The reality, rather, lies somewhere in between. Because fundamental public values and preferences have been partially
shaped by business, some of the responsiveness we observe simply
reflects an indirect source of business power. At the same time, much of
the responsiveness is genuine as well. Business unity coexists, but only
uneasily, with the precepts and requirements of democracy.

Additional Coding Rules Used to Uncover
Positions of the U.S. Chamber of Commerce

If the U.S. Chamber of Commerce declared positions on multiple bills, but each of them had highly comparable language, I count only one of them.[1] Sometimes within a given debate the Chamber supported one bill and opposed another; in these cases both bills are included as separate items. If the Chamber declared positions on two (or, on rare occasions, three) bills that would accomplish different tasks, and the bills subsequently were combined into a single piece of legislation, then each of them is included separately. Bills that were identical or nearly identical to policy proposals on which the Chamber took a position during the immediately preceding or succeeding Congress are included in the analysis, even if the archival evidence did not uncover any statement by the Chamber on the particular bill at hand.

For the occasions in which the Chamber says that it "generally supports" a bill or "supports with reservations," I code the Chamber as favoring the bill. A bill that the Chamber "opposes unless amended" is counted along with other opposed bills, but if the Chamber's requested amendments were added, the opposed bill is coded as dying at that point and the Chamber is coded as being neutral on the new bill. Similarly, if the Chamber announced that it will support a bill if amended, I coded the Chamber as neutral unless the proposed amendments were adopted, in which case the bill is coded as being supported. This

---

1. This happened most often when companion bills to accomplish the same function were introduced in both the House and the Senate. As a criterion for determining how to code two different bills in a policy area, I sought to determine whether both of them could potentially be enacted as separate laws (thereby suggesting two agenda items) or whether their overlap would eventually force Congress to choose between them (thereby indicating one agenda item).

happened most often for budgetary items, in which the Chamber did not express an overall position but rather recommended a specific cut. These items are included if Congress voted on an amendment to cut approximately the amount requested by the Chamber.

For most of the items in the analysis, the Chamber either endorsed or opposed an entire bill. If the Chamber declared a position on one or more specific provisions within a bill receiving congressional action, those provisions count as individual agenda items only if they either originated as independent bills or else received separate votes at some point during that Congress. For example, when the Chamber did not espouse an overall position on a bill but supported one particular provision, I code the provision if it received a separate vote, such as an amendment to add it or strike it.[2] The coding of provisions in this way means that one bill could produce multiple agenda items; as a practical matter, no bill ever yields more than three items through the coding of specific provisions. An exception to the coding rule for amendments outlined above occurs if an amendment did not really address a separable component but rather either weakened or strengthened the central thrust of the bill. If the Chamber opposed a bill and announced support for an amendment to weaken it, to take one instance, then the amendment does not merit a separate agenda item.

2. The reason for this coding rule is that without separate consideration for a provision, one cannot assess its level of congressional and presidential support independent from support for the bill in which it is embedded. Most of the agenda items (86 percent) are entire bills, while the remainder (14 percent) are provisions. The Chamber of Commerce did, however, express positions on many provisions that are not included in the analysis because those provisions were never acted upon separately by Congress.

The Potential for Feedback between Policy and Opinion

The models estimated in chapters 5–7 posit legislative action as the dependent variable and public opinion as an independent variable. On substantive grounds, a case could be made for keeping legislative action tightly linked in time with public opinion. Politicians monitor public opinion continuously, not only through polls but also through communications received from constituents and informal discussions with staff, advisors, colleagues, and reporters. The actual elapsed time between public opinion changing and politicians learning about it is likely to be short. Measuring public opinion too far in the past may obscure any responsiveness that exists.

Methodologically, though, if public opinion is not measured with some kind of lag, an empirical analysis could be flawed. In particular, if contemporaneous covariation between policy and opinion were used to estimate the models in chapters 5–7, any simultaneity in the data would lead to biased coefficients. This is not a problem for the two election variables. By measuring the results of the last election, those variables automatically precede in time the lawmaking measure and thus put the direction of causality into clear relief. The Congress and president that made policy in 1953, for example, were elected in 1952. Hence any linkage between the 1952 election and policy decisions in 1953 represents the former causing the latter rather than vice versa.

For the two indicators of public opinion, matters become more complicated. Given its sizable contemporaneous correlation with law-making of 0.47, public mood especially should be investigated further. Chapter 5 hypothesizes that public mood causes legislative action, but there might be theoretical reasons to expect a feedback effect whereby legislative action drives public mood. For my purposes, a positive feedback relationship would be the most vexing problem. A positive feedback relationship could result if officeholders "educate" their constituents after decisions have already been reached, or if the public through other means comes to support the policies government has adopted (Weissberg 1976; Nadel 1972). Depending upon the origins of the policies, this possibility could undermine or even contradict the theoretical propositions developed in this book.

For example, suppose that business leaders convince government officials to enact certain policies, and subsequently those officials use all communication tools at their disposal to sell the policies to the public at large. That process could produce positive contemporaneous co-variation between public mood and policymaking. Such a relationship would mean something very different from the causal process I have advanced. It would indicate that business manipulates public opinion by using policies, combined with government's efforts to justify those policies to the citizenry, as mediators.

In addition to its interest for theoretical reasons, mutual causation between public mood and policy decisions may pose statistical problems for any single-equation regression approach. With policy as the dependent variable, the coefficient on public mood would be biased upward if the estimation simultaneously captures an unmodeled feedback effect that is *positive in sign*. The problem with contemporaneous relationships is that they cannot distinguish between this scenario and the one I have proposed. The positive contemporaneous covariation between public mood and policymaking is equally consistent with either of them.

Of course, a negative feedback relationship is also possible. Durr (1993) and Wlezien (1995) build upon Easton (1965), Schlesinger (1986), and Stimson (1991) in proposing that kind of relationship (see also McFarland 1991). Durr and Wlezien find that policy moving in one ideological direction causes public opinion to shift in the opposite direction. The public, that is, appears to react negatively to policy enactments that push too far in one direction. Because contemporaneous relationships entangle the potential causal linkages between public mood and policymaking, any negative feedback could make the positive effect of public mood on policymaking appear weaker than it really is.

Given that I know how each variable changes over time, however, I can leverage that information to assess the direction of causality. If one variable moves and then another follows, we can assume—barring unusual circumstances—that the former has caused the latter. Suppose that policymaking becomes liberal only after public mood has already shifted toward liberalism. In this case, we would infer that public mood causes policymaking. If the latter were to change before the former, we would infer instead the existence of a feedback effect whereby policy causes opinion. In addition, the data might support the existence of both or neither causal processes.

Estimating relationships where the two variables are offset by some period can allow one to determine empirically the direction of causality. The time series techniques developed by Box and Jenkins (1976), well known for providing a coherent framework to examine causality, incorporate and estimate these lagged relationships. The Box-Jenkins strategy begins by removing each series' dependence upon its own past values. After doing so, the relationships between the resulting variables can be assessed without the confounding effects of spurious trending or drifting.

The Box-Jenkins procedures should be useful for the data being studied. The annual periodicity of the public mood and policymaking measures, though, poses a challenge for assessing causality. Suppose, to take one possibility, that a change in one variable produces a response in the other occurring over the span of a few weeks or months. This response might be absorbed into the zero-order correlation and mistakenly appear to be a contemporaneous effect. As a practical matter, the zero-order correlation between the two variables could not provide any definitive evidence on the direction of causality.

Because public mood is aggregated from individual surveys, this problem can be mitigated by calculating public mood over a different interval than the policy variable. I therefore recalculated public mood to include all those surveys conducted during the last two quarters of one calendar year and the first two quarters of the following year. For example, the first observation of the new variable incorporates surveys taken between July 1, 1952, and June 30, 1953. When rescored in this way, opinion can be offset from policy by six months instead of an entire year. This rescoring should allow a better estimation of causal relationships since temporal linkages that are not contemporaneous yet unfold in a period less than a full year can be picked up by the six-month stagger.

Following the Box-Jenkins approach, I began by prewhitening both series. Public mood was transformed by calculating the residuals from a $(1,0,0)$ ARIMA model with $\phi = 0.80$[1] while policy outcomes fit a $(1,0,0)$

---

1. The version of public mood presented in Stimson, MacKuen, and Erikson (1995), which covered 1955–1990, fits a $(1,1,0)$ model. The version used here, spanning a longer period from July 1, 1952, to June 30, 1996, fits a $(1,0,0)$ model.

model with $\phi = 0.55$.[2] I then assessed the relationship between the prewhitened series by calculating the cross-correlation function, which is provided in table B.1. I expect to find a positive effect of opinion on policy. For the feedback effect of policy on opinion, I do not predict a sign on the correlations.

For the negative lags in table B.1 indicating that policy leads opinion—the feedback effect—none of the correlations reach statistical significance.[3] Those correlations do, however, exhibit a clear pattern of negative signs. If feedback exists, then most likely policy that is favorable to business subsequently causes opinion to actually become *less* favorable to business (more liberal) in the next period. Such a process would be consistent with studies by Wlezien (1995) and Durr (1993), who present evidence for the public's negative reaction to policy initiatives that continue too long in one direction.

When we switch to positive lags whereby opinion leads policy—the causal direction I am proposing—the correlations are all positive in sign. When opinion precedes policy by 0.5 years (six months), the

Table B.1 Public Mood and Policy Decisions: The Cross-Correlation Function

LAG IN YEARS	CORRELATION	STANDARD ERROR
−4.5	−0.07	0.16
−3.5	−0.30	0.16
−2.5	0.05	0.16
−1.5	−0.21	0.15
−0.5	−0.06	0.15
+0.5	0.45*	0.15
+1.5	0.22	0.15
+2.5	0.20	0.15
+3.5	0.06	0.16
+4.5	0.16	0.16

N = 44
* $p < .05$
Note: The table provides the cross-correlation function for prewhitened series of public mood and policy decisions from 1953 to 1996. Public mood is calculated from July 1 through June 30 while policy decisions cover the calendar year. Negative lags mean that policy leads opinion while positive lags mean that opinion leads policy. Lag +0.5 indicates that opinion precedes policy by six months, lag +1.5 indicates one year and six months, etc.

2. Ten lags were used for identification and diagnostics. Both residual series produce correlograms indicating white noise and also generate nonsignificant Box-Ljung Q(10) statistics of 6.50 and 5.95, respectively. Given that I am entertaining causality in both directions, I employ a unique filter for each series.

3. The table presents only the first five lags, but the same patterns hold if we examine ten lags.

correlation between the prewhitened series is 0.45 and is statistically significant. This finding is consistent with a process of representation whereby policymakers alter their decisions in response to changes in public mood.

Two conclusions follow from this analysis. First, the evidence indicates that feedback is probably either nonexistent or else is *negative*. This result eliminates the primary threat to inference within a single-equation regression approach. Any positive effect of opinion on policy, the findings here suggest, is unlikely to be exaggerated due to simultaneity bias. That is, most likely either feedback does not exist at all or else the feedback effect is negative in sign and cannot cause upward bias in the coefficient on public mood. Ordinary least squares regression thus offers a sufficient technique for determining whether public mood affects policymaking.

As for the second conclusion, the cross-correlation function adds evidence that when opinion leads policy, the two variables have the expected positive relationship. The temporal ordering achieved through the lag structure provides leverage on causality such that opinion is causing policy. Temporal ordering of this sort is also employed for the regression analysis reported in earlier chapters. Consistent with the findings of table B.1, public mood is staggered to lead policy by six months.

The six-month offset strikes a reasonable balance between the substantive motivation, which calls for a tight temporal linking between opinion and policy, and the methodological concerns, which suggest some kind of lag on opinion. This measurement strategy is used for the models of chapters 5–7. Policy decisions within a given calendar year are predicted using public mood from the first two quarters of that year and the last two quarters of the previous year. The same July 1–June 30 period is used for the second public opinion indicator, public attitudes toward corporations.

REFERENCES

Abelson, Donald E. 1996. *American think-tanks and their role in U.S. foreign policy.* New York: St. Martin's Press.

Abramowitz, Alan I., and Kyle L. Saunders. 1998. Ideological realignment in the U.S. electorate. *Journal of Politics* 60:634–52.

Akard, Patrick J. 1992. Corporate mobilization and political power: The transformation of U.S. economic policy in the 1970s. *American Sociological Review* 57:597–615.

Allen, Michael Patrick. 1992. Elite social movement organizations and the state: The rise of the conservative policy-planning network. *Research in Politics and Society* 4:87–109.

Allen, Michael Patrick, and John L. Campbell. 1994. State revenue extraction from different income groups: Variations in tax progressivity in the United States, 1916 to 1986. *American Sociological Review* 59:169–86.

Alexander, Herbert E. 1984. *Financing politics: Money, elections, and political reform.* Washington, D.C.: CQ Press.

Andres, Gary. 1985. Business involvement in campaign finance: Factors influencing the decision to form a corporate PAC. *PS: Political Science and Politics* 18:215–19.

Andrews, David M. 1994. Capital mobility and state autonomy: Toward a structural theory of international monetary relations. *International Studies Quarterly* 38:193–218.

Arendt, Hannah. 1965. *On revolution.* New York: Viking.

Arnold, R. Douglas. 1990. *The logic of congressional action.* New Haven: Yale University Press.

Aschauer, David A. 1990. *Public investment and private sector growth.* Washington, D.C.: Economic Policy Institute.

Bachrach, Peter, and Morton S. Baratz. 1963. Decisions and non-decisions: An analytical framework. *American Political Science Review* 57:632–42.

Bailey, Stephen Kemp. 1950. *Congress makes a law: The story behind the Employment Act of 1946.* New York: Columbia University Press.

Balz, Daniel J. 1976. The Chamber and the NAM: A marriage of convenience. *National Journal* (August 7): 1102–7.

Bauer, Raymond A., Ithiel de Sola Pool, and Lewis Anthony Dexter. 1963. *American business and public policy: The politics of foreign trade.* New York: Atherton Press.

Baumgartner, Frank R., and Bryan D. Jones. 1993. *Agendas and instability in American politics.* Chicago: University of Chicago Press.

Baumgartner, Frank R., Bryan D. Jones, and Michael C. MacLeod. Forthcoming. The evolution of legislative jurisdictions. *Journal of Politics.*

Beck, Nathaniel, and Jonathan N. Katz. 1996. Nuisance vs. substance: Specifying and estimating time-series cross-section models. *Political Analysis* 6:1–36.

Bennett, W. Lance. 1990. Toward a theory of press-state relations in the U.S. *Journal of Communication* 40:103–25.

Berle, Adolph A. 1963. *The American economic republic.* New York: Harcourt, Brace & World.

Bernstein, Marvin D. 1955. *Regulating business by independent commission.* Princeton: Princeton University Press.

Berry, Jeffrey M. 1998. *The interest group society.* 3d ed. New York: Longman.

———. 1999. *The new liberalism: The rising power of citizen groups.* Washington, D.C.: Brookings Institution Press.

Best, Samuel J. 1999. The sampling problem in measuring public mood: An alternative solution. *Journal of Politics* 61:721–40.

Block, Fred. 1977. The ruling class does not rule. *Socialist Revolution* 33:6–28.

Blumenthal, Sidney. 1986. *The rise of the counter-establishment: From conservative ideology to political power.* New York: Times Books.

Bond, Jon R., and Richard Fleisher. 1990. *The president in the legislative arena.* Chicago: University of Chicago Press.

Bowles, Samuel, and Herbert Gintis. 1986. *Democracy and capitalism: Property, community, and the contradictions of modern social thought.* New York: Basic Books.

Box, George E. P., and Gwilym M. Jenkins. 1976. *Time series analysis: Forecasting and control.* San Francisco: Holden Day.

Brady, David W., John F. Cogan, Brian J. Gaines, and Douglas Rivers. 1996. The perils of presidential support: How the Republicans took the House in the 1994 midterm elections. *Political Behavior* 18:345–67.

Brady, David W., Brandice Canes-Wrone, and John F. Cogan. 1999. Out of step, out of office: Legislative voting behavior and House election outcomes. Typescript. Stanford University.

Browne, William P. 1988. *Private interests, public policy, and American agriculture.* Lawrence: University of Kansas Press.

Bryner, Gary C. 1993. *Blue skies, green politics: The Clean Air Act of 1990.* Washington, D.C.: CQ Press.

Burris, Val. 1992. Elite policy-planning networks in the United States. *Research in Politics and Society* 4:111–34.

Burstein, Paul. 1998. *Discrimination, jobs, and politics: The struggle for equal employment opportunity in the United States since the New Deal,* rev. ed. Chicago: University of Chicago Press.

Cammisa, Anne Marie. 1998. *From rhetoric to reform? Welfare policy in American politics.* Boulder, Colo.: Westview Press.

Campbell, John L., and Michael Patrick Allen. 1994. The political economy of revenue extraction in the modern state: A Time-series analysis of U.S. income taxes, 1916–1986. *Social Forces* 72:643–69.

Cater, Douglass. 1964. *Power in Washington: A critical look at today's struggle to govern in the nation's capital.* New York: Random House.

Chapman, Keith, and David F. Walker. 1991. *Industrial location: principles and policies.* 2d ed. Oxford: Blackwell.

Chandler, Alfred D., Jr. 1980. Government versus business: An American phenomenon. In *Business and public policy,* edited by John T. Dunlop. Cambridge: Division of Research, Graduate School of Business Administration, Harvard University.

Childs, Harwood Lawrence. 1930. *Labor and capital in national politics.* Columbus, Ohio: Ohio State University Press.

Clawson, Dan, and Mary Ann Clawson. 1987. Reagan or business? Foundations of the new conservatism. In *The structure of power in America,* edited by Michael Schwartz. New York: Holmes & Meier.

Clawson, Dan, Alan Neustadtl, and Mark Waller. 1998. *Dollars and votes: How business campaign contributions subvert democracy.* Philadelphia: Temple University Press.

Cobb, Roger W., and Charles D. Elder. 1983. *Participation in American politics: The dynamics of agenda-building.* 2d ed. Baltimore: Johns Hopkins University Press.

Cohen, Joshua, and Joel Rogers. 1983. *On democracy: Toward a transformation of American society.* Harmondsworth: Penguin.

Collie, Melissa P. 1985. Voting behavior in legislatures. In *Handbook of legislative research,* edited by Gerhard Loewenberg, Samuel C. Patterson, and Malcolm E. Jewell. Cambridge: Harvard University Press.

Collins, Robert M. 1981. *The business response to Keynes, 1929–1964.* New York: Columbia University Press.

Converse, Philip. 1964. The nature of belief systems in mass publics. In *Ideology and discontent,* edited by David Apter. New York: The Free Press, 206–61.

———. 1990. Popular representation and the distribution of information. In *Information and democratic processes,* edited by John A. Ferejohn and James H. Kuklinski. Urbana: University of Illinois Press, 369–90.

Cox, Ronald W., ed. 1996. *Business and the state in international relations.* Boulder, Colo.: Westview Press.

Crawford, Kenneth Gale. 1939. *The pressure boys: The inside story of lobbying in America.* New York: Julian Messner.

Crenson, Matthew A. 1971. *The unpolitics of air pollution.* Baltimore: Johns Hopkins University Press.

Dahl, Robert A. 1958. A critique of the ruling elite model. *American Political Science Review* 52:463–69.

———. 1961. *Who governs?* New Haven: Yale University Press.

Danielian, Lucig H, and Benjamin I. Page. 1994. The heavenly chorus: Interest group voices on TV news. *American Journal of Political Science* 38:1056–1078.

Davis, Frank L. 1993. Balancing the perspective on PAC contributions: In search of an impact on roll calls. *American Politics Quarterly* 21:205–22.

Deakin, James. 1969. *The lobbyists.* Washington, D.C.: Public Affairs Press.

Deutsch, Karl W. 1963. *The nerves of government.* New York: The Free Press.

Delli Carpini, Michael, and Scott Keeter. 1996. *What Americans know about politics and why it matters.* New Haven: Yale University Press.

Devine, Joel A. 1984. State and state expenditure: Determinants of social investment and social consumption spending in the postwar United States. *American Sociological Review* 50:150–65.

Domhoff, G. William. 1967. *Who rules America?* Englewood Cliffs, N.J.: Prentice-Hall.

———. 1978. *The powers that be: Processes of ruling class domination in America.* New York: Random House.

———. 1983. *Who rules America now?* New York: Touchstone.

———. 1990. *The power elite and the state: How policy is made in America.* New York: Aldine de Gruyter.

Donnelly, Harrison H. 1978. Organized labor found 1978 a frustrating year, had few victories in congress. *Congressional Quarterly Weekly Report* (December 30):3539–42.

Downs, Anthony. 1957. *An economic theory of democracy.* New York: Harper.

Dryzek, John S. 1996. *Democracy in capitalist times: Ideals, limits, and struggles.* New York: Oxford University Press.

Durr, Robert H. 1993. What moves policy sentiment? *American Political Science Review* 87:158–70.

Durst, Samantha L., and James T. Thurber. 1989. Studying Washington think tanks: In search of definitions and data. Paper presented at the Annual Meeting of the American Political Science Association in Atlanta, Georgia.

Dye, Thomas R. 1978. Oligarchic tendencies in national policy-making: The role of private policy-planning organizations. *Journal of Politics* 40:309–31.

———. 1995. *Who's running America: The Clinton years.* Englewood Cliffs, New Jersey: Prentice-Hall.

Easterbrook, Gregg. 1986. Ideas move nations. *Atlantic Monthly* (January):66–80.

Easton, David. 1965. *A framework for political analysis.* Englewood Cliffs, N.J.: Prentice-Hall.

Edsall, Thomas Byrne. 1984. *The new politics of inequality.* New York: W. W. Norton.

Edwards, George C., III. 1989. *At the margins: Presidential leadership of Congress.* New Haven: Yale University Press.

Edwards, George C., III, Andrew C. Barrett, and Jeffrey Peake. 1997. The legislative impact of divided government. *American Journal of Political Science* 41:545–63.

Edwards, George C., III, William Mitchell, and Reed Welch. 1995. Explaining presidential approval: The significance of issue salience. *American Journal of Political Science* 39:108–34.

Eismeier, Theodore J., and Philip H. Pollack III. 1988. *Business, money, and the rise of corporate PACs in American elections.* New York: Quorum.

Eisner, Marc Allen. 1993. *Regulatory politics in transition.* Baltimore: Johns Hopkins University Press.

Elkin, Stephen L. 1985. Pluralism in its place: State and regime in liberal democracy. In *The democratic state,* edited by Roger Benjamin and Stephen L. Elkin. Lawrence: University of Kansas Press, 179–211.

Engler, Robert. 1961. *The politics of oil: A study of private power and democratic directions.* Chicago: University of Chicago Press.

Epstein, Edwin M. 1969. *The corporation in American politics.* Englewood Cliffs, N.J.: Prentice-Hall.

Erikson, Robert S. 1990. Economic conditions and the congressional vote: A review of the macrolevel evidence. *American Journal of Political Science* 34:373–99.

Erikson, Robert S., Michael B. MacKuen, and James A. Stimson. Forthcoming. *The macro polity*. Cambridge: Cambridge University Press

Erikson, Robert S., and Gerald C. Wright. 1997. Voters, candidates, and issues in congressional elections. In *Congress reconsidered*, 6th ed., edited by Lawrence C. Dodd and Bruce I. Oppenheimer. Washington, D.C.: CQ Press.

Erikson, Robert S., Gerald C. Wright, and John P. McIver. 1993. *Statehouse democracy: Public opinion and policy in the American states*. Cambridge: Cambridge University Press.

Fan, David P. 1988. *Predictions of public opinion from the mass media: Computer content analysis and mathematical modeling*. New York: Greenwood Press.

Ferguson, Thomas, and Joel Rogers. 1986. *Right turn: The decline of the Democrats and the future of American politics*. New York: Hill and Wang.

Fiorina, Morris. 1981. *Retrospective voting in American national elections*. New Haven: Yale University Press.

Fisher, Burton R, and Stephen B. Witney. 1951. *Big business as the people see it: A study of a socio-economic institution*. Ann Arbor: Survey Research Center, Institute for Social Research, University of Michigan.

Fones-Wolf, Elizabeth A. 1994. *Selling free enterprise: The business assault on labor and liberalism, 1945–60*. Urbana: University of Illinois Press.

Freeman, John R. 1983. Granger causality and the time series analysis of political relationships. *American Journal of Political Science* 27:327–58.

———. 1989. *Democracy and markets: The politics of mixed economies*. Ithaca: Cornell University Pres.

Frendreis, John P., and Richard W. Waterman. 1985. PAC contributions and legislative behavior: Senate voting on trucking deregulation. *Social Science Quarterly* 66:401–12.

Frieden, Jeffry A. 1991. Invested interests: The politics of national economic policies in a world of global finance. *International Organization* 45:425–51.

Friedrich, Robert J. 1982. In defense of multiplicative terms in multiple regression equations. *American Journal of Political Science* 26:797–833.

Fritz, Sara. 1978. Hard times for labor. *U.S. News & World Report* (July 10):23.

Froman, Lewis A. Jr. 1967. *The congressional process: Strategies, rules, and procedures*. Boston: Little, Brown.

Gais, Thomas L., Mark A. Peterson, and Jack L. Walker. 1984. Interest groups, iron triangles, and representative institutions in American national government. *British Journal of Political Science* 14:161–85.

Galambos, Louis. 1975. *The public image of big business in America, 1880–1940*. Baltimore: Johns Hopkins University Press.

Gans, Herbert J. 1979. *Deciding what's news: A study of CBS Evening News, NBC Nightly News, Newsweek, and Time*. New York: Pantheon Books.

Garrett, Geoffrey. 1998. *Partisan politics in the global economy*. Cambridge University Press.

Geer, John G. 1996. *From tea leaves to opinion polls: A theory of democratic leadership*. New York: Columbia University Press.

Gimpel, James. 1996. *Legislating the revolution: The Contract with America in its first 100 Days.* Needham Heights, Mass.: Allyn & Bacon.

Gitelson, Alan R., Robert L. Dudley, and Melven J. Dubnick. 1998. *American government.* 5th ed. Boston: Houghton Mifflin.

Goldman, Patricia A. 1972. U.S. chamber works to erase negative image and improve grass-roots clout. *National Journal* (April 1): 558–70.

Goldstein, Kenneth M. 1999. *Interest groups, lobbying, and participation in America.* Cambridge: Cambridge University Press.

Gordon, Al. 1975. U.S. Chamber: It speaks through members. *Congressional Quarterly Weekly Report* (November 15): 2457–63.

Graber, Doris A. 1989. *Mass media and American politics.* 3d ed. Washington, D.C.: CQ Press.

Gramsci, Antonio. 1971 [1929–1935]. *Selections from the prison notebooks.* Edited and translated by Quintin Hoare and Geoffrey Nowell Smith. New York: International Publishers.

Granger, Clive W. J., and Paul Newbold. 1974. Spurious regressions in econometrics. *Journal of Econometrics* 26:1045–66.

Gray, Virginia, and David Lowery. 1997. Reconceptualizing PAC formation: It's not a collective action problem, and it may be an arms race. *American Politics Quarterly* 25:319–46.

Grier, Kevin B., Michael C. Munger, and Brian E. Roberts. 1994. The determinants of industry political activity, 1978–1986. *American Political Science Review* 88:911–26.

Griffin, Larry J., Joel A. Devine, and Michael Wallace. 1982. Monopoly capital, organized labor, and military expenditures: Military Keynesianism in the United States, 1949–1976. *American Journal of Sociology* 88:S113–S154.

Guth, James L., John C. Green, Lyman A. Kellstedt, and Corwin E. Smidt. 1995. Faith and the environment: Religious beliefs and attitudes on environmental policy. *American Journal of Political Science* 39:364–82.

Hall, Donald R. 1969. *Cooperative lobbying: The power of pressure.* Tuscon: University of Arizona Press.

Harris, Richard A. 1989. Politicized management: The changing face of business in American politics. In *Remaking American politics,* edited by Richard A. Harris and Sidney M. Milkus. Boulder, Colo.: Westview Press.

Hartz, Louis. 1955. *The liberal tradition in America: An interpretation of American political thought since the Revolution.* New York: Harcourt, Brace.

Heclo, Hugh. 1978. Issue networks and the executive establishment. In *The new American political system,* edited by Anthony King. Washington, D.C.: American Enterprise Institute.

Heidenheimer, Arnold J., Hugh Heclo, and Carolyn Teich Adams. 1990. *Comparative public policy: The politics of social choice in America, Europe, and Japan.* 3d ed. New York: St. Martin's Press.

Heinz, John P., Edward O. Laumann, Robert L. Nelson, and Robert H. Salisbury. 1993. *The hollow core: Private interests in national policymaking.* Cambridge: Harvard University Press.

Hellebust, Lynn, ed. 1996. *Think tank directory: A guide to nonprofit public policy research organizations.* Topeka, Kan.: Government Research Service.

Hellebust, Lynn, ed. 1996. *Think tank directory: A guide to nonprofit public policy research organizations.* Topeka, Kan.: Government Research Service.

Herrnson, Paul S. 1998. *Congressional elections: Campaigning at home and in Washington.* 2d ed. Washington, D.C.: CQ Press.

Herrnson, Paul S., and Clyde Wilcox. 1994. Not so risky business: PAC activity in 1992. In *Risky business? PAC decisionmaking in congressional elections,* edited by Robert Biersack, Paul Herrnson, and Clyde Wilcox. Armonk, N.Y.: M. E. Sharpe.

Hibbs, Douglas A. 1987. *The American political economy: Macroeconomics and electoral politics.* Cambridge: Harvard University Press.

Hicks, Alexander. 1984. Elections, Keynes, bureaucracy and class: Explaining U.S. budget deficits, 1961–1978. *American Sociological Review* 49:165–82.

Hicks, Alexander, and Duane Swank. 1984. On the political economy of welfare expansion. *Comparative Political Studies* 17:81–119.

Hicks, John D. 1961. *The populist revolt.* Lincoln: University of Nebraska Press.

Himmelstein, Jerome L. 1990. *To the right: The transformation of American conservatism.* Berkeley: University of California Press.

Holbrook, Thomas M. 1994. Campaigns, national conditions, and U.S. presidential elections. *American Journal of Political Science* 38:973–98.

Hrebenar, Ronald J., and Ruth K. Scott. 1982. *Interest group politics in America.* Englewood Cliffs, New Jersey: Prentice-Hall.

Huckfeldt, R. Robert, and John Sprague. 1995. *Citizens, politics, and social communication: Information and influence in an election campaign.* Cambridge: Cambridge University Press.

Jackson, Brooks. 1988. *Honest graft: Big money and the American political process.* New York: Alfred A. Knopf.

Jacobs, David. 1988. Corporate economic power and the state: A longitudinal assessment of two explanations. *American Journal of Sociology* 93:852–81.

Jacobs, David C. D. 1998. *Business lobbies and the power structure in America: Evidence and arguments.* Westport, Conn.: Quorum Books.

Jacobson, Gary C. 1997. *The politics of congressional elections.* 4th ed. New York: Longman.

Jacobs, Lawrence R. 1993. *The health of nations: Public opinion and the making of American and British health policy.* Ithaca, N.Y.: Cornell University Press.

Jacobson, Louis. 1995. Tanks on the roll. *National Journal* (July 8):1767–71.

Jacoby, Sanford, ed. 1991. *Masters to managers: Historical and comparative perspectives on American employers.* New York: Columbia University Press.

Jenkins-Smith, Hank C., Gilbert K. St. Clair, and Brian Woods. 1991. Explaining change in policy subsystems: Analysis of coalition stability and defection over time. *American Journal of Political Science* 35:851–80.

Jennings, M. Kent, and Richard G. Niemi. 1974. *The political character of adolescence: The influence of families and schools.* Princeton: Princeton University Press.

Jones, Bryan D. 1994. *Reconceiving decision-making in democratic politics: Attention, choice, and public policy.* Chicago: University of Chicago Press.

Jones, Charles O. 1975. *Clean air.* Pittsburgh: University of Pittsburgh Press.

———. 1994. *The presidency in a separated system.* Washington, D.C.: The Brookings Institution.

Jones, Woodrow Jr., and K. Robert Keiser. 1987. Issue visibility and the effects of PAC money. *Social Science Quarterly* 68:170–76.

Kelley, Stanley. 1956. *Professional public relations and political power.* Baltimore: Johns Hopkins University Press.

Kellstedt, Paul, Gregory E. McAvoy, and James A. Stimson. 1995. Dynamic analysis with latent constructs: The Kalman DYMIMIC specification. *Political Analysis* 5:113–50.

Kennedy, Peter. 1985. *A guide to econometrics.* 2d ed. Cambridge: MIT Press.

Kernell, Samuel. 1997. *Going public: New strategies of presidential leadership.* 3d ed. Washington, D.C.: CQ Press.

Kirkland, Richard I, Jr. 1981. Fat days at the Chamber of Commerce. *Fortune* (September 21):144–58.

Kolko, Gabriel. 1963. *The triumph of conservatism.* New York: The Free Press.

Kollman, Ken. 1998. *Outside lobbying: Public opinion and interest group strategies.* Princeton: Princeton University Press.

Knoke, David. 1979. Stratification and the dimensions of American political orientations. *American Journal of Political Science* 23:772–91.

Kondracke, Morton. 1980. The Heritage model. *New Republic* (December 20): 1–3.

Krooss, Herman E. 1970. *Executive opinion: What business leaders said and thought on economic issues, 1920s–1960s.* Garden City, N.Y.: Doubleday & Company, Inc.

Kuttner, Robert. 1985. What's the big idea? Inside the Democratic think tanks. *The New Republic* (November 18):23–6.

Ladd, Everett Carll, with Charles D. Hadley. 1975. *Transformations of the American party system: Political coalitions from the New Deal to the 1970s.* New York: W. W. Norton.

Lanouette, William J. 1982. Chamber's ponderous decision making leaves it sitting on the sidelines. *National Journal* (July 24):1298–1301.

Levitan, Sar A., and Martha R. Cooper. 1984. *Business lobbies: The public good and the bottom line.* Baltimore: Johns Hopkins University Press.

Lewis, Charles. 1998. *The buying of the Congress: How special interests have stolen your right to life, liberty, and the pursuit of happiness.* New York: Avon Books.

Light, Paul C. 1985. *Artful work: The politics of social security reform.* New York: Random House.

Lindblom, Charles E. 1977. *Politics and markets: The world's political-economic systems.* New York: Basic Books.

———. 1982. The market as prison. *Journal of Politics* 44:324–36.

Lipset, Seymour Martin. 1996. *American exceptionalism: A double-edged sword.* New York: W. W. Norton.

Lipset, Seymour Martin, and William Schneider. 1983. *The confidence gap: Business, labor, and government in the public mind.* New York: The Free Press.

Loomis, Burdett A. 1983. A new era: Groups and the grass roots. In *Interest group politics,* edited by Allan J. Cigler and Burdett A. Loomis. Washington, D.C.: CQ Press.

Loomis, Burdett A., and Eric Sexton. 1995. Choosing to advertise: How interests decide. In *Interest group politics,* 4th ed., edited by Allan J. Cigler and Burdett A. Loomis. Washington, D.C.: CQ Press, 193–214.

Lowi, Theodore S. 1964. American business, public policy, case studies and political theory. *World Politics* 16:677–715.

———. 1979. *The end of liberalism: The second republic of the United States.* 2d ed. New York: W. W. Norton.

Lukes, Stephen. 1974. *Power: A radical view.* London: Macmillan.

Maass, Arthur. 1951. *Muddy waters: The army engineers and the nation's rivers.* Cambridge: Harvard University Press.

MacKuen, Michael B, Robert S. Erikson, and James A. Stimson. 1992. Peasants or bankers? The American electorate and the U.S. economy. *American Political Science Review* 86:597–600.

Manes, Susan. 1990. Up for bid: A common cause view. In *Money, elections, and democracy: Reforming congressional campaign finance,* edited by Margaret Latus Nugent and John R. Johannes. Boulder, Colo.: Westview Press.

Martin, Cathie J. 1991. *Shifting the burden: The struggle over growth and corporate taxation.* Chicago: University of Chicago Press.

———. 1995. Nature or nurture? Sources of firm preference for national health reform. *American Political Science Review* 89:898–913.

———. 2000. *Stuck in neutral: Business and the politics of human capital investment policy.* Princeton: Princeton University Press.

Masters, Marick F., and Gerald D. Keim. 1985. Determinants of PAC participation among large corporations. *Journal of Politics* 47:1158–73.

Mayer, William G. 1992. *The changing American mind: How and why American public opinion changed between 1960 and 1988.* Ann Arbor: University of Michigan Press.

Mayhew, David R. 1974. *Congress: The electoral connection.* New Haven: Yale University Press.

———. 1991. *Divided we govern: Party control, lawmaking, and investigations, 1946–1990.* New Haven: Yale University Press.

McConnell, Grant. 1966. *Private power and American democracy.* New York: Alfred A. Knopf.

McCrone, Donald J., and James H. Kuklinski. 1979. The delegate theory of representation. *American Journal of Political Science* 23:278–300.

McFarland, Andrew S. 1991. Interest groups and political time: Cycles in America. *British Journal of Political Science* 21:257–84.

———. 1992. Interest groups and the policymaking process: Sources of countervailing power in America. In *The politics of interests: Interest groups transformed,* edited by Mark P. Petracca. Boulder, Colo.: Westview Press.

McGann, James G. 1992. Academics to ideologues: A brief history of the public policy research industry. *PS: Political Science and Politics* 25:733–40.

McGuire, William J. 1969. The nature of attitudes and attitude change. In *Handbook of social psychology,* 2d ed., edited by G. Linzey and E. Aronson. Reading, Mass.: Addison-Wesley, 136–214.

McLelland, David S., and Charles E. Woodhouse. 1966. American business leaders and foreign policy: A study in perspectives. *American Journal of Economics and Sociology* 25:267–80.

McQuaid, Kim. 1982. *Big business and presidential power: From FDR to Reagan.* New York: Morrow.

———. 1994. *Uneasy partners: Big business in American politics, 1945–1990.* Baltimore: Johns Hopkins University Press.

Miliband, Ralph. 1969. *The state in capitalist society.* New York: Basic Books.

Mill, John Stuart. [1859] 1989. *On liberty*. In *On liberty with the subjection of women and chapters on socialism*. Cambridge: Cambridge University Press.

Mills, C. Wright. 1956. *The power elite*. New York: Oxford University Press.

Mintz, Beth, and Michael Schwartz. 1985. *The power structure of American business*. Chicago: University of Chicago Press.

———. 1987. Sources of intercorporate unity. In *The structure of power in America: The corporate elite as a ruling class*, edited by Michael Schwartz. New York: Holmes & Meier.

Mitchell, Neil J. 1989. *The generous corporation: A political analysis of economic power*. New Haven: Yale University Press.

———. 1997. *The conspicuous corporation: Business, public policy, and representative democracy*. Ann Arbor: University of Michigan Press.

Mitchell, Neil J., Wendy L. Hansen, and Eric M. Jepsen. 1997. The determinants of domestic and foreign corporate political activity. *Journal of Politics* 59:1096–1113.

Mizruchi, Mark S. 1992. *The structure of corporate political action: Interfirm relations and their consequences*. Cambridge: Harvard University Press.

Moore, W. John. 1992. Wichita pipeline. *National Journal* (May 16):1168–74.

Morgan, Bob. 1981. Conservatives: A well-financed network. *Washington Post* (January 4):A1.

Morone, James A. 1998. *The democratic wish: Popular participation and the limits of American government*, rev. ed. New Haven: Yale University Press.

Mucciaroni, Gary. 1990. *The political failure of employment policy, 1945–1982*. Pittsburgh: University of Pittsburgh Press.

Motermans, Ton. 1993. The abdication of national policy autonomy: Why the macroeconomic regime has become so unfavorable to labor. *Politics and Society* 21:133–67.

Mundo, Philip A. 1992. *Interest groups: Cases and controversies*. Chicago: Nelson-Hall.

Murray, Charles. 1984. *Losing ground: American social policy, 1950–1980*. New York: Basic Books.

Nadel, Mark. 1972. Public opinion and public policy. In *American democracy: Theory and reality*, edited by Robert Weissberg and Mark V. Nadel. New York: John Wiley & Sons.

Nagel, Jack H. 1975. *The descriptive analysis of power*. New Haven: Yale University Press.

Neustadl, Alan. 1990. Interest group PACsmanship: An analysis of campaign contributions, issue visibility, and legislative impact. *Social Forces* 69:549–64.

Offe, Claus. 1984. *Contradictions of the welfare state*. Cambridge: MIT Press.

Oleszek, Walter J. 1989. *Congressional procedures and the policy process*. 3d ed. Washington, D.C.: CQ Press.

Olson, Mancur, Jr. 1965. *The logic of collective action*. Cambridge: Harvard University Press.

Ornstein, Norman J., Thomas E. Mann, and Michael E. Malbin. 1996. *Vital statistics on Congress 1995–1996*. Washington, D.C.: Congressional Quarterly.

Page, Benjamin I. 1978. *Choices and echoes in presidential elections: Rational man and electoral democracy*. Chicago: University of Chicago Press.

———. 1996. *Who deliberates? Mass media in modern democracy*. Chicago: University of Chicago Press.

Page, Benjamin I., and Robert Y. Shapiro. 1983. Effects of public opinion on policy. *American Political Science Review* 77:175–90.

———. 1992. *The rational public: Fifty years of trends in Americans' policy preferences.* Chicago: University of Chicago Press.

Page, Benjamin I., Robert Y. Shapiro, and Glenn R. Dempsey. 1987. What moves public opinion? *American Political Science Review* 81:23–43.

Peschek, Joseph G. 1987. *Policy-planning organizations: Elite agendas and America's rightward turn.* Philadelphia: Temple University Press.

Peterson, Mark A. 1990. *Legislating together: The White House and Capitol Hill from Eisenhower to Reagan.* Cambridge: Harvard University Press.

Petty, Richard E., and John T. Cacioppo. 1981. *Attitudes and persuasion: Classic and contemporary approaches.* Dubuque, Iowa: Brown.

Pitkin, Hanna F. 1967. *The concept of representation.* Berkeley: University of California Press.

Poole, Keith, and Howard Rosenthal. 1997. *Congress: A political-economic history of roll call voting.* New York: Oxford University Press.

Poulantzas, Nicos. 1969. The problem of the capitalist state. *New Left Review* 58:67–78.

———. 1973. *Political power and social classes.* London: New Left Books.

Prechel, Harland. 1990. Steel and the state: Industry politics and business policy formation, 1940–1989. *American Sociological Review* 55:648–68.

Prewitt, Kenneth, and Alan Stone. 1973. *The ruling elites: Elite theory, power, and American democracy.* New York: Harper & Row.

Prothro, James W. 1954. *The dollar decade: Business ideas in the 1920s.* Baton Rouge: Louisiana State University Press.

Quinn, Dennis P. 1988. Investment incentives: A Five-country test of the Lindblom hypothesis. *Research in Corporate Social Performance and Policy* 10:87–111.

Quinn, Dennis P., and Robert Y. Shapiro. 1991. Business political power: The Case of taxation. *American Political Science Review* 85:851–74.

Reagan, Michael D. 1963. *The managed economy.* New York: Oxford University Press.

Redford, Emmette S. 1969. *Democracy in the administrative state.* New York: Oxford University Press.

Reich, Robert B. 1992. *The work of nations: Preparing ourselves for 21st century capitalism.* New York: Vintage Books.

Ricci, David. 1993. *The transformation of American politics: The new Washington and the rise of think tanks.* New Haven: Yale University Press.

Rich, Andrew. 1999. *Think tanks and American policy making: The politicization of expertise and ideas.* Draft of Ph.D. Dissertation. Yale University.

Rose, Arnold M. 1967. *The power structure.* New York: Oxford University Press.

Salama, John S., III. 1984. *Ominous politics: The new conservative labyrinth.* New York: Farrar, Straus.

Schattschneider, E. E. 1960. *The semisovereign people: A realist's view of democracy in America.* New York: Holt, Rinehart and Winston.

Schlesinger, Arthur M. 1986. *The cycles of American history.* Boston: Houghton Mifflin.

Schwartz, Michael. 1987. *The structure of power in America: The corporate elite as a ruling class.* New York: Holmes & Meier.

Sethi, S. Prakash. 1977. *Advocacy advertising and large corporations.* Lexington, Mass.: Heath.

Sharp, Elaine B. 1994. The dynamics of issue expansion: Cases from disability rights and fetal research controversy. *Journal of Politics* 56:919–39.

———. 1999. *The sometime connection: Public opinion and social policy.* Albany: State University of New York Press.

Silk, Leonard and David Vogel. 1976. *Ethics and profits: The crisis of confidence in American business.* New York: Simon and Schuster.

Simon, William. 1978. *A time for truth.* New York: Berkley.

Smith, Eric R. A. N., and Peverill Squire. 1990. The effects of prestige names in question wording. *Public Opinion Quarterly* 54:97–116.

Smith, James A. 1991. *The idea brokers: Think tanks and the rise of the new policy elite.* New York: The Free Press.

Smith, Mark A. 1997. The nature of party governance: Connecting conceptualization and measurement. *American Journal of Political Science* 41:1042–56.

———. 1999. Public opinion, elections, and representation within a market economy: Does the structural power of business undermine popular sovereignty? *American Journal of Political Science* 43:842–63.

Smith, Steven S. 1989. *Call to order: Floor politics in the House and Senate.* Washington, D.C.: The Brookings Institution.

Smith, Tom. 1987. The welfare state in cross-national perspective. *Public Opinion Quarterly* 51:.

Soley, Lawrence C. 1991. Right thinking conservative think tanks. *Dissent* (Summer): 418–20.

Sorauf, Frank J. 1988. *Money in American elections.* Glenview, Ill.: Scott, Foresman.

———. 1992. *Inside campaign finance: Myths and realities.* New Haven: Yale University Press.

Stefancic, Jean and Richard Delgado. 1996. *No mercy: How conservative think tanks and foundations changed America's social agenda.* Philadelphia: Temple University Press.

Steinmo, Sven. 1993. *Taxation and democracy: Swedish, British, and American approaches to financing the modern state.* New Haven: Yale University Press.

Stern, Philip M. 1992. *Still the best Congress money can buy.* Washington, D.C.: Regnery Gateway.

Stimson, James A. 1991. *Public opinion in America: Moods, cycles, and swings.* Boulder, Colo.: Westview.

———. 1999. *Public opinion in America: Moods, cycles, and swings.* 2d ed. Boulder, Colo.: Westview.

Stimson, James A., Michael B. MacKuen, and Robert S. Erikson. 1995. Dynamic representation. *American Political Science Review* 89:543–65.

Stone, Peter H. 1981. Conservative brain trust. *New York Times* (May 10):F18.

Sutton, Francis X., Seymour E. Harris, Carl Kaysen, and James Tobin. 1956. *The American business creed.* Cambridge: Harvard University Press.

Swank, Duane. 1992. Politics and the structural dependence of the state in democratic capitalist nations. *American Political Science Review* 86:38–54.

Tedlow, Richard S. 1979. *Keeping the corporate image: Public relations and business, 1900–1950.* Greenwich, Conn.: JAI Press.

Thurber, James A. 1991. Dynamics of policy subsystems in American politics. In *Interest group politics,* 3d ed., edited by Allan J. Cigler and Burdett A. Loomis. Washington, D.C.: CQ Press.

Truman, David. 1951. *The governmental process.* New York: Knopf.

Tulis, Jeffrey. 1987. *The rhetorical presidency.* Princeton: Princeton University Press.

Useem, Michael. 1984. *The inner circle.* New York: Oxford University Press.

Verba, Sidney, Kay Lehman Schlozman, and Henry E. Brady. 1995. *Voice and equality: Civic voluntarism in American politics.* Cambridge: Harvard University Press.

Victor, Kirk. 1993. Deal us in. *National Journal* (April 3): 805–9.

Vogel, David. 1978. Why businessmen distrust their state. *British Journal of Political Science* 8:45–78.

———. 1989. *Fluctuating fortunes: The political power of business in America.* New York: Basic Books.

———. 1995. *Trading up: Consumer and environmental regulation in a global economy.* Cambridge: Harvard University Press.

Wahlke, John C., Heinz Eulau, William Buchanan, and Leroy C. Ferguson. 1962. *The legislative system: Explorations in legislative behavior.* New York: John Wiley and Sons.

Wayne, Stephen J., G. Calvin Mackenzie, David M. O'Brien, and Richard L. Cole. 1997. *The politics of American government.* 2d ed. New York: St. Martin's Press.

Weir, Margaret. 1992. *Politics and jobs: The boundaries of employment policy in the United States.* Princeton, N.J.: Princeton University Press.

Weir, Margaret, Ann Shola Orloff, and Theda Skocpol, eds. 1988. *The politics of social policy in the United States.* Princeton: Princeton University Press.

Weissberg, Robert. 1976. *Public opinion and popular government.* Englewood Cliffs, N.J.: Prentice-Hall.

West, Darrell M., and Burdett A. Loomis. 1998. *The sound of money: Voices of influence in a high-tech age.* New York: W. W. Norton.

Whitt, J. Allen. 1982. *Urban elites and mass transportation.* Princeton: Princeton University Press.

Wiebe, Robert H. 1995. *Self-rule: A cultural history of American democracy.* Chicago: University of Chicago Press.

Williams, John T., and Brian K. Collins. 1997. The political economy of corporate taxation. *American Journal of Political Science* 41:208–44.

Wilson, Graham K. 1981. *Interest groups in the United States.* Oxford: Clarendon Press.

———. 1985. *The politics of safety and health: Occupational safety and health in the United States and Britain.* Oxford: Clarendon Press.

———. 1990. *Business and politics: A comparative introduction.* 2d ed. Chatham, N.J.: Chatham House Publishers.

Wilson, James Q. 1973. *Political organizations.* New York: Basic Books.

———. 1980. The politics of regulation. In *The politics of regulation,* edited by James Q. Wilson. New York: Basic Books.

Wilson, Woodrow. 1913. *The new freedom: A call for the emancipation of the generous energies of a people.* New York: Doubleday, Page and Company.

Wlezien, Christopher. 1995. The public as thermostat. *American Journal of Political Science* 39:981–1000.

Wright, John R. 1985. PACs, contributions, and roll calls: An organizational perspective. *American Political Science Review* 79:400–14.

Zaller, John. 1992. *The nature and origins of mass opinion.* New York: Cambridge University Press.

I N D E X